3/12/82 James C. Cowen

INDIANA SOURCES FOR GENEALOGICAL RESEARCH IN THE INDIANA STATE LIBRARY

By
Carolynne L. (Wendel) Miller

THE FAMILY HISTORY SECTION
INDIANA HISTORICAL SOCIETY
1984

Copyright 1984
Carolynne L. (Wendel) Miller

Copies of this publication may be obtained from the Indiana Historical Society, 315 W. Ohio Street, Indianapolis, Indiana 46202.

FOREWORD

In 1962 the Detroit Society for Genealogical Research published the author's *Aids for Genealogical Searching in Indiana*. It was revised in 1970.

The resources listed in this volume are primarily those housed in the Genealogy Division of the Indiana State Library, Indianapolis, Indiana. Therefore, this guide does not serve as an exhaustive study of Indiana resources.

The first two editions of "*Aids*" included a listing of major histories for Indiana counties in the Indiana Division of the State Library. This does not. It is contemplated that separate publications of county histories, atlases, plat books, and directories will be prepared in the future.

The author, Carolynne L. Wendel Miller, who supervised the Genealogy Division of the Indiana State Library, retired September 1, 1982.

ACKNOWLEDGEMENTS

Dorothy Riker, past editor of *The Hoosier Genealogist*, and author and editor of numerous historical and genealogical publications; and

Rebah Fraustein, CG, editor of *The Hoosier Genealogist*, for their advice and bibliographic recommendations.

Willard Heiss, Fellow of ASG, NGS, and UGS, renowned Quaker authority, and editor of *Genealogy*, for his encouragement and assistance in publication.

Staff of Genealogy Division, Indiana State Library, and especially Diane Sharp, for their assistance.

Jean Singleton Weimer, former supervisor of the Indiana Division, Indiana State Library, for the selected list of Indiana church records.

Eric Pumroy, Head, Manuscripts Department, Indiana Historical Society Library, for the update of the manuscript information in the Society's library.

Staff of the Archives Division, Commission on Public Records, for the list of major genealogical sources in the State Archives.

THE AUTHOR

Carolynne Wendel Miller, head of the Genealogy Division of the Indiana State Library, retired August 20, 1982. Her first library experience was at the Crown Point, Indiana, Public Library where she worked while still attending high school. She was on the staff of the State Library for thirty-six years, starting as a page in the Genealogy Division in 1946 when she was enrolled as a freshman at Butler University. She continued to work in the Genealogy Division while a student at Butler, and while working toward a masters degree in Library Science at Indiana University. All of her thirty-six years of service at the Indiana State Library was in the Genealogy Division with the exception of a brief period when she worked in the Reference and Loan Division. She was made head of the Genealogy Division in 1956.

Following World War II the United States experienced an accelerated interest in both American and family history. This interest continued to grow at a phenomenal pace throughout the years. Carolynne, as head of the Genealogy Division, addressed the growing demand for services in the field. This interest in family history brought forth a mass of publications, books, magazines, pamphlets on the subject, from which she selected appropriate materials to build up and round out the library's genealogical collection. Through the years this was a task which she did exceptionally well, making the Indiana State Library genealogy collection one of the finest in the Midwest.

She worked closely with patriotic, hereditary, and religious organizations. Many Indiana county records were microfilmed under her supervision. This was done in conjunction with the Indianapolis Public Library through the Eugene Haslet Darrach Memorial Fund. Cemetery records were added to the collection and many items of national interest as well as books relating to genealogy in other states throughout the United States, and in foreign countries were acquired. She introduced extensive indexing projects which made information in the Genealogy Division more accessible to patrons.

In co-operation with the Indiana Historical Society she was able to increase the number of hours the division was open to the public, and to enlarge the staff so more services would be available to the public.

Carolynne's cheerful disposition, her winning smile, and her keen knowledge of her chosen field will be greatly missed by her many patrons and by the staffs of the Indiana State Library and the Indiana Historical Society. For her devoted and longtime service to the citizens of the State of Indiana, Governor Robert D. Orr named her a "Sagamore of the Wabash."

Hazel Hopper

CONTENTS

	Page
History	9
Libraries	10
Indiana State Library	10
Indiana Historical Society	10
Archives, Commission on Public Records	11
Indiana Periodicals	13
Land Records	14
Military and Pension Records	16
Court and Vital Statistics Records	18
Censuses	19
Mortality Schedules	20
Cemetery Records	21
Church Records	22
General Indiana Sources	28
Abbreviations	32
County Listings, Arranged Alphabetically by County	33

INDIANA SOURCES FOR GENEALOGICAL RESEARCH

HISTORY

Indiana, known as the Hoosier State, had its early experience with Indians and fur traders. Three forts were established in Indiana in the early 1700's; Post Miami (Fort Wayne), Ouiatanon (near Lafayette), and Post Vincennes.

Indiana's major participation in the Revolutionary War was the George Rogers Clark activity in the late 1700's, when Clark took possession of the posts of Kaskaskia and Cahokia in southern Illinois and Vincennes.

By the enactment of the 1787 Ordinance, the Northwest Territory was established. In 1790 most of Indiana, and a portion of Illinois, formed Knox County with Vincennes serving as the governmental seat. In addition to Knox, St. Clair, Randolph, and Wayne were the counties comprising the Northwest Territory, but only Knox remains as a present part of Indiana.

The Indiana Territory was formed by an Act of Congress in 1800. In 1805 when the Michigan Territory was formed, Wayne "county" became a part of it, and in 1809 when the Illinois Territory was formed, St. Clair and Randolph counties became a part of the Illinois Territory.

When Indiana was admitted to the Union as a state in 1816 there were fifteen organized counties: Knox, Clark, Dearborn, Harrison, Wayne, Jefferson, Franklin, Warrick, Gibson, Washington, Switzerland, Perry, Jackson, Posey, and Orange. Corydon, the county seat of Harrison County, was its capital.

Indiana with its present capital at Indianapolis now comprises 92 counties.

LIBRARIES

The INDIANA STATE LIBRARY in Indianapolis was organized in 1825. It maintains two collections helpful to the genealogical researcher: Indiana and Genealogy. The Indiana Division has a unique collection of materials relating to the state, including the county and town histories, church records, directories, and newspapers.

The Genealogy Division of the State Library accommodates over 35,000 volumes and pamphlets and an expanding microform collection. Co-operation with the Indianapolis-Marion County Public Library, the Genealogical Society of Utah, and the Indiana Historical Society, has enhanced the Division's resources.

Many PUBLIC LIBRARIES IN INDIANA have some resources to aid the genealogist. The libraries of Anderson, Bloomington, Columbus, Evansville, Fort Wayne, Franklin, Michigan City, New Albany, Noblesville, Peru, South Bend, Terre Haute, and Valparaiso are some of those that maintain separate historical/genealogical sections in their libraries. The Fort Wayne-Allen County Public Library is known nationally for its genealogical holdings.

BRANCH LIBRARIES OF THE CHURCH OF JESUS CHRIST OF LATTER DAY SAINTS are available in Indiana. Arrangements to borrow genealogical references from the library in Salt Lake City can be made directly through the local branches.

FRANKLIN COLLEGE has a fine Baptist collection; DePauw University, a Methodist collection; Earlham College, a Quaker library; Goshen College, a Mennonite collection; and Hanover College, Presbyterian material. Vincennes University's Byron R. Lewis collection is a unique source of early French Catholic records.

The SOCIETY OF INDIANA PIONEERS houses its records at the State Library and Historical Building in Indianapolis. Membership consists of those descendants who had pioneer ancestors in Indiana.

The INDIANA HISTORICAL SOCIETY and its library are located in the State Library and Historical Building. The Society, a private, not-for-profit organization, was founded in 1830 to preserve and disseminate information about the state's past. The Society supports numerous historical activities, a library containing many outstanding research collections, a prolific publications program, and a dynamic genealogical section. For additional information about the Society's past, see the comprehensive, illustrated *A History of the Indiana Historical Society, 1830-1980*, by Lana Ruegamer. The August and October 1979 issues of *Genealogy* contain an article by Tom Rumer, "Genealogical Sources in the Indiana Historical Society Library".

The following information on the Society's library was prepared by Eric Pumroy, Head, Manuscripts Department.

The Indiana Historical Society Library (William Henry Smith Memorial) is a repository of rare books, manuscripts, pictures, maps, and ephemera relating to the history of Indiana and the Old Northwest. Among its more important collections are published accounts of explorations and travels through the middle west; Indiana county and town histories and atlases; early midwestern and Indiana maps; and approximately 100,000 pictures and photographs of Indiana people and scenes.

Of particular value for genealogical research is the library's manuscript collection, which consists of nearly two million items. Although traditionally the library concentrated its collecting on the territorial and early statehood periods, it now also has extensive collections relating to twentieth century Indiana, with particular strengths in the areas of black, Jewish, and ethnic history. Among the library's more prominent collections are the papers of territorial governor William Henry Harrison; politicians William H. English, Henry S. Lane, Conrad Baker, and Charles W. Fairbanks; nineteenth century bankers Calvin Fletcher and Samuel Merrill; authors Lew Wallace and Booth Tarkington; territorial soldiers Samuel Vance and John Armstrong; and fur trader Francis Vigo.

In addition the library has a large collection of letters, diaries, account books, and business records of numerous ordinary families from all parts of the state, particularly from the nineteenth century. Although these collections generally do not include vital records, they frequently contain other information which would be useful for filling in a family history. A general store account book, for example, will list the names of all of the store's customers, the amount each paid, and often a list of items purchased; a family's letters and diaries will normally include discussions of the activities of relatives and neighbors. Although the library does not index each name which appears in a collection of family papers, collections are indexed under the names of the counties and towns which appear prominently in the papers.

The library also contains several collections specifically valuable for genealogical research:

WILLIAM H. ENGLISH COLLECTION, 1741-1928. 119 boxes.

In addition to English's personal papers relating to his political career in the mid-nineteenth century, the collection also includes a large amount of material he collected for his historical research. Of particular interest to genealogists are the biographical materials he compiled on nearly all of Indiana's territorial officials, nineteenth century state legislators, and delegates to the 1851 state constitutional convention. The collection also includes photographs of many of these officials.

SOCIETY OF FRIENDS RECORDS. 111 microfilm rolls.

The Library has a nearly complete collection of the records of nineteenth century Indiana Friends meetings on microfilm. The meeting minutes include records of marriages, births and deaths, removals, and new members. These records were abstracted and indexed in *Abstracts of the Records of the Society of Friends in Indiana*, edited by Willard Heiss. (1962-1977, 7 vols.)

MARION COUNTY RECORDS, 1822-1928. 129 microfilm rolls.

Marion County (Indianapolis) Commissioners and court records, predominately from the mid-nineteenth century. Of particular value are probate court records and naturalization records.

HENDRICKS COUNTY RECORDS, 1824-1905. 23 microfilm rolls.

The collection includes deed, court, marriage, tax, voting, and commissioners records prior to 1850, and will and probate records to 1900.

The ARCHIVES OF INDIANA, once a part of the Indiana State Library, separated from the library in 1979. It is now a part of the Indiana Commission on Public Records.

The staff of the Archives Division, Commission on Public Records, prepared the following information and list of major genealogical sources housed in the State Archives.

The Archives preserves the permanent government records of the state for their legal and administrative values. Only secondarily are records preserved for research values. No government record was ever created for exclusive genealogical use. However, since genealogists seek information on name, place, time, and relationship, primarily as vital statistics, most government records have significant genealogical value. The list that follows reflects only highly used records of genealogical value in the Archives. Many lesser known records among the 32 million items that exist in the Archives also reflect name, place, and relationship. Since August, 1980 a column in the *Indiana History Bulletin* lists activities and holdings in the Archives. The Archives accessions, maintains, preserves and makes available for use state and selected local government records. It has no private or institutional records.

Major Genealogical Sources, Archives Division.

NAME INDEX: Extensive WPA project card file indexing names found in many (but not all) record series in the Archives prior to 1850.

LAND RECORDS: Bound volumes, microfilm and manuscripts document the sale of land to individuals from the federal government through the federal land offices in Indiana, 1804-1876. State land records record the sale of Michigan Road, Seminary, and Swamp lands.

INDIANA CIVIL WAR VOLUNTEERS: Card file may include the name of soldier, rank, company, regiment, period of original enlistment, place and date of enrollment, place and date of muster, age, physical description, nativity, occupation, date, place and manner of leaving the service. Information on promotions and wounds received may also be entered.

INDIANA LEGION (Civil War State Militia): Card file may include the name, company, periods of active duty and age. It is possible in somes cases to ascertain the county and town where the unit was organized.

CIVIL WAR SUBSTITUTES: Card file of Indiana citizens who hired substitutes. The name of the individual, the name of the substitute, and the unit to which the substitute was assigned are given.

VETERANS' GRAVES REGISTRATION FILE: Card file of veterans. Holdings include 51 of 92 counties. The cards generally give name, war in which served, unit, cemetery location, and some cards may give birth and death dates and next of kin.

VETERANS' ENROLLMENTS OF 1886, 1890 and 1894: Arranged by county. There are individual books for each township. The records list the veteran's name, his company and regiment, the state from which he served, and the number of children under 16. Information is given on wounds, medical problems, and current physical condition. (Duplicate copies of the enrollment were filed with the Clerk of Court in each county in Indiana).

INDIANA MILITIA INDEX 1872-1896: Card file includes name, rank, and unit.

INDIANA MEXICAN WAR VOLUNTEER INDEX 1846-1848: Card file includes name, rank, muster in and muster out dates for five Indiana volunteer regiments.

INDIANA BLACK HAWK WAR MILITIA INDEX May-July 1832: Card file includes name, rank, unit, term of enlistment and by whom enlisted.

FEDERAL CENSUS OF MANUFACTURERS 1820-1880: Microfilm of the decennial Census of Manufacturers arranged by county and township.

FEDERAL CENSUS OF AGRICULTURE 1850-1880: Microfilm of the decennial Census of Agriculture arranged by county and township.

GOLD STAR ROLL OF HONOR 1914-1918: Bound volumes arranged alphabetically by names of men and women who died during World War I. The manuscript was source material for the publication, *Gold Star Honor Roll 1914-1918*. Further details can be found in the February 1982 *Indiana History Bulletin*.

REGISTERS OF VISITORS TO THE NATIONAL ENCAMPMENT OF THE GRAND ARMY OF THE REPUBLIC AT INDIANAPOLIS—September 4-9, 1893: Thirty-three volumes, each devoted to an Indiana Civil War volunteer regiment or battery, gives veteran's name, company and regiment or battery, and usually his town and state of residence in 1893. See the June 1982 *Indiana History Bulletin*.

INDIANA SPANISH-AMERICAN WAR VOLUNTEERS: Microfilm of registration cards. Information given includes name, unit, age, physical description, birthplace, occupation, and muster in and muster out dates.

INDIANA PERIODICALS

Many of the genealogical and historical societies in Indiana distribute a publication of their organization. No attempt is made to list them in this volume. Some specific titles are included in the county bibliography. Genealogical queries also appear in several Indiana newspapers. Anita Milner's *Newspaper Indexes, A Location and Subject Guide for Researchers*, 1982 revision, will prove helpful.

Mary K. Meyer's *Directory of Genealogical Societies in the U.S.A. and Canada*, 3rd ed., 1983, lists addresses for county genealogical agencies. The American Association for State and Local History's *Historical Societies and Agencies in the United States and Canada*, 12th edition, 1982, gives addresses of county societies.

Listed below is a sampling of the numerous publications in the state.

The Hoosier Genealogist, Indiana Historical Society, 1961-

Genealogy, Indiana Historical Society, 1973-

Indiana History Bulletin, Indiana Historical Bureau, 1923-

Indiana Historical Society Publications, Indiana Historical Society, 1897-

Indiana Magazine of History, Indiana University, 1904-

Black History News and Notes, Indiana Historical Society, 1979-

Indiana Genealogical Informer, Malinda Newhard, Harlan, Indiana, 1979-1982.

Tri-State Trader, Mayhill Publications, 1968-
    (Index to genealogical queries, 1968-).

Sycamore Leaves, Wabash Valley Genealogical Society, 1971-

Hoosier Journal of Ancestry, 1969-

LAND RECORDS

Prior to 1800, the major land owned by individuals in Indiana was at Vincennes and in Clark's grant. Between 1779 and 1783, the Vincennes court granted land to every American immigrant who wanted land, usually 400 acres. A list of some of these persons receiving land appears in House Document 198, 23rd Congress. A list of militia donations of 100 acres at Vincennes in 1790 is contained in House Document 455, 25th Congress. According to Logan Esarey's *A History of Indiana*, there were five series of Vincennes land claims.

The *Vincennes Donation Lands* by Leonard Lux was printed in 1949 in volume 15 of the *Indiana Historical Society Publications*. The *American State Papers* also contain documents relating to the Vincennes district lands. The 1972 publication, *Grassroots of America*, is an alphabetical surname index to the eight volumes of public lands and the volume of claims.

The *George Rogers Clark Papers, 1771-1784*, appear in volumes 8 and 19 of the Virginia Series and volumes 3 and 4 of the *Collections of the Illinois Historical Library*. The Indiana State Library collection also includes the *Official Plat Book of Clark's Grant in Clark County, Indiana, 1789-1810*, by William Clark. Series J and K of the *Draper Manuscripts* contain George Rogers Clark papers. (See the Military Section for additional Clark notations).

In 1795 the first treaty with the Indians affecting the ceding of lands in Indiana was signed; this opened for settlement a strip of land in southeastern Indiana known as the "wedge" or "gore". After the land was surveyed, the Cincinnati Land Office was opened in 1801 for land sales.

In 1804, the Vincennes Land Office was established and opened in 1805. Only a few of these land office records remain. Margaret Waters compiled and published in 1948 and 9, the two volume set, *Indiana Land Entries*. Volume 1 pertains to the Cincinnati District and volume 2, to the Vincennes District. The former volume gives land descriptions for the period 1801-1840 in Dearborn, Fayette, Franklin, Jay, Ohio, Randolph, Switzerland, Union, and Wayne counties. Volume 2, 1807-1877, land in Daviess, Gibson, Knox, Lawrence, Martin, Monroe, and Pike. These compilations do not include all recordings in the districts. Volume 1 and volume 2, part 1, were reprinted in 1977.

Later treaties resulted in the opening of land offices in Jeffersonville (1807), Brookville (1819), Terre Haute (1820), Fort Wayne (1823), and LaPorte (1833).

Many of the entries from the Jeffersonville Office appear in a publication by Ball State University, *Original Returns, Federal Land Sales in Indiana*. There are two volumes with a surname index and includes land in Brown, Bartholomew, Decatur, Ripley, Franklin, and Jennings counties.

The Brookville Office was moved to Indianapolis in 1825. Ball State University abstracted from microfilm the *Original Federal Land Sales, Township 21 North Sold at Indianapolis* and *Original Federal Land Sales, Township 20, North*, sold at Indianapolis. The counties included are Clinton, Tipton, Madison, Delaware, Boone, Hamilton, and Randolph. The staff of the Genealogy Division indexed both compilations by surname.

The Terre Haute Office was moved to Crawfordsville prior to 1828. The LaPorte Office was moved to Winamac in 1839.

The State Library prepared a surname index to the film, *Records of General Land Offices Located in Indiana*, Acts of 1847, 1850, and 1852. The index was prepared from the first reel of the twelve reel set and relates only to Indiana. The index gives the land office, registration number, warrant number, act, and number of acres, and are principally military land warrants.

The Genealogy Division staff indexed *Letter From the Secretary of the Treasury, Transmitting Sundry Statements of the Commissioner of the General Land Office, of the Quantity of Land Sold Under the Provisions of the Act of the 24th April 1820*...(House Doc., 2nd Session, 16th Congress). It includes land offices at Vincennes, Jeffersonville, and several Ohio and Missouri district offices.

A vital resource to research in Indiana's formative years is *Indiana Boundaries, Territory, State, and County*, compiled by George Pence and Nellie C. Armstrong in 1933 and reprinted in 1967. Black and white maps accompany legal statute citations and boundary formations and changes. The 1933 edition appeared as volume 19 of the *Indiana Historical Collections*. In 1982, "A Special Sampling from Outline Maps of Indiana Boundaries" was reprinted by the Family History Section of the Indiana Historical Society.

Indiana acquired a section of land called the "New Purchase" from the Indians through the Treaty of St. Mary's in 1818. In 1820 this "new purchase" was divided by expanding the boundaries of Randolph, Franklin, and Jennings counties. The remaining land was organized into two counties named Delaware and Wabash. Confusion often arises because these two counties are not the current counties of Delaware and Wabash. The "new purchase" counties had no county seat nor governmental jurisdiction, but were governed concurrently by the surrounding counties. For Wabash, this meant Vigo, Owen, and Monroe counties and in 1822 by Parke and Putnam counties. Legal jurisdiction of Delaware of the "new purchase" was by Jackson, Jennings, Franklin, Ripley, Wayne, Randolph, and Fayette. In 1821 sole jurisdiction for one year was under Bartholomew county. In 1822 it was granted to Randolph where it remained until 1827, when the present Delaware county was formed.

Subsequent changes in the current Delaware county boundaries formed still another area with no county organization, but named the same as a present county. In 1831, legislation provided that all land remaining unorganized from the previous Delaware be known as Adams county. This county of Adams had no connection with the present Adams county formed in 1835 from Allen and Randolph.

Mrs. Immogene B. Brown abstracted information from the land records of Indiana as recorded in the district land offices and worked from the original land descriptions prepared by the surveyors, recorded by congressional townships, and transposed them to the civil county. This *Land Records of Indiana* is a series of five volumes and includes the civil counties of Madison, Delaware, Jackson, Brown, and Martin.

Clifford Neal Smith's *Federal Land Series,* volume 1, 1788-1810, volume 2, 1799-1835, and volume 3, 1810-1840, give some Vincennes and Jeffersonville land office records. Volume 4, part 1 relates to grants in the Virginia Military District of Ohio.

Most of the land in Indiana was bought and individual purchases are recorded by the county recorders in the specific county where the land was purchased. Many grantor and grantee records appear on microfilm in the Genealogy Division of the Indiana State Library. This bibliography will indicate the Indiana county records available in the State Library's Genealogy Division at the time of publication.

MILITARY AND PENSION RECORDS

The largest collection of war records in the genealogy section concerns the rosters of Revolutionary War soldiers. Some War of 1812 and Mexican War rosters are also included in the genealogical files. Service records of Indiana men in the Civil War and later wars are kept in the State Archives, Commission on Public Records.

Beard, Reed, *The Battle of Tippecanoe, Historical Sketches*....4th ed. 1911. 134pp. (Indexed by Genealogy Division). Reprinted 1977 of 1889 edition.

Beckwith, H. W., ed. "General George Rogers Clark's Conquest of the Illinois," *Collections of The Illinois State Historical Library.* Vol. 1, 1903.

Brumbaugh, Gaius M., *Revolutionary War Records,* Vol. 1, Virginia. Virginia Army and Navy Forces and Bounty Land Warrants for Virginia Military District of Ohio, and Virginia Military Scrip....1936. 707pp.

Cannon, Jouett T., "Index to Military Certificates, 1787, etc.," *The Register of The Kentucky State Historical Society.* 1924. (Majority of certificates given for service in Clark's and Logan's expeditions of 1786 and 1787).

A Census of Pensioners for Revolutionary or Military Services: With Their Names, Ages, and Places of Residence... Under the Act for Taking the Sixth Census [1840]. 1841. 195pp. (Indexed by states in Genealogy Division). Reprinted 1967. (Also Index of 1840 Pensioners compiled 1965 by Church of Jesus Christ of Latter Day Saints).

DAR, *Roster of Revolutionary Ancestors of the Indiana Daughters of the American Revolution.* 1976/77?. 2 vols.

———, *A Roster of the Revolutionary Ancestors of Forty Five DAR Chapters of Indiana and Kentucky.* n.d. 87pp.

Delinquent List of Militia in the 30th Regiment, Indiana Militia for 1831. 12pp.

English, William H., *Conquest of the Country Northwest of the River Ohio, 1778-1783 and Life of Gen. George Rogers Clark*....1896. 2 vols.

Funk, Orville L., *Revolutionary War Era in Indiana.* 1975. 37pp.

General Index to Compiled Military Service Records of Revolutionary War Soldiers. microfilm.

"George Rogers Clark's Illinois Regiment," *The Hoosier Genealogist,* volume 19, #2, June, 1979.

Harding, Margery H., *George Rogers Clark and His Men, Military Records, 1778-1784.* Ky. Hist. Soc. 244pp.

Holliday, Murray, "The Battle on the Mississinewa," *Indiana History Bulletin,* volume 45, no. 12, Dec. 1968.

"Illinois Regiment, A List of the Officers, Non-Commissioned Officers, and Privates of 'The Illinois Regiment'...," *Yearbook, Kentucky Society, Sons of the American Revolution.* 1896.

Index to War of 1812 Pension Applications Files. microfilm.

Indiana Revolutionary, 1812, and Indian Wars, Invalid Pensions. [12pp.].

Indiana Revolutionary War Soldiers, Survivors of Revolutionary War. Recopied by DAR, 1980. 15pp. (Report made to Senate, 1834, List of Pensioners under Acts of 1828 and 1832).

Indiana State Museum, George Rogers Clark Bicentennial Celebration, papers of the George Rogers Clark Bicentennial Celebration Descendants Committee, including correspondence, lineage charts, family histories, and other material submitted by descendants of George Rogers Clark's family and of men who served with Clark during the American Revolution, and genealogical material collected by the committee. 1978/79. manuscript.

Letter from the Secretary of War, Transmitting a Report of the Names, Rank, and Line, of Every Person Placed in the Pension List...1818. Repr. 1955. 672pp. (Index by Genealogy Division).

List of Pensioners on the Roll, January 1, 1883....1883. (47th Congress, 2nd Sess., Senate Ex. Doc. 84). 5 vols. (Indiana is in vol. 4). Reprinted 1970. (Genealogy Division indexed volume 4, Indiana).

Long, John T., "The Illinois Regiment", *Yearbook, Illinois Society, Sons of the American Revolution,* 1896.

McDermott, John F.,...*The French, the Indians, and George Rogers Clark in the Illinois Country.* 1977.

McGhee, Lucy K., *Indiana Revolutionary Soldiers, War of 1812 and Indian Wars Pension List.* [1955?]. v.p.

Morris, Mrs. Harvey, *Indiana Revolutionary Soldiers Buried in Indiana.* 1925. Recopied by DAR, 1980. n.p.

Muster-in Roll of Capt. John Wheeler, Company B. in the 20th Regiment (3rd Brigade) of Indiana Foot Volunteers Commanded by Colonel William L. Brown...July 22 at Lafayette...1978. 22pp.

National Genealogical Society, *Index of Revolutionary War Pension Applications in the National Archives.* Bicentennial Ed. (rev. & enl.). 1976. 658pp. (Special publication 40).

O'Byrne, Mrs. Roscoe C., *Roster of Soldiers and Patriots of the American Revolution Buried in Indiana.* 1938-1980. 3 vols. (Volume 1 reprinted 1968). (1974, 1975 indexes by Sarah G. Ticuson; 1975, 1976 indexes by Jane E. Darlington).

O'Byrne, Mrs. Roscoe C., *Revolutionary War Pension Abstracts of Indiana Soldiers.* 1935-1938. 7 vols.

Pay Rolls of Militia in the Battle of Tippecanoe, Photostats from National Archives, 1939. 34pp. (Index by Genealogy Division).

Perry, Oran, Adj. Gen., *Indiana in the Mexican War.* 1908. 496pp.

Photostatic Copies of Muster, Pay and Receipt Rolls of Indiana Territory Volunteers or Militia of the Period of the War of 1812, Deposited in the Office of the War Department of the U.S. Adjutant General's Office. 1926. 4 vols. (Index by Genealogy Division).

Pirtle, Capt. Alfred, *The Battle of Tippecanoe.* 1900. 158pp. (Filson Club Publication No. 15).

Report From the Secretary of War, in Obedience to Resolutions of the Senate of the 5th and 30th of June, 1834, and the 3rd of March, 1835, in Relation to the Pension Establishment of the United States. 1835. (Senate Doc. 514, 1st Sess., 23rd Congress). 3 vols. (Indexed by states in Genealogy Division. Vol. 3 contains Indiana). Reprinted 1968.

Report of the Adjutant General of the State of Indiana [W.H.H. Terrell] Containing Indiana in the War of the Rebellion, and Statistics and Documents, [1865-1869]. 8 vols. (Rosters of soldiers, 1861-1865; indexed in Archives).

Revolutionary War Pension and Bounty Land Warrant Application Files, Selected Records. microfilm.

Sanford, Wayne L., *"Bivouac of the Dead"*, (The Hoosier Dead at Andersonville). [1981?]. [184pp.].

Seineke, Kathrine W., *The George Rogers Clark Adventure in the Illinois.* 1981. 650 pp.

Turner, Ann, comp., *Guide to Indiana Civil War Manuscripts.* Indiana Civil War Centennial Commission. 1965. 402pp.

Waters, Margaret R., *Revolutionary Soldiers Buried in Indiana, 300 Names Not Listed in the Roster....* 1949. 154pp. (Also Supplement, 485 *Names...* 1954. 165pp.). Reprinted 1970.

Wolfe, Barbara E.S., *Index to Revolutionary Soldiers of Indiana and Other Patriots.* 1977. 130pp.

COURT AND VITAL STATISTICS RECORDS

Legislation effecting the recording of birth and death statistics in Indiana was instituted in the late 1800's. Beginning about 1882, original birth and death certificates are recorded with the county health officers. Births after 1907 and deaths after 1899 are also filed at the Indiana State Board of Health in Indianapolis.

A law regulating marriages was first adopted in 1788. Consequently marriages were usually kept from the date of formation of the county, with original certificates remaining in the custody of the county clerks. The first annual state wide index of marriages in Indiana occurred in 1958. This material is compiled by the State Board of Health in the *Indiana Marriage Index*. It indexes marriages by bride and groom, indicating the county of license, marriage, and date. Annual indexes from 1958 to 1965 are in book form and those from 1966 to 1981 are on microfilm at the Indiana State Library.

The Researchers of Indianapolis in 1981 compiled *Indiana Marriages Thru 1820: In the Counties of Washington, Jefferson, Clark, Scott, Jackson, Jennings, Switzerland, Ripley* in a 52 page booklet. Abstracts of many early marriages appear in the serial, *The Hoosier Genealogist*, and are reprinted in the three volumes of *Indiana Source Book*. A computerized index was published in 1983.

In the 1940's the Works Progress/Projects Administration indexed many of the births and deaths for the period 1882-1920, and marriages, primarily fom 1850 to 1920. About two thirds of the Indiana counties were included. The original reports were filed with the county welfare offices, and a copy deposited in the Indiana State Library. The 1940's also produced a WPA filming program whereby court records of some of the southern Indiana counties were microfilmed.

During the 1930-1940 decade a survey of extinct county records and their locations was made, producing the U.S. Historical Records Survey of Indiana's *Guide to Public Vital Statistics Records in Indiana* and the *Inventory of the County Archives of Indiana*. The former cites the laws regarding vital statistics, indicates dates of records available at the county offices, and is arranged by county. The latter is likewise arranged by county and lists which original county records were filed in the specific county office. Unfortunately, only 22 of the surveys were published, the others remain in manuscript format in the State Archives, except for Hancock and Wayne which were not surveyed. No individual names are given, and since the 1940's many changes have occurred in the location and existence of the original documents.

To supplement the WPA recording of vital and court records and those copied by persons and groups, the Indiana State Library microfilmed many of these court records in the 1950's and 1960's. This was done with the financial assistance of the Eugene Haslet Memorial Library of the Indianapolis-Marion County Public Library.

Currently, the State Library receives positive microfilm copies of Indiana county records via a cooperative program with the Commission on Public Records, Indiana Historical Bureau, Indiana Historical Society, and the Genealogical Society of Utah. This program is acronymized CRIMP (County Records of Indiana Microfilm Project).

Vera Mae Moudy has compiled three useful volumes: *Directory, Marriage Record Information in Genealogy Dept...Indiana State Library*, (50pp.); *Directory, Land Record Information in Genealogy Dept...*, (15pp.); and *Directory, Wills and Estates Information in Genealogy Dept...*,(18pp.) All were published in the early 1980's.

In 1981, the Indiana Historical Society published the 172 pages, *An Index to Indiana Naturalization Records Found in Various Order Books of the Ninety-Two Local Courts Prior to 1907*.

The July 1974 issue of *Genealogy*, edited by Willard Heiss, devotes most of the issue to "Courthouse Research in Indiana". Following a general historical description are the various court record descriptions and the county official having jurisdiction of the record. Similar county court record data is relayed by John Newman, State Archivist, in "Using County Records in Writing Your Community's History", *Local History Today, 1980*. The July 1981 issue of *Genealogy* has an excellent article by John Newman "Managing Your Research in Indiana Court Records".

The April 1975 issue of *Genealogy* has a list of Indiana courthouse fires.

CENSUSES

Indiana made early provision for a state census, but no general state-sponsored censuses listing names was made. A few portions of a particular township of a county have been discovered in the county treasurers' offices.

Territorial censuses for the most part list only total statistics. The first census for the Indiana Territory was 1800. Few of the early censuses are known to exist.

In 1980, the Indiana Historical Society published *Census of Indiana Territory For 1807*, compiled by Rebah Fraustein. In 1974 a copy of the census for Exeter and Harrison townships of Harrison county for 1810 were discovered at Corydon. This schedule was reproduced in *The Hoosier Genealogist* in June 1976.

The first federal population schedule for Indiana which does include all names is the 1820. It was reproduced in 1966 and reprinted in 1975 by the Indiana Historical Society. Compiled by Willard Heiss, it is titled *1820 Federal Census for Indiana*. Mrs. C.E. Cox of Ellensburg, Washington, published a compilation of the 1820 census and Accelerated Indexing Systems of Utah also printed the 1820 and 1830 census indexes for Indiana. When using the 1820 schedules, note that Daviess county is missing and Delaware and Wabash were still the "new purchase" counties.

Index, 1830 Federal Population Census for Indiana was published in 1981 by the Indiana Historical Society.

Index, 1840 Federal Population Census, Indiana was published in 1975. Compiled by the Indiana State Library and published by the Indiana Historical Society, microfiche copies are available. Several county indexes from the filmed 1840 census schedules were prepared by the staff of the Genealogy Division of the State Library and are listed in the county bibliographies.

The 1850 census, indexed by head of household by the Indiana State Library, is a 21 volume xerox copy housed in the Genealogy Division. Accelerated Indexing System's publication of the Indiana 1850 census was printed in 1976. Many county 1850 indexes have been prepared by local county historical and genealogical societies, but only a few are filed in the Indiana State Library and therefore are not listed in this bibliography.

No complete 1860 census index has been compiled. Again several local reports have been made, and the State Library indexed the 1860 census for blacks, Indians, and Chinese. In xerox form, the *Report of Blacks and Mulattos as Enumerated in the 1860 Federal Population Census of Indiana*, was compiled by Mrs. Ruth M. Slevin. It consists of 212 pages and was completed in 1981. Mrs. Slevin also gathered material for the seven pages of names for the *Index to Indians in 1860 Federal Population Census of Indiana*.

No 1870 index is known, except for scattered county reports.

In addition to the 1880 Soundex index, a partial index by Mrs. Ruth M. Slevin is: *Index to Blacks, Indians, Chinese, Mulattoes in Indiana 1880 Census*. It is 676 pages and in xerox format at the State Library.

Indiana's 1900 federal population census is indexed by soundex. The 1910 enumeration is not.

Copies of all federal population censuses for Indiana are available for research in the Indiana State Library.

The 1816 Indiana Constitution made provision for an enumeration of all white male inhabitants above the age of 21, the first in 1820 and then to be taken every five years after, for apportionment. These were known as "Enumeration of Persons over 21 Years for the Year 1820". The records which have survived are for Crawford, Gibson, Jackson, Jennings, Knox, Monroe, Orange, Perry, Posey, Ripley, Vanderburgh, Washington, and Wayne counties. The records are filed in the State Archives.

The 1850 Constitution changed the schedule to every six years. The township assessors were responsible for the enumerations and to submit a copy to the Auditor of the State, who in turn was to abstract and publish the lists in two Indianapolis newspapers. None of the Auditor's records were ever found. The 1865 Act indicated that the township trustee was to also obtain the specific age of every male over 21; and the 1877 Act added negroes to the list. The various laws required reports to be filed with the county auditors. If any schedules still exist, they should be at the local courthouses. The Indiana State Archives has very few of these reports.

A few "Veterans Enrollments for 1886, 1890, and 1894" are housed in the State Archives.

MORTALITY SCHEDULES

Mortality schedules were taken by the federal marshals during the census years of 1850, 1860, 1870, and 1880. They were taken in the summer months and list persons who died prior to May 31st during the census year—i.e., June 1, 1849-May 31, 1850. Each entry lists the name, sex, color, age, free or slave, married or widowed, place of birth, month in which person died, occupation, cause of death, number of days ill. For the 1880 schedule, the birthplaces of the parents are also shown.

A complete surname index for all schedules was made by the Indiana State Library. This *Index to Indiana Mortality Schedules of Indiana, 1850, 1860, 1870, 1880*, consists of eight volumes. A microfilm copy of the schedules and the index is in the Genealogy Division.

Lowell M. Volkel transcribed and indexed in 1971, the 1850 mortality information in a three volume set: *1850 Indiana Mortality Schedule*.

CEMETERY RECORDS

Inscriptions from many of the Indiana cemeteries are filed in the Indiana State Library. Records are far from complete. There is no central recording of inscriptions and no state agency responsible for the gathering of this data. Individual persons as well as members of patriotic, hereditary, genealogical, and historical societies have provided much of the tombstone data that is on file. Cemetery inscriptions available in the Genealogy Division are listed in the county bibliography.

The Genealogy Division staff compiled an "Indiana Cemetery Locator File." It is an alphabetical, by name of cemetery, file showing the location of the cemetery and the book number in the Division where the inscriptions are listed.

Virgil A. Jewell's *Cemeteries of Indiana, A Checklist*, prepared in 1970, and the *1961 Cemetery Directory* by the Cemetery Association of Indiana, although not complete, provide useful listings. The Genealogy Division collection also houses the 5th and 6th editions of the *International Cemetery Directory*. The 6th edition was printed in 1974.

The "Veterans Grave Registration File," a project sponsored by the American Legion and the Indiana Adjutant General's Office in the 1940's appears on thirteen reels of microfilm. The original card file is in the State Archives. The information contained in this file is in varying degrees of completeness and may include the name, war in which served, birth and death dates, next of kin, and cemetery where buried. This includes soldiers who fought in wars prior to and including World War I and who are buried in Indiana. Counties for which records are available are: Adams, Blackford, Brown, Cass, Clark, Clay, Crawford, Daviess, DeKalb, Delaware, Elkhart, Floyd, Gibson, Grant, Greene, Harrison, Howard, Huntington, Jasper, Jay, Johnson, Knox, Kosciusko, LaGrange, Lake, LaPorte, Lawrence, Madison, Marion, Marshall, Martin, Miami, Monroe, Montgomery, Morgan, Orange, Owen, Parke, Pike, Posey, Pulaski, St. Joseph, Spencer, Starke, Steuben, Sullivan, Tipton, Vanderburgh, Vermillion, Vigo, and Washington.

CHURCH RECORDS

Obituaries of Methodist, Baptist, and Presbyterian ministers appear in many church minutes and conference reports, some of which are indexed in a card file in the State Library's Indiana Division.

The July 1975 issue of *Genealogy* lists some of these church record collections housed in the Indiana Division.

A two volume set of abstracted obituaries and marriages was prepared by Mabel Millikan and Margaret Waters from the Methodist, *Western Christian Advocate*.

William W. Sweet's *Circuit-Rider Days in Indiana* is helpful in locating data on early Methodist ministers.

Willard Heiss' *A List of All the Friends Meetings That Exist or Ever Have Existed in Indiana, 1807-1955*, indicates the Quaker meeting by county, date of formation, parent meeting, etc.

Heiss also abstracted the six volumes of *Abstracts of the Records of the Society of Friends in Indiana*, published by the Indiana Historical Society. It is identified as volume 7 of Hinshaw's *Encyclopedia of American Quaker Genealogy*. An index was printed in 1977. Microfiche copies are available. Robert S. Boone in 1978 compiled a 162 page *Additions, Corrections and Comments: Abstracts of the Records of the Society of Friends in Indiana, Parts One-Six*.

A few other items include: Society of Friends, *Some Marriage and Birth Records of Indiana Yearly Meetings* (Duck Creek, Spiceland, Milford, New Garden, Whitewater Monthly Meeting); the *Indiana Conference of the Methodist Church*, 1912-1930, 1939-1968, of marriages and funerals conducted by Rev. Harrison G. Ramsey; *A Preliminary Guide to Church Records Repositories*, 1969, 108 pages, arranged by denomination, state and repository; and the microfilm, *Quaker Records, as Filmed From Cards Filed at Swarthmore College, Swarthmore, Pennsylvania*, by Hinshaw.

The following bibliography on church history in the Indiana Division was compiled by Jean Singleton Weimer, who was supervisor of the Division at the time of compilation, 1982. It is provided here with Indiana Division book numbers as a guide to those wishing to pursue additional church history information.

BAPTIST

Ball, Timothy Horton, *The Lake of the Red Cedars; or Will it Live: Thirty years in Lake...state of Indiana*. Crown Point, Indiana, 1880. 357 p. I 286 B187L.

Bethel Association, *History of the first century of the Bethel Baptist Association of Indiana*. n.p. 1937. IP 286 #60.

Dobbs, C.E.W., *The first half century of the Mission Baptist Association...Indianapolis*. The Indiana Baptist, 1883. 43 p. IP 286 #43.

Haskins, Herman Hartwell, *The activities of the Baptists in the "Northwest Territory", 1815-1850*. 1918. 58 p. (Harvard Univ. Thesis). I 286 H 35la.

Howe, Joseph Edwin, *Hist. of the Perry Co. Baptist Assoc*. Cannelton, Ind. [1922] 36 p. I 286 H856h.

Kimbrough, Bradley Thomas, *Jubilee in '53. The sesquicentennial hist. of the Long Run Assoc. of Baptists*. Louisville, Ky., Long Run Assoc..., 1953 [125 p.] I 286 K 49j.

Laslie, Theophilus Alexander Hall, *Laslie's history of the General Baptists*. Popular Bluff Mo., General Baptist publishing house, 1938. 421 p. I 286 L 345L.

Montgomery, David B., *General Baptist history*. Evansville, Courier Co., 1882. 408 p. I 286 M 787g.

Oliphant, P.T., *Brief hist. of the White River Assoc. of Primitive Baptists covering a period of 107 years [1821-1928]*. Indianapolis, The Speedway Press, 1928 20 p. IP 286 #86.

Stewart, I.D., *The history of the Freewill Baptists, for half a century with an introductory chapter*. Dover, Freewill Baptist Printing Establishment, William Burr, printer, 1862. 1 vol. I 286 S 849L.

Stott, William Taylor, *Indiana Baptist history, 1798-1908*. [Franklin, Ind., 1908] 381 p. I 286 S 888.

Tibbets, Joshua C., *History of the Coffee Creek Baptist Association (Southern Indiana): an account of present churches*. Cincinnati, 1883. I 286 T 552.

———, *History of the Coffee Creek Baptist Association...to 1882. Rev....to 1930*. [Seymour, Ind., Seymour Daily Tribune printers, 1930]. 191 p. I 286 T 552.

Weatherbolt, Lavina Bryant, *History of the Perry County Association of Baptists [1958]* 12 p. IP 286 #114.

Catholic

Alerding, Herman Joseph, *Diocese of Fort Wayne, 1857-September 22, 1907; a book of historical reference 1669-1907*. Fort Wayne, 1907. 541 p. I 282 A 369d.

———, *A history of the Catholic Church in the diocese of Vincennes*. Carlon & Hollenbeck, 1883. 636 p. I 282 V 767.

Blanchard, Charles, ed., *History of the Catholic Church in Indiana*. Edited and compiled by Col. Charles Blanchard. Logansport, Ind., A.W. Bowen & Co., 1898. 2 vols. I 282 B639.

Carr, Michael W., *A history of catholicity and Catholic institutions in Indianapolis*. Carlon & Hollenbeck, 1887. 90 p. IP 282 #52.

———, *History of catholicity in New Albany and Jeffersonville, and Floyd and Clark Counties, Indiana*. Indianapolis, Carlon & Hollenbeck, 1890. 74 p. IP 282 #51.

———, *A history of catholicity in Richmond and Wayne County, Indiana*...Indianapolis, Carlon & Hollenbeck, 1889. 74 p. IP 282 #5.

Chancery Office, *Military personnel from the Diocese of Indianapolis, compiled at the Chancery Office*. Indianapolis, Chancery Office, 1944. 124 p. I 282 C 363m.

Indiana Catholic and Record, *The Diocese of Indianapolis, 100 years, the Indiana Catholic and Record, 25 years*. Indianapolis, The Indiana Catholic Press, 1935. 116 p. IF 282 I 385c.

McAvoy, Thomas Timothy, *The Catholic Church in Indiana 1789-1834*. New York, Columbia University Press, 1940. 226 p. I 282 M 116c.

———, *The history of the Catholic Church in the South Bend area*. South Bend, Aquinas Library and Book Shop, 1953. 25 p. IP 282 #60.

McNamara, William, *The Catholic Church in the northern Indiana frontier 1789-1844*. Washington, D.C., Catholic University of America, 1931. 84 p. I 282 M 169c.

Pagani, Humbert P., *200 years of Catholicism in Indiana: an authentic history of the Diocese of Indianapolis, formerly the Diocese of Vincennes*. Indianapolis, 1934. 34 p. IP 282 #23.

Schroeder, Sister Mary Carol, *The Catholic Church in the Diocese of Vincennes, 1847-1877*. Washington, D.C. The Catholic University of America Press, 1946. 227 p. I 282 S 381e.

Wilson, George Robert, *"Pioneers of the Catholic faith in Dubois County" to which are added personal reminiscences of the writer*. 1930. 61 p. I 922 W 748p.

Church of God

Cole, Mary, *Trials and triumphs of faith*. Anderson, Indiana. Gospel Trumpet Co., 1914. 300 p. I 922 C 689t.

Smith, Frederick George, *Brief sketch of the origin, growth, and distinctive doctrine of the Church of God reformation movement*. Anderson, Ind., Gospel Trumpet Co., 1926. 46 p. IP 289.9 #12.

Church of the Brethren

Church of the Brethren, *History of the Church of the Brethren in Indiana by historical committees of the districts*. Winona Lake, Ind., Light and Life Press, 1952. 508 p. I 289.9 H 673.

Holsinger, Henry R., *Holsinger's history of the Tunkers and the Brethren Church, 1901*. Reprinted 1962 L.W. Shultz, North Manchester, Ind. I 289.9 H 756h.

Opperman, Owen, *A brief sketch of the Brethren, generally known as "Dunkards" of northern Indiana*. Goshen, Ind., News Printing Co., 1897. 45 p. IP 289.9 #15.

Winger, Otho, *History of the Church of the Brethren in Indiana*. Brethren publishing house, 1917. 479 p. I 289.9 W 769hi.

Congregational

Hyde, Nathaniel Alden, *Congregationalism in Indiana*. Indianapolis, 1895. 70 p. IP 285.8 #5.

Whitehead, Herbert L., *History of Indiana Congregationalism*. 1919. 18 p. IP 285.8 #10.

Disciples of Christ

Book, William Henry, ed., *Indiana pulpit.* Standard Publishing Co., 1912. 343 p. I 252 B 724.

Cauble, Commodore Wesley, *Disciples of Christ in Indiana; achievements of a century.* Indianapolis, Meigs Publishing Co., [c 1930] 305 p. I 286.6 C 371d.

Disciples of Christ. Eel River Conference, *History...from its organization to the present time—August 15, 1902... together with biographical sketches of ministers and laymen.* Huntington, Ind., News Publishing Co., 1902. 160 p. I 286.6 D 611h.

Lollis, Lorraine, *The shape of Adam's Rib, a lively history of women's work in the Christian Church.* St. Louis, Mo., Bethany Press [c 1970] 219 p. I 286.6 L 837s.

McAllister, Lester Grover, *Journey in faith; a history of the Christian Church (Disciples of Christ).* St. Louis, Mo., Bethany Press [c 1975] 505 p. I 286.6 M 114j.

Shaw, Henry K., *Hoosier Disciples: a comprehensive history of the Christian Churches (Disciples of Christ) in Indiana.* St. Louis, Bethany Press for the Association of the Christian Churches in Indiana, 1966. 535 p. I 286.6 S 534h.

Evangelical

Baumgartner, Samuel Henry, *Indiana Conference of the Evangelical Association.* Cleveland, Ohio, Indiana Conference, 1915-1924. 2 vols. I 289.9 B 347i.

Schorg, Albert, *Geschichte der Deutschen Evangelischen Synode von Nord-Amerika.* St. Charles, Mo., Deutschen Evangelischen Synode von Nord-Amerika, 1889. 137 p. I 289.9 S 374g.

Evangelical United Brethren Church. See also United Brethren in Christ, Methodist

Wiseman, James C., *History of the United Brethren Churches of Harrison County, Indiana* [Fairview, Indiana?] 1972. 23 p. IP 289.95 #18.

Freewill Baptist

Stewart, I.D., *The history of the Freewill Baptists, for half a century.* Dover, Freewill Baptist Printing Establishment, William Burr, printer, 1862. 1 vol. I 286 S 849h.

Society of Friends

Edgerton, Walter, *A history of the separation in Indiana Yearly Meeting of Friends; which took place in the winter of 1842 and 1843.* Cincinnati, A. Pugh, printer, 1856. 352 p. I 289.6 E 23h.

Elliott, Errol Thomas, *Quakers on the American frontier; a history of western migrations.* Richmond, Indiana, Friends United Press [c 1969] 434 p. I 289.6 E 46q.

Friends, Society of Western Yearly Meeting, *Semi-centennial anniversary.* Plainfield, 1908. I 289.6 W 527a.

Friends, Society of Whitewater Monthly Meeting, *History of Whitewater Monthly Meeting of Friends.* 1899. 4 p. IP 289.6 #69.

Furnas, Seth E., *A history of Indiana Yearly Meeting by Seth E. Furnas, Sr.* Indiana Yearly Meeting, Religious Society of Friends general conference, 1968. 110 p. I 289.6 F 987h.

Hadley, Evan, *Historical sketch of the settlement of Friends and the establishment of meetings in central Indiana, read at a reunion meeting held at White Lick meeting house, Morgan County, Indiana...1890.* Mooresville, 1890. 8 p. IP 289.6 #25.

Heiss, Willard Calvin, *A brief history of Western Yearly Meeting of Conservative Friends and the separation of 1877.* Indianapolis, John Woolman Press, 1963. 37 p. IP 289.6 #48.

———, *A list of all the Friends meetings that exist or ever have existed in Indiana, 1807-1955.* Indianapolis, 1959. 64 p. I 289.6 H 473.

Parker, Ida, *The Hicksite separation.* Earlham College, June 12, 1907. 24 p. IP 289.6 #50.

Pluris, Gerene Osborn, *Booklet about Friends in Orange County, Indiana. Helpful truth about the Friends or Quakers.* [Paoli, Ind., Stout's Print Shop, 1958] 69p. IP 289.6 #102.

Ratcliff, Richard Pickering, *Our special heritage; the sesquicentennial publication of Indiana Yearly Meeting of Friends.* New Castle, Ind., Community Printing Company, 1970. 165 p. I 289.6 R 233o.

Trueblood, David Elton, *The people called Quakers.* New York, Harper & Row [1966] 298 p. I 289.6 T 866p.

LUTHERAN

Defenderfer, C. Robert, *Lutheranism at the crossroads of America.* [History of Indiana synod.] 1948. 67 p. I 284.1 D 313L.

Evangelical Lutheran Synod of Northern Indiana, *Our church, a history of the Synod of northern Indiana of the Evangelical Lutheran Church.* Edited by William L. Tedrow. Ann Arbor, Michigan, Register Pub. Co., 1894. 295 p. I 284.1 E 92o.

Graebner, Alan, *Uncertain saints; the laity in the Lutheran church—Missouri Synod 1900-1970.* Westport, Conn., Greenwood Press [c 1975] 284 p. I 284.1 G 734u.

Rehmer, R.F., *Lutherans in pioneer Indiana.* Lafayette, Ind., Commercial Printing Corp., 1972. 23 p. IP 284.1 #69 1972.

Reve, J.L., *Kurzgesasste geschichte der Lutheritchen Kirche Amerikas von Dr. J.L. Reve...* 2d ed. Burlington, Iowa, German Literary Board, 1915. 391 p. I 284.1 R 449k.

Schulze, Andrew, *Race against time; a history of race relations in the Lutheran Church—Missouri Synod from the perspective of the author's involvement 1920-1970.* Valparaiso, Ind., The Lutheran Human Relations Association of America [c 1972] 153 p. I 284.1 S 391r.

Sheatsley, Clarence Valentine, *History of the Evangelical Lutheran joint synod of Ohio and other states from the earliest beginnings to 1919.* Columbus, Ohio, Lutheran book concern, 1919. 312 p. I 284.1 S 539.

Wagner, Martin L., *Chicago synod and its antecedents.* Wartburg Pub. House Press, 1909. 271 p. I 284.1 W 134c.

MENNONITE

Horsch, John, *The Mennonites, their history, faith and practice.* Elkhart, Indiana, Mennonite Pub. Co., 1893. 40 p. IP 289.7 #1.

Wenger, John Christian, *Glimpses of Mennonite history.* Scottdale, Pa., Mennonite Publishing House, 1940. 126 p. I 289.7 W 474 g.

———, *The Mennonites in Indiana and Michigan.* Scottdale, Pa., Herald Press [1961] 470 p. I 289.7 W 474m.

Yoder, Raymond Mark, *Indiana literaries.* Scottdale, Pa., Mennonite Pub. House [1936?] 184 p. I 289.7 Y 54i.

METHODIST, Methodist Episcopal, Methodist Protestant

Detzler, Jack J., *The history of the Northwest Indiana Conference of the Methodist Church 1852-1951.* Nashville, Tenn., Parthenon Press, [c 1953] 200 p. I 287.6 D 484h.

Heller, Herbert Lynn, *Indiana Conference of the Methodist Church, 1832-1956.* [Greencastle] Historical Society of the Indiana Conference [1956] 452 p. I 287.6 H 474i.

Herrick, Horace Nelson, *History of the North Indiana Conference of the Methodist Episcopal Church.* Indianapolis, W.K. Stewart, 1917-[1957] 2v. I 287.6 H 566h.

Rottingham, Elizabeth Kristine, *Methodism and the frontier; Indiana proving ground.* New York, Columbia University Press, 1941. 231 p. I 287 N 919m.

Beggs, Stephen R., *Pages from the early history of the West and Northwest with especial reference to the history of Methodism.* Cincinnati; Methodist Book Concern, 1868. 325 p. I 287.6 B 416p. M.E.B.

Finley, James Bradley, *Sketches of Western Methodism: biographical, historical and miscellaneous. Illustrative of pioneer life.* Cincinnati, Methodist Book Concern, 1854. 551 p. I 287.6 F 513 s.

Golder, Christian, *Geschichte der zentral deutschen Konferenz einschliesslich der Anfangsgeschichte des deutschen Methodismus. Herausgegeben nach Anordnung der Konferenz von C. Golder, John H. Horst, J.G. Schall....* Cincinnati, O., Jennings & Graham [1907?] 447 p. I 287.6 G 618g.

[Goodwin, Thomas A.], *The evolution of American Methodism or, The Methodist Episcopal Church, as it was, as it is, and as it is to be.* [Indianapolis, 1898?] 32 p. IP 287.6 #109.

Holliday, Fernandez C., *Indiana Methodism, being an account of the introduction, progress, and present position of Methodism in the state.* Cincinnati, Hitchcock and Walden, 1873. 360 p. I 287.6 H 739.

Smith, John C., *Reminiscences of early Methodism in Indiana.* Indianapolis, J.M. Olcott, 1879. 322 p. I 287.6 S 648.

Smith, John Lewis, *Indiana Methodism, a series of sketches and incidents, grave and humorous, concerning preachers and people of the West.* Valparaiso, Ind., 1892. 482 p. I 287.6 S 652i.

Sweet, William Warren, *Circuit-rider days in Indiana.* Indpls., W.K. Stewart Co., 1916. 344 p. I 287.6 S 974c.

Coous, John C., *A brief history of the Methodist Protestant Church in Indiana.* 1939. 73 p. I 287.7 C 775b.

Moravian

Couillard, Vernon Williams, *The early Moravian settlement in Bartholomew County, Indiana.* [Indianapolis] Butler University, 1939. 61 p. I 284.6 C 854e.

Gipson, Lawrence Henry, *The Moravian Indian Mission on White River; diaries and letters, May 5, 1799 to Nov. 12, 1806, translated from the German.* Indianapolis, Indiana Historical Bureau, 1938. 674 p. I 284.6 G 514 m.

Church of the New Jerusalem

Field, G., *Memoirs, incidents and reminiscences of the early history of the New Church in Michigan, Indiana, Illinois, and adjacent states; and Canada.* Toronto, Carswell, 1879. 368 p. I 289.4 F 453m.

Presbyterian

Allen, William T., *The Presbytery of Indianapolis.* 1951. 97 p. I 285 A 432p.

Allison, George William, *Forest, fort, and faith. Historical sketches of the Presbytery of Fort Wayne, organized January 1, 1845.* Issued centennial year, 1945. 55 p. IP 285 #113.

———, *History of Fort Wayne Presbytery 1891-1945, prepared in connection with its centennial.* Fort Wayne, 1945. 109 p. I 285 A 439.

Darby, W.J., *Cumberland Presbyterianism in southern Indiana being a history of Indiana Presbytery and an account of the proceedings of its fiftieth anniversary held at Princeton, Indiana, April 13-18, 1876.* 1876. 124 p. I 977.2 I 385 v. 4'2.

Dickey, John M., *Brief history of the Presbyterian Church in the state of Indiana.* Madison, 1828. 24 p. IP 285 #33.

Edson, Hanford Abram, *Contributions to the early history of the Presbyterian Church in Indiana, together with biographical notices of pioneer ministers.* Cincinnati, Winona Publishing Co., 1898. 281 p. I 285 E 24.

Glasgaw, William Melancthon, *History of the Reformed Presbyterian Church in America: with sketches of all her ministry, congregations, missions, institutions, publications, etc.* Baltimore, Hill & Hawey, 1888. 788 p. I 285.5 G 548h.

Gray, Beulah Brazelton, *The saga of three churches; a history of Presbyterianism in Petersburg, 1821-1953.* [Petersburg, Indiana, 1953?] 177 p. I 285 G 788s.

Presbyterian Church. Presbytery of Indianapolis, *The Presbytery of Indianapolis [a history]* [Indianapolis] 1951. 97 p. IP 285 #167.

Presbyterian Church. Presbytery of Logansport, *Celebration of the fiftieth anniversary of the Presbytery of Logansport, 1870-1920.* 1920. 32 p. IP 285 #98.

Rudolph, L.C., *Hoosier Zion; the Presbyterians in early Indiana.* New Haven, Yale University Press, 1963. 218 p. I 285 R 917h.

Stewart, D., *Historical discourse of Whitewater Presbytery.* Indianapolis, Baker, Schmidlap and Co., 1876. 32 p. I 977.2 I 385 v.4#10.

Whallon, Edward Payson, *History of the Presbytery of Vincennes.* Published by the Presbytery. Indianapolis, W.A. Patton, 1888. 52 p. IP 285 #36.

Protestant Episcopal

Center, Robert J., *Our heritage; a history of the first seventy-five years of the Diocese of Northern Indiana.* [South Bend, Ind., Petersen Printing Corporation, 1973] 96 p. I 283 C 397o.

UNITED BRETHREN IN CHRIST

Condo, Adam Byron, *History of the Indiana Conference of the United Brethren in Christ, with a brief review of the events leading up to the organization of the conference in 1830.* 1926. 422 p. I 289.95 c 746h.

Wilmore, Augustus Cleland, *History of the White River Conference of the Church of the United Brethren in Christ, containing an account of the antecedent annual conferences.* Dayton, O., United Brethren Publishing House, 1925. 504 p. I 289.95 W 744h.

GENERAL INDIANA SOURCES

The majority of these remaining materials relating to the State of Indiana are found in the Indiana Division of the Indiana State Library and the Indiana Historical Society Library. An asterisk indicates in Genealogy Division.

The State Library's collection includes county and town histories, plat books, atlases, maps, gazetteers, directories, and church histories. A biographical card file of prominent Indianans and a newspaper index beginning in 1898 of noteworthy persons, firms, and events, give valuable assistance in tracing a family lineage. An index of Indiana post offices, 1800-1920, lists when and where (county) the post office was established, changed, or discontinued, and the name of the first postmaster.

Files of Indiana newspapers are housed in the Newspaper Section of the Indiana State Library. Individual newspapers are not listed in this bibliography.

Histories of Indiana patriotic, hereditary, genealogical, or county historical societies are not noted.

The following resources are listed only as guides and do not provide a comprehensive inventory on any one subject.

Alvord, Clarence W., ed., "Kaskaskia Records, 1778-1790," *Collections of the Illinois State Historical Library*, vol. 5, Virginia Series, vol 2. 1909. 681pp.*

American State Papers, Documents, Legislative and Executive of the Congress of the United States, in Relation to the Public Lands...[1789-1837]. 8 vols.

Baker, J. David, *The Postal History of Indiana*. 1976. 2 vols. (Volume 2 lists post offices and postmasters, 1800-1890).

Barnhart, John D. and Carmony, Donald F., *Indiana, From Frontier to Industrial Commonwealth*. 1954, 1979. 4 vols.

A Biographical Directory of the Indiana General Assembly, vol. 1, 1816-1899. 1980. 610pp.*

A Biographical History of Eminent and Self-Made Men of the State of Indiana...1880. 2 vols.

Buley, R. Carlyle, *The Old Northwest: Pioneer Period, 1815-1840*. 1950. 2 vols.

Carter, Clarence E., *The Territorial Papers of the United States*. (Vols. 2-3, Territory Northwest of the River Ohio, 1787-1803; vol. 7, Territory of Indiana, 1800-1810; vol. 8, Territory of Indiana, 1810-1816).

Coombs, Leonard A., *American Indian Genealogical Research in the Indiana State Library: A Selected Bibliography*. [1980]. 23pp.*

Cox, Evelyn, *Ancestree Climbing in the Midwest: Illinois, Indiana, Iowa, Kansas, Missouri, and Nebraska*. 1977. 138pp.*

DAR, Family Bible Records. n.p.*

————, *Bible and Family Records of Families in Indiana*. Comp. by Janet C. Cowen, 1972. 217pp.*

————, *Bible and Family Records of Jasper, Clark, Lake, Posey, Cass, Crawford, Randolph, Dubois, Henry, DeKalb, Montgomery, Jennings, Steuben, and Morgan Counties, Indiana*. 1976. 241pp.*

————, *Bible and Family Records, Indiana State Book, 1977; Allen, Clay, Crawford, Dearborn, Dubois, Fayette, Jasper, Lake, Marion, Montgomery, Morgan, Perry, Posey, Putnam, Tippecanoe, Steuben, Washington, and Wayne Counties*...1977. 179pp.*

Dunn, Jacob P., *Indiana and Indianans*. 1919. 5 vols. [Vol. 3-5, biographical].

————, *Memorial and Genealogical Record of Representative Citizens of Indiana*. 1912. 778pp.

Evans, Madison, *Biographical Sketches of the Pioneer Preachers of Indiana*. [1864]. 422pp.

"Governors' Messages and Letters," *Indiana Historical Collections*, volumes 7, 9, 12, 34, 38, 43, 44. 1922-. (Series covers administrations of William Henry Harrison, Thomas Posey, Jonathan Jennings, Ratliff Boon, William Hendricks, James Brown Ray, Noah Noble, David Wallace, and Samuel Bigger).

History of Indiana. (Vol. 1, Indiana to 1816, The Colonial Period. By John D. Barnhart and Dorothy Riker. 1971. Vol. III, Indiana in the Civil War Era, 1850-1880. By Emma Lou Thornbrough. 1965. Repr. 1977. Vol. IV, Indiana in Transition; 1880-1920. By Clifton J. Phillips. 1968. Vol. V, Indiana Through Tradition and Change, 1920-1945. By James H. Madison. 1982).

Hixson, W.W. and Co. [*Plat Books of Indiana Counties*]. [1920?]. 6 vols.

Illustrated Historical Atlas of the State of Indiana. 1876. 462pp. (Gives maps of counties showing townships as of 1876; also plans of some cities and towns). Repr.: *Maps of Indiana Counties in 1876.* Indiana Historical Society. 1968, 1979.*

Index to Poll Books of Elections [1809, 1812]. Typed by Indiana State Library from original poll lists housed in William H. English Collection.*

Indiana Biography Series. Clippings from Indiana newspapers, 1922—. 91 vols. (Indexed in Indiana Division; still in process).

Indiana Source Book. Ed. by Heiss and Riker. 3 vols. (Genealogical material reprinted from *The Hoosier Genealogist,* 1961-1966; 1967-1972; 1973-1978).*

Internal Revenue Assessment Lists of Indiana, 1862-1866. microfilm*

Jarboe, Betty M., *Obituaries, A Guide to Sources.* 1982. 370pp.*

Kemper, G.W.W., *A Medical History of the State of Indiana.* 1911. 393pp.

Knollenberg, Bernhard, "Pioneer Sketches of the Upper Whitewater Valley", *Indiana Historical Society Publications,* vol. 15, no. 1, 1945. 171pp.

Leahy, Ethel C., *Who's Who on the Ohio River and Its Tributaries.* 1931. 868pp.

McCay, Betty L., *Sources for Genealogical Searching in Indiana.* 1969, 1973. 24pp.*

McCord, Shirley, "State Senators of Indiana, 1851-1967"; "Members of the Indiana House of Representatives, 1851-1967", *Indiana History Bulletin,* vol. 45, 46. 1968, 1969.

Memoirs of the Lower Ohio Valley, Personal and Genealogical.... 1905. 2 vols.

Miller, Carolynne L., "Early Post Office Guide to Indiana, 1816-1825", (Part B, *The Value of Guides to Genealogical Records in the U.S. and Canada...,* Part III, State Library. World Conference on Records, Salt Lake City, Area I, 2 & 3c, 1969. (Also in *The Hoosier Genealogist,* vol. 11, #1, Jan.-Mar., 1971).*

Miller, John W., *Indiana Newspaper Bibliography.* Historical Accounts of all Indiana Newspapers Published from 1804 to 1980 and Locational Information for all Available Copies, Both Original and Microfilm. 1982. 538pp.*

Monks, Leander J., *Courts and Lawyers of Indiana.* 1916. 3 vols.

Morris, Mrs. Harvey, *Pioneer Women of Indiana.* 1922-25.*

Newhard, Malinda E.E., *Divorces Granted by the Indiana General Assembly Prior to 1852.* 1981. 31pp.*

———, *A Guide to Genealogical Records in Indiana.* 1979. 156pp.*

———, *Name Changes Granted by the Indiana General Assembly Prior to 1852.* 1981. 28pp.*

Philbrick, Francis S., "The Laws of Indiana Territory, 1801-1809", *Collections of the Illinois State Historical Library,* vol. 21, 1930. Repr. 1931. (Also Louis Ewbank's "The Laws of Indiana Territory, 1809-1816", *Indiana Historical Collections,* vol. 20, 1934).*

Reed, George I., *Encyclopedia of biography of Indiana.* 1895. 2 vols.

Researchers, *Indiana, Her Counties, Her Townships, and Her Towns.* 1979. 20pp.*

Riker, Dorothy, "Executive Proceedings of the State of Indiana, 1816-1836," *Indiana Historical Collections,* vol. 29, 1947. 911pp. (Lists early county officials, appointments of officers in the Indiana militia, etc.).

———, *Genealogical Sources.* Genealogical Material Reprinted From the *Indiana Magazine of History.* 1979. 456, [14]pp.*

Riker, Dorothy and Gayle Thornbrough, "Indiana Election Returns, 1816-1851," *Indiana Historical Collections,* vol. 40, 1960. 493pp.

Roll, Charles, *Indiana, One Hundred and Fifty Years of American Development....* 1931. 5 vols.

St. Louis Genealogical Society, *Tracing Family Trees in Eleven States: Missouri, Illinois...Indiana....* 1970, 1980 printing. 209 and 272pp., resp.*

Scott, John, *The Indiana Gazetteer...1826.* Repr. 1954. (Vol. 18, *Indiana Historical Society Publications*).

Sidwell, Studio, [*Plat Books of Indiana Counties*]. [1925-1941]. [92] pts.

Smith, William H., *The St. Clair Papers....* 1882, 2 vols.

Thompson, Donald E., *Preliminary Checklist of Archives and Manuscripts in Indiana Repositories.* 1980. 68pp.

Thornbrough, Gayle and Dorothy Riker, "Journals of the General Assembly of Indiana Territory, 1805-1815," *Indiana Historical Collections,* vol. 32, 1950. 1106pp.

Trissal, Francis M., *Public Men of Indiana* [1860-1920]...[1922-3]. 2 vols.

Wabash College, *Indiana Authors and Their Books.* 1949, 1974, 1981. 3 vols. (Vol. 1, 1816-1916, comp. by R.E. Banta; vol. 2, 1917-1966, comp. by Donald E. Thompson; vol. 3, 1967-1980, comp. by Donald E. Thompson).

Walters, Betty L., *Furniture Makers of Indiana, 1793-1850.* 1972. (*Indiana Historical Society Publications,* vol. 25, no. 1).

Wiggins and Weaver's Ohio River Directory for 1871-72.... 1871. 419pp.

Wilson, George R., *Early Indiana Trails and Surveys.* 114pp. Repr. (*Indiana Historical Society Publications,* vol. 6, no. 3, 1919).*

Wilson, George R. and Gayle Thornbrough, "The Buffalo Trace", *Indiana Historical Publications,* vol. 15, no. 2, 1946.*

Wolfe, Barbara, *Index of Genealogical Gleanings from Indiana Magazine of History.* 1977. 35pp.*

———, *Index to Yearbook of the Society of Indiana Pioneers, 1921-1977.* 1977. [260pp.].*

Hoyt, Arabelle C., *Index to Yearbook of the Society of Indiana Pioneers, 1977.**

*Yearbook of the Society of Indiana Pioneers, 1921- .**

Woollen, William W., *Biographical and Historical Sketches of Early Indiana.* 1883. 568pp.

Woollen, William W., D.W. Howe, and J.P. Dunn, "Executive Journal of Indiana Territory, 1800-1816," *Indiana Historical Society Publications,* vol. 3, no. 3, 1900. 187pp. (Lists early county officials, etc. and appointments of officers in Indiana militia).

The Research Publications of Connecticut reproduced as Series III of the *County Histories of the Old Northwest* the Indiana Segment. It represents 262 titles in 293 volumes on 67 reels of microfilm.

Genealogical Indexing Associates of West Bountiful, Utah, prepared a computerized *Indiana Biographical Index.* This comprehensive index of biographical sketches includes hundreds of thousands of names of Indianans whose biographies appear in miscellaneous Indiana historical works. Microfiche editions are available for distribution.

COUNTY LISTINGS

ABBREVIATIONS

This bibliography cites the author, title in abbreviated form (i.e., county name and other nonpertinent words in the title were omitted), date of publication, size, and format.

The format indicates whether microfilm, miCrofilm, and the book number for the entry as it appears in the collection of the Genealogy Division of the Indiana State Library.

A few commissioners records housed in the Indiana Historical Society Library are also listed.

No book number is given for a few items since they had not yet been processed at time of publication.

All book numbers in the Genealogy Division are preceded by a G, Geneal., or IPL G. The latter symbol (IPLG) signifies that the item is a part of the Eugene Haslet Darrach Memorial Library housed in the Genealogy Division. The G or Genealogy symbol has not been reproduced in this paper.

n.d.	no date
v.p.	various pagination
p.f.	pamphlet collection; book numbers in the pamphlet collection may also be preceded by a "pam".
f	folio
q	quarto (oversize)
n.p.	no pagination
pp.	pages (a comma will separate various noted pagination)
microfilm	item appears on microfilm
miCrofilm	item is a part of the CRIMP microfilm collection (County Records of Indiana Microfilm Project—still in progress)
WPA	Works Progress/Projects Administration compilation (volume numbers are not indicated for the series of county vital records)
THG	The Hoosier Genealogist
IMH	Indiana Magazine of History
NP	New purchase

ADAMS COUNTY

Formed 1835; organized 1836 from[1] Allen, Randolph · · · County Seat—Decatur

Births:

Works Progress Administration, Index to birth records, 1882-1920.	*977.201 A219u

Deaths:

WPA, Index to death records, 1882-1920.	977.201 A219u

Deeds:

Deed indexes, 1837-1902.	microfilm

Marriages:

WPA, Index to marriage records, 1845-1920.	977.201 A219u
Marriages, 1836-1844.	microfilm
Marriages, 1836-1844 (The Hoosier Genealogist, vol. 18 #4, Dec. 1978).	977.2 H789
Marriage returns, 1882-1891.	microfilm
WPA, Index to supplemental records, marriage applications, 1840-1897.	977.201 A219u
DAR, Marriage license...[1836-1845]. Copied by Electa Lochner. 1973?. 8pp.	p.f. 977.201 A219 no. 1

Probates:

Probates, 1838-1846; indexes, 1847-1900.	microfilm

Wills:

Wills, 1839-1899.	microfilm
DAR, Will books...1837-1888....Cop. by Electa I.B. Lochner. 1971. 109pp.	977.201 A219L
Heller, Dick D., Jr...., Index of files, administrationships...1841-1968. 1970. 259pp.	977.201 A219h

Cemetery & Church:

DAR, Cemetery records....1957-1961. 3 vols.	977.201 A219d
...Cemetery inscriptions. Cop. by Mrs. Ervin Lochner? 1965. n.p.	977.201 A219
Scharpenberg, Louis, A Visit to our cemeteries (Adams & Allen counties). 7pp.	p.f. 977.201 Auncat. no. 1
Grether, Rev. George, German Reformed Zion Congregation records, Decatur.... 4pp.	p.f. 977.201 Auncat. no. 2
Lochner, Electa I.B., First records of Salem Magley, St. Lukes Honduras, Zion Friedheim and First Methodist churches, Decatur....1970. 58,145pp.	977.202 D291L

Miscellaneous:

Adams Co. Hist. Soc., 1979 Hist. of Adams county....Ed. by Dick D. Heller. 1980. 786pp.	q977.201 A219ni
Tract book, 1824-1854.	microfilm
...Early tax lists, 1839, 1842, 1843. [1975]. [105pp.]	977.201 A219a
Lochner, Electa I.B., Virgil Dick, and Dick Heller, Tract book...with index of deeds. 1971. 149pp.	977.201 A219da

---

[1] In listing parent counties, unorganized areas attached to these counties are included as part of them.

* All materials listed in this section are filed in the Genealogy Division of the Indiana State Library unless otherwise designated.

ALLEN COUNTY

Formed 1824 from Randolph, Delaware (N.P., unorganized)[2] County Seat—Fort Wayne

Births:

WPA, Index to birth records, 1887-1920.	977.201 A425u
WPA, Supplementary index to birth records, 1882-1896.	977.201 A425u

Deaths:

WPA, Index to death records, 1896-1920.	977.201 A425u
WPA, Supplementary index to death records, 1870-1896.	977.201 A425u

Deeds:

Deeds, 1824-1842.	microfilm

Marriages:

DAR, Early marriage records...1824-1849, [1849-1874]. Comp. by Josephine Ehle. [1935, 1948]. 2 vols.	977.201 A425o
WPA, Index to marriage records, 1824-1920.	977.201 A425u
WPA, Index to supplemental record, marriage transcript...[1893-1896]. [In back of each marriage volume].	977.201 A425u
Marriage records...1931-1936. Comp. by Ft. Wayne Pub. Lib. 1971. 4 vols.	977.201 A425o 1931-1936
Marriages, 1824-1837 (THG, vol. 5 #1, Jan.-Feb. 1965).	977.2 H789
Wilkens, Cleo G., Misc. marriage notices as found in Ft. Wayne...newspapers, 1840-1850, 1875-1876. 1964. 13pp.	977.201 A425wim

Probates:

Probate order book, 1825-1844.	microfilm

Wills:

DAR, Will record...[1831-1900]. 1936, 1962-64. 2 vols.	977.201 A425w
Wills, 1831-1855.	microfilm

Cemetery:

Allen Co. Gen. Soc., Adams-Jefferson township cemeteries. 1983. 241pp.	977.201 A425a
____, Marion-Pleasant, Lafayette-Aboite cemeteries. 1981. 207pp.	977.201 A425mp
____, Wayne township cemeteries. 1982. 366 pp.	977.201 A425wa
DAR, A Collection of cemetery inscriptions....Comp. by Alberta M. Flint. [1932]. 317pp.	977.201 A425d
Harter, Stuart, Cemetery readings of Ell River and Riverview cemeteries....1980. 179pp.	977.201 A425har
Cemetery records, pt. 1 (Albright, Brenton Chapel, Fogwell, Kelsey, Schlemmer cemeteries; from *Lines*, vols. 2, 3, 4).	p.f. 977.201 Auncat. no. 2
Lower, Dorothy M., The Patriots sketches of the known soldiers of the American Revolution buried in Allen county....1976. 53pp.	973.34 I385L
Madison-Monroe Township cemeteries....Comp. by Allen Co. Genealogical Soc....1980. 173pp.	977.201 A425m
Newhard, Malinda, Cemetery inscriptions...Maumee, Milan, Scipio & Springfield townships. 1978. 246pp.	977.201 A425n
____,... Veterans burial records, 1906-1929. 1981. 142pp.	977.201 A425na

---

[2] "In 1820 the legislature disposed of the entire tract purchased at [the Treaty of] St. Mary's by enlarging Randolph, Franklin, and Jennings counties and by dividing the remainder into two counties—Delaware, east of the second principal meridian and Wabash, west of it. These so-called counties did not have the usual county organization. They were put under the jurisdiction of adjoining counties, and new counties were formed within their boundaries...." (Pence, George, and Nellie C. Armstrong, *Indiana Boundaries, Territory, State, and County, Indiana Historical Collections,* vol. 19, Ind. Hist. Bureau, 1933, repr. 1967).

Census:

Banet, Charles, French immigrants...1850-1870, compiled from the population schedules for the 7th, 8th, and 9th censuses of the U.S. for Allen County. [1981] 265pp. — 977.201 A425 ban

Harter, Fayne E., 1850 federal census....1968. 521pp. — 977.201 A425h

U.S. Bureau of the Census, Index to the sixth census...1840. Comp. by Cleo G. Wilkens. 1958. 29pp. — 977.201 A425wil

Church:

Allen Co. Gen. Soc...., Survey of church records....1981. 48pp. — 977.201 A425sc

Bloomfield, Virginia F., First Baptist Church records, Fort Wayne...1837-1931. 1969. 189pp. — 977.202 F745b

___, First Presbyterian Church records, Fort Wayne...1858-1959. 1971. 2 vols. — 977.202 F745bf

DAR, Baptism records, 1900-1972. East Liberty. E.U.B. Church, south of Monroeville....[1973]. 20pp. — p.f. 977.202 M753 no. 1

Harter, Fayne E., Milan Evangelical Lutheran church records (Barnett Chapel) of Milan Township....1975. 55pp. — 977.201 A425ha

Heffelfinger, Taft, The Genesis of the Huntertown United Methodist church and area history. [1979]. 68pp. — 977.202 H947h

Lomont, Gladys, Records of St. Louis Catholic Church, Besancon, Indiana, 1865-1907....1980. 173pp. — 977.202 B554Lo

Court & Commissioners:

Alien record, 1839-1844 [in probate record B]. — microfilm

Circuit court order book, 1824-1835. — microfilm

Commissioners records, 1824-1850. — microfilm

Mortuary & Obituaries:

Fort Wayne...P.L., Peltier Funeral home, Fort Wayne...coffin sales, 1862-1877. 1969. 286pp. — 977.202 F745f

___, Index to obituary records as found in the News-Sentinel and the Journal-Gazette, Fort Wayne...1966-1970. 1971. 291pp. — 977.202 F745i

___, Index to obituary records as found in the Journal-Gazette, Fort Wayne...1938-1949: Journal Gazette on strike Jul. 8, 1945-Aug. 19, 1945; obituaries copied from the News-Sentinel on these dates. 1976. 449pp. — 977.201 A425f

___, Tri-state obituaries (Indiana-Ohio-Michigan). (1970-1976). 6 vols. — 977.2 T819t

Newhard, Malinda E.E., E.C. Carrington family records and funeral register 1892-1922, Harlan, Indiana....1976. — 929.2 C318n 1976

Palmer, Louise M., Index to Tri-state obituaries (Indiana, Ohio, Michigan) From the Fort Wayne Journal Gazette, 1977. 1978. 99pp. — 977.2 P174i

___, Index to Tri-state obituaries (Indiana, Ohio, Michigan) From the Fort Wayne Journal Gazette, 1978. 1979. 101pp. — 977.2 P174ia

Scheumann funeral home, mortuary records, 1899-1951. Ft. Wayne P.L. 1971. 331pp. — 977.201 A425s

Wilkens, Cleo G., Obituary records as found in Fort Wayne...newspapers, 1841-1900. 1962. 434pp. — 977.201 A425wi

School:

[St. Mary's Catholic Boys School (Fort Wayne, Ind.)], Graduate register of commercial class, St. Mary's Catholic Boys school, 1905-1938 (Bound with "St. Mary's Commercial Course, Complete roster of graduates, 1898-1938). [1981?]. 57pp. — 977.202 F745sbg

———, Records of St. Mary's Catholic Boys school...1898-1927. [1981?] 24pp.   977.202 F745sbr

[St. Mary's Catholic Girls School (Fort Wayne, Ind.)], Grade school record of St. Mary's Catholic Girls school...1898-1923. [1981?] 72pp.   q977.202 F745sgc

———, Graduate and post graduate record of St. Mary's Catholic Girls school...1903-1930. [1981?]. 71pp.   977.202 F745sgd

Miscellaneous:

Bloomfield, Virginia F., Genealogical records of German families..., 1918. 1974. 185, 48pp.   977.201 A425bl

Cavanaugh, Karen B., ...Bibliography of genealogical and historical references in the genealogy department of the Allen County Public Library. 1982. 28pp.   977.201 A425c

———, A Genealogist's guide to the Ft. Wayne, Indiana, Public Library. 1980. 92pp.   16.9772 C377ge

DAR, Bible records. Comp. by Josephine C. Ehle. 1951. 74pp.   977.201 A425b

Edwards, Melba, Zanesville, Indiana history, 1849-1976. 1976. 253pp. (Also Wells County)   977.202 Z28e

Lines. Published by Allen Co. Gen. Soc. of Indiana (scattered issues).   p.f. 977.201 Auncat. no. 1

Newhard, Malinda E.E., Index to Tri-state ancestry as it appeared in the News-Sentinel, Fort Wayne, Indiana, 1973-4.   977.2 N548i

Rondot, Alfred B., Place or town of origin of Allen County...French surnames, 1800-1900, found in the Courchaton, Haute Saone, France register, 1670-1852. 1980. [18pp.]   977.201 A425ron

Trentadue, Helene B., Program and narration of Monroeville, Indiana's centennial, 1851-1951. 33pp.   p.f. 977.202 Muncat. no. 1

WPA, Index to supplemental record, 1928 personal and poll tax records.   977.201 A425u

BARTHOLOMEW COUNTY

Formed 1821 from Jackson, Delaware (N.P., unorganized)　　　　　　　County Seat—Columbus

Births:

Delayed births prior to 1941	*miCrofilm
WPA, Index to birth records, 1883-1920.	977.201 B287u

Deaths:

WPA, Index to death records, 1882-1920.	977.201 B287u

Deeds:

Deed indexes, [1822]-1939 (1900-1922, grantor only).	microfilm
Deed indexes, [1822]-1887; deeds, 1822-1886; tax title deeds, 1865-1962; sheriff's deeds, 1869-1921; land and property, clerk's record, 1822-1836.	miCrofilm
Partition deed record, 1880-1890	miCrofilm
Holmes, Maurice, Early landowners.... 1975. 42, 46pp.	977.201 B287h

Marriages:

Marriages, 1821-1850	microfilm
Marriages, 1821-1921; returns, 1882-1890.	miCrofilm
WPA, Index to marriage records, 1850-1920.	977.201 B287u
(also)	miCrofilm
WPA, Index to marriage transcript records, 1882-1920.	977.201 B287u
DAR, ...Marriage license application affidavits, 1849, 1852, 1863-1867, 1884-1886. 1979. v.p.	977.201 B287bm
Marriages, 1821-1832 (THG, vol. 7 #5, Sept.-Oct. 1967) and marriage licenses [1863-1867] (THG, vol. 19 #1, Mar. 1979).	977.2 H789
Ridlen, Colleen A., ...Early marriage returns, 1821-1838. 1977. 44pp.	977.201 B287ri

Probates:

Probates, 1821-1843; indexes, 1857-1900.	microfilm
Probates, 1822-1918; order books, 1826-1918.	miCrofilm
Partitions, 1853-1872.	miCrofilm
Probates, 1821-1829 (THG, vol. 7 #5-6, Sept.-Oct., Nov.-Dec. 1967).	977.2 H789

Wills:

Wills, 1844-1900.	microfilm
Wills, 1844-1921.	miCrofilm
Holmes, Maurice, Will records...1822-1908. 1976. 368pp.	977.201 B287ho

Cemeteries:

Bartholomew Co. Hist. Soc., Cemetery records, 1939—. 2 vols. (11 pts.).	977.201 B287i
DAR, ...Cemeteries. 1959-74. 42 pts.	977.201 B287d
____, Listing of burials in Hope Moravian cemetery, March 14, 1928 thru July 27, 1966. Cop. by Mildred Harrod. 1979. 60 pp.	977.202 H791L
Gabbert family cemetery....1975. 1 pp.	p.f. 977.201 Buncat. no. 6
Hutslar, Jack, Cemetery located NE part of Columbus Twp....on Hawcreek.... 1 pp.	p.f. 977.201 Buncat. no. 3
Jonesville and Jones or Yeley cemeteries. Cop. by Mary F. Urbahns. 1971-72. 14, 2 pp.	977.201 B287b
Huffer, John, War veterans graves in Newbern cemetery...6 pp.	p.f. 977.201 Buncat. no. 5

* The term MiCrofilm signifies the CRIMP collection (County Records of Indiana Microfim Project)

Kinnett, Lucille B., Wisner cemetery...Harrison Twp..1973. 1 pp.	p.f. 977.201 Buncat. no. 4
Talkington, Edgar, Parkerson cemetery....1955. 4 pp.	p.f. 977.201 Buncat. no. 1

Church:

DAR, The Beginning of East Columbus Methodist Church....1979. 10, [2]pp.	p.f. 977.201 Buncat. no. 11
_____, [Hope Methodist church...]. benevolent report....1907-1908; directory and financial report...[1919-1920]....1979. [6 pp.]	p.f. 977.201 Buncat. no. 12
_____, St. John's church...membership, deaths, marriages,births. 1980. 16pp.	p.f. 977.201 Buncat. no. 13
_____, Index, baptism, marriage, and death records, St. Paul's Lutheran Church.... 1978. 136pp. (Bound with a short historical sketch, St. Paul's Lutheran Church... [2]pp. and St. Paul's Lutheran Cemetery..., comp. by M.F. Urbahns, [20]pp.)	977.201 B287da
_____, The Methodist Church of Hope, Indiana. Cop. by George E. Utterback. 1955. [14]pp.	977.202 H791u
_____, Quarterly conference records of the St. Louis Circuit of the Methodist Church. Cop. by Mildred D. Harrod. [1978]. 44, 10pp.	977.201 B287q
_____, Methodist, Hope and St. Louis church records....[Cop. by Mrs. Helen L. Coffin]. [1976?]. [3-109pp.]	977.201 B287me
Hawcreek Baptist Church...organized September 22, 1926....Cop. by Mildred D. Harrod. 1979. 129pp.	977.201 B287haw

Court:

DAR, Index, Civil Court order book "B" 1833-1840....1977. 47pp.	p.f. 977.201 Buncat. no. 8
_____, Complete record "A" March 1821, June 1821, October 1823 to September 1833....[1876]. [14pp.]	p.f. 977.201 Buncat. no. 9
_____, Letters of administration, 1824-1827....[1976]. [4pp.]	p.f. 977.201 Buncat. no. 10
Common pleas complete record, 1853-1872	miCrofilm
Index to commissioners records, 1821-1855	microfilm
Holmes, Maurice, Court record, 1822-52. 1977. 376pp.	977.201 B287hoc

Land:

Tract Book V, 1841	microfilm
DAR, Original tract book....Comp. by Jane F. Murphy. [1976/7]. 126pp.	977.201 B287m

Mortuary & Obituaries:

DAR, Obituaries and miscellaneous items abstracted from Columbus... newspapers, 1872-1884. Comp. by Jane F. Murphy. 1978/79. 150pp.	977.201 B287mu
Murphy, Jane F., J.D. Emmons Funeral home records, Columbus, Ind., 1891-1901. 1982. 128pp.	977.202 C726j

Naturalization:

Declaration of intention, 1852-1914	miCrofilm
Naturalization records, 1856-1916	miCrofilm
Naturalization records....[1976]. 26pp.	977.201. B287n
DAR, Miscellaneous naturalizations....1978 [25] pp.	977.201 B287dau

Miscellaneous:

Amanns, Mark, Index of a portion of the 1900 census...Ohio, Nineveh, Rockcreek townships. [1982?] 15, [1] pp.	977.291 B287am
Bartholomew County historical society's scrap book no. 10, Trans. by Jane F. Murphy. 1980 182, [17] pp. (A collection of newspaper articles...).	977.201 B287bh
DAR, Bartholomew...veterans: American Revolution, War of 1812, Mexican War, Spanish American War. 1979-[1980]. 4, 3, 7, 9pp. (also miCrofilm)	p.f. 977.201 B287bv

Directory of Bartholomew County...(May 14, 1821). 3 pp.   p.f. 977.201 Buncat. no. 2

Negro register, 1853-1855   miCrofilm
    (also in THG, Vol. 17 #2, June 1977)   977.2 H789

George Pence manuscript collection, (From Bartholomew County Hist. Soc.).   microfilm

Road record, 1821-1851.   microfilm

Stott, Russell, History of Ohio Ridge. 1972. 4pp.   p.f. 977.201 Buncat. no. 14

Darlington, Jane E., ...Auditor's duplicate of taxes for 1843....[1981?] [47 pp.]   977.201 B287db

BENTON COUNTY

Formed 1840 from Jasper   County Seat—Fowler

Births:

WPA, Index to birth records, 1822-1920. (also incomplete microfilm copy).	977.201 B478u

Deaths:

WPA, Index to death records, 1882-1920.	977.201 B478u

Deeds:

Deed indexes, 1840-1895.	microfilm

Marriages:

Marriages, 1841-1858.	microfilm
Marriages, 1840-1858 (THG, vol. 15 #1, Jan.-Mar. 1975).	977.2 H789
WPA, Index to marriage records, 1850-1922.	977.201 B478u
WPA, Index to supplemental record, marriage applications, [1846-1905].	977.201 B478u
Slevin, Ruth M., ...Marriages...1840-1858. [1974?]. 6, 5pp.	977.201 B478s

Probates:

Probates, 1840-1852; indexes, books 1-5, n.d.	microfilm

Wills:

Wills, 1857-1897.	microfilm

Others:

Ind. Junior Hist. Soc., [Dunnington cemetery...]. 1978. 16pp.	p.f. 977.201 B478i
___, ...Cemetery records, 4 pts.	p.f. 977.201 B478 no. 1
Fleming cemetery, York twp....(And Blue Ridge, from Barce, History of Benton county....1930, vol. 1). 5pp.	p.f. 977.201 Buncat. no. 1
Tract book, 1832-1875.	microfilm
Wilkinson, W.C., Federal census, 1860, Oxford....1974. [11pp.]	p.f. 977.202 098f

BLACKFORD COUNTY

Formed 1838; organized 1839 from Jay   County Seat—Hartford City

Deaths:

Deaths, 1882-1930; Hartford City, 1900-1907, Montpelier, 1915-1951.	microfilm

Deeds:

Affidavits for land transactions...in possession of Marion P. Bonham, abstracter, Hartford City....1972. 5 vols.	q977.201 B628b
Beeson, Cecil, ...Deed book A [1836-1844]. 1960. n.p.	977.201 B628d

Marriages:

Beeson Cecil, Marriage records..., 1877-1888. 1977. 148pp.	977.201 B628be
Marriage license record books, 1839-1857. Comp. by Guy Mahorney: 1857-1877. Comp. by Cecil Beeson. 1957-9. 2 vols.	977.201 B628m

Probates:

Beeson, Cecil, Probate docket book, 1839-1849....[10]pp.	p.f. 977.201 B628 no. 5

[handwritten] Probate Court Judgement Dockets 1846-1861   *[handwritten]* Film

Wills:

Beeson, Cecil, Will records...1842-1895. 1959 [25]pp.	p.f. 977.201 B628 no. 7
___, [Wills...1839-49]. (From Probate docket book). [6]pp.	p.f. 977.201 Buncat. no. 1

Cemetery & Church:

Beeson, Cecil, Cemetery records (incomplete).	microfilm
___, '76 and Blackford County....[and] (Revolutionary War heroes buried in Blackford..., by John A. Bonham). 1974. 24pp.	p.f. 977.201 B628 no. 11
___, "Fitting tribute to soldier dead" [A list of names of soldiers buried in the IOOF Cemetery, Hartford City...1911]. 6, 7pp.	p.f. 977.201 Buncat. no. 3
___, I.O.O.F. cemetery, section 4, Harrison twp....[10pp.]	p.f. 977.201 Buncat. no. 4
...Cemeteries records. [19—]. [ca 799pp.]	977.201 B628bc
Cemeteries and other miscellaneous records.	microfilm
I.O.O.F. Cemetery, Hartford City, Indiana (1960-1981). 46pp. (See also 977.201 B628bc for records prior to 1920 and "microfilm" for records to 1960).	q977.202 H328io
[Church of Jesus Christ of Latter Day Saints], ...Cemetery records. 11pts.	p.f. 977.201 B628 no. 8
[Shroyer, Mary], History of the Millgrove United Methodist Church. 1972. [2], 9pp.	p.f. 977.202 M653s
[The Tombstone inscription of William H. Beedy who died August 3, 1883, and the death announcements of Benjamin Bird...and Martin Griffin...]. 1pp.	p.f. 977.201 Buncat. no. 6

Census:

Enumeration...males over 21 years of age....(Scattered townships for 1854, 1856, 1860, 1871, 1877, 1883, 1889, 1895). 4pts.	p.f. 977.201 B628 no. 1
Registration book, 1914, Precinct 5, Ward 4, Licking Twp....1967. 6, 2pp.	p.f. 977.201 B628 no. 9
Indiana State Library, ...1840 census. 1970. 3pp.	p.f. 977.201 B628 no. 10

History:

Beeson, Cecil, Some Blackford...families. 9pp.	p.f. 977.201 Buncat. no. 2
___, [Some Blackford County...soldiers]. [7pts.] (William Montgomery, William Hicks, John T. Fair, Weedin H. Shields & John Mills, John Twibell, John Saxon, Thomas Miles).	p.f. 977.201 Bunact. no. 5
___, Misc. records...plus index. 1978. [471pp.]	977.201 B628bee

41

___, Miscellaneous books submitted for filming [includes Beeson genealogy, 1895 city directory, Hartford City, Montpelier, Merchants day book of Hartford City, 1850-1, etc.]. microfilm

___, Newspaper items from the Hartford City Telegram, (Hartford City, Indiana). 1972. 402pp. (and 1974 ed. 43, 4pp). 977.202 H328b

___, Indiana newspaper index, Hartford City Telegram..., 1902-1914. microfilm

___, Miscellaneous records, Board of commissioners'...4 pts. (First log court house...; Hartford City census, 1857; Merchant's Day book, 1850; Poll book of an election...Hartford City, Oct. 1854). v.p. p.f. 977.201 B628 no. 4

[Day book, Dec. 1847-Oct. 1848, Henley and Campbell Store, Hartford (now Hartford City), Indiana, Blackford County. Cop. by Cecil Beeson. 1972.] [4pp.] p.f. 977.202 Huncat. no. 1

Flashbacks II, Blackford county history. n.d. 24pp. p.f. 977.201 B628 no. 12

Land:

Tract book...1836-1853. Cop. by Cecil Beeson. 1959. 39pp. p.f. 977.201 B628 no. 6

Tract book [1836-1853] (THG, #6, Nov.-Dec. 1962 and #1, #2, Jan.-Feb., Mar.-Apr. 1963). 977.2 H789

Mortuary & Obituaries:

Allen County Public Library, Index to J. Will Baxter Mortuary records, Hartford City, Indiana, Jan. 8, 1906-June 26, 1925. 1983. 205pp.

Beeson, Cecil, W.H. Cox, Funeral directory, Hartford City, Indiana, Feb. 22, 1892-Dec. 29, 1905. 1978. 45pp. 977.202 H328be

___, Obituaries....[293pp.] q977.201 B628beo

Miscellaneous:

Beeson, Cecil, Assessor's list, Jackson Township, 1855...1863; Washington Twp., 1857; Licking Twp., 1860. 1959. [4pts.] p.f. 977.201 B628 no. 2

Asylum for the poor...records, 1886-1959. 1 vol. q977.201 B628a

Commissioners book 1, 1839-1847. Cop. by Cecil Beeson. 23pp. p.f. 977.201 B628 no. 3

BOONE COUNTY

Formed 1830 from Hendricks, Marion   County Seat—Lebanon

Births:

WPA, Index to birth records, 1882-1920.   977.201 B724u

WPA, [Index to supplemental birth records, 1882-1920, A-K, incomplete].   977.201 B724u

Deaths:

WPA, Index to death records, 1882-1920.   977.201 B724u

Deeds:

Deed indexes, 1856-1901; heretofore recorded, 1835-1929.   microfilm

Marriages:

Marriages, 1831-1854.   microfilm

Marriages, 1831-Aug. 1844 (THG, vol. 19 #1, March 1979).   977.2 H789

Stark, Ralph W., Marriage licenses issued...1831-1844. 1970. [32pp.], 29pp.   977.201 B724s

WPA, Index to marriage records, 1842-1920.   977.201 B724u

WPA, Index to supplemental records, marriage transcript, 1882-1907.   977.201 B724u

Ridlen, Colleen A., ...Early marriage records, 1831-1848. 1977. 40pp.   977.201 B724r

Probates:

Probates, 1846-1852; indexes, 1852-1901.   microfilm

Wills:

Wills, 1853-1904.   microfilm

Cemetery & Church:

Hoyt, Mrs. Leo, [Cemetery records...]. (Eagle Village cemetery, Eagle Twp.]. 7pp.   p.f. 977.201 B724 no. 4

Sluder, Adron B., Soldiers buried in cemeteries, Eagle Twp....and Pleasant View, Union Twp. [1962]. 8pp.   p.f. 977.201 B724 no. 5

Williamson, Wallace F., Sugar Plain cemetery, an index. Located in northwestern Boone county...in connection with the Sugar Plain Friends monthly meeting. 1964. [26pp.]   p.f. 977.201 B724 no. 7

Warren, Mrs. Dan., [Cemetery records...]. 1965. 2pts. (Pt.1, Mechanicsburg; pt. 2, Family cemetery—Gipson Myers, Wilson families).   p.f. 977.201 B724 no. 8

Hanna, Mary F., "Mud Creek" cemetery....1965. 19pp.   p.f. 977.201 B724 no. 9

Harvey, Ruth C., Census of the "Old Porter cemetery", Jamestown....[1966]. 2pp.   p.f. 977.201 B724 no. 10

DAR, Records from Cedar Hill cemetery, Lebanon....1953. 10pp.   p.f. 977.201 B724 no. 11

West, Mrs. Richard L., Burials in McCord (abandoned) cemetery about one mile southeast of Whitestown....1971. [3 pp.]   p.f. 977.201 B724 no. 12

Boebinger, Greg, Sheets cemetery, Zionsville....[1971?]. [3]pp.   p.f. 977.201 B724 no. 13

Harvey, E.S., Johns cemetery...Union Twp....1975. 6pp.   p.f. 977.201 Buncat. no. 9

Stark, Ralph W., Thorntown's colored cemetery remembered. [5pp.]   p.f. 977.201 Buncat. no. 10

Stover, Barbara T., Old section, Salem Church cemetery, Eagle Twp....7pp.   p.f. 977.201 Buncat. no. 11

Bridge, Harold A., The Cason cemetery, county road W500 at Prairie Creek, Section 8, Washington Twp...[1975?] [8]pp.   p.f. 977.201 B724 no. 16

Stark, Ralph W., Cedar Hill cemetery...Lebanon....1972. 10pp.   p.f. 977.202 L441 no. 1

Our heritage in Oak Hill cemetery, Lebanon....One hundred years of community service, 1872-1972. 1972. n.p.   p.f. 977.202 L441. no. 2

McKinley, Mrs. Thryza, [Boone County...cemetery records]. 2pts. (Johns cemetery, Sugar Grove cemetery).   p.fl. 977.201 Buncat. no. 1

Chelf, Mrs. Connie, Gravestones in Regular Eagle Creek Baptist Church cemetery, Old Eagle Creek cemetery....1960. 3, 2pp.   p.f. 977.201 Buncat. no. 2

Schofield, Mrs. Wm. E., The Old McCord cemetery...Worth Twp....2pp.   p.f. 977.201 Buncat. no. 3

"Soldiers silent at Cedar Hill cemetery". (Clipping, May 27, 1963). 1pp.   p.f. 977.201 Buncat. no. 4

Harmon, Walter H., People buried in Sheets cemetery southwest of Zionsville. 1pp.   p.f. 977.201 Buncat. no. 5

The Book of records for Union Church commenced in...1838....32pp.   p.f. 977.201 Buncat. no. 6

Stark, Ralph W., Simeon Sedwick family burial plot [Union Twp.]. 1974. 1pp.   p.f. 977.201 Buncat. no. 7

Funkhouser, Jewell C., Lutheran cemetery, Worth twp....1978. 23pp.   977.201 B724f

___, Pleasant View cemetery, now called Hutton Memorial...Eagle Twp...[1979]. 16pp.   977.201 B724fu

Houk, Andrew K., Cemeteries in Jackson Twp....1971. [3pp.]   p.f. 977.201 B724h

Schuetz, Kay, "Old Eagle" or Cox cemetery....1977. [2], 2pp.   p.f. 977.201 B724sc

Schuetz, Katherine, Zionsville cemetery...originally known as Bishop cemetery. 1975/77. [30]pp.   977.202 Z79s

Ind. Hist. Soc., [Cemetery records....] (Cedar Hill, Lebanon). 1945. [5pp.]   p.f. 977.201 B724 no. 1

Martindale, Harry H., Tombstone records in the Howard graveyard...: tombstone records of Howards, Hurts, and related families, Old Union churchyard, Jackson Twp...: tombstone inscriptions in Herndon graveyard, on old Larkin H. Hurt farm, Jackson Twp....[1947?]. [6]pp.   p.f. 977.201 B724 no. 2

Herr, Ben, [Cemetery records...]. 5pts. (pt. 1, Gravestones, Mt. Tabor, Jones, Dickerson, Howard & Smith; pt. 2, Mount Union, Robison, Milledgeville, Griffith, Chitwood, & Leap; pt. 3-5, Dickerson, Howard, Pitzer, Poplar Grove).   p.f. 977.201 B724 no. 3

Evans, Nellie E., "Boone County" publication: cemeteries. [1978?]. vol. 1, 43pp.   977.201 B724e

Miscellaneous:

Boone, your county magazine. (Scattered issues for 1975-76).   p.f. 977.201 Buncat. no. 8

Combination atlas map of Boone....1878, Rep. 1974. 56pp.   f977.201 Buncat. no. 1

Ind. State Library, Index to 1840 census....1971. 27pp.   977.201 B724i

Harmon, Walter H., Census 1850....n.d. 45pp.   p.f. 977.201 B724 no. 15

Mills, Keith, Zionsville mortuary records...1893-1923. [1962?]. 73pp.   p.f. 977.201 B724 no. 6

Tract books 1-2, 1825-1854, 1822-1852.   microfilm

BROWN COUNTY

Formed 1836 from Bartholomew, Jackson, Monroe   County Seat—Nashville

Births:

Delayed records, births prior to 1941.	miCrofilm

Deaths:

Deaths, 1882-1899.	microfilm

Deeds:

Deed indexes, 1873-1900.	microfilm
Brown, Immogene B., Land records of Indiana. 5 vols. (Vol. 4, Brown County).	977.2 B878L

Marriages:

Marriages, 1836-1901.	microfilm
1836-1923.	miCrofilm
Marriages, 1836-1855 (THG, vol. 17 #4, Dec. 1977).	977.2 H789
Slevin, Mrs. Ruth, Early marriage records...1836-1852. 2pts.	p.f. 977.201 B877 no. 2
Slevin, Ruth M., ...Marriage records, 1853-1901....1972. 101, 101pp.	977.201 B881sl
DAR, Marriage records...(1836-1879). 1973/4. 163pp.	977.201 B881d
DAR, ...Marriages, 1880-1886. 1974. 14, 5, 6pp.	977.201 B881da
DAR, Marriage records (1880-1917)....1975. 179pp.	977.201 B881daa
Ridlen, Colleen A., ...Early marriage records, 1836-1859. 1980. 41pp.	977.201 B881ri

Probates:

Probates, 1850-1853 [book contains a few guardian bonds, 1839-1856]; indexes, 1864-69, 1874-1901.	microfilm
Probates, 1837-1926.	miCrofilm

Wills:

Wills, 1845-1914.	microfilm
1845-1875, 1877-1957.	miCrofilm
Slevin, Ruth M., Brown County...will records...1845-1914. 1972. 60pp.	977.201 B881s
Index of estates. n.d.	miCrofilm
Index wills...1836-1875....[2pp.] (missing 1982)	p.f. 977.201 Buncat. no. 8

Cemetery & Church:

Burkhart cemetery or Catholic cemetery....1pp.	p.f. 977.201 Buncat. no. 2
Curry, George L., Sprunica cemetery record (Hamblen Twp.); Mount Zion cemetery (Hamblen Twp...). 3, 3pp.	p.f. 977.201 Buncat. no. 5-6
Hoffine, Mrs. Nota, Spiker cemetery. 1pp.	p.f. 977.201 Buncat. no. 7
Taylor, Dwight, Unidentified graveyard....1975. 4pp.	p.f. 977.201 Buncat. no. 9
Mertens, Nova M., Cemetery records...: Coon or Fleenor, Bean Blossom or Georgetown, and Oak Ridge church and cemetery. [1950, 1952.] 17pp. (Cop. from Ind. Mag. of Hist., vols. 46, 48).	p.f. 977.201 Buncat. no. 10
___, Oak Ridge cemetery, Jackson Twp....[1973?]. 5pp.	p.f. 977.201 B877 no. 4
___, Records of Georgetown (Bean Blossom) Presbyterian Church....1951. 9pp.	p.f. 977.201 Buncat. no. 3
Meyer, A.H., Duncan cemetery (Peoga, Indiana...). 1973. [2pp.]	p.f. 977.201 B877 no. 3
Ind. Hist. Soc., [Cemetery records...]. 1941. 6pts.	p.f. 977.201 B877 no. 1
Reeve, Helen H., ...Cemeteries. 1977. 365pp.	977.201 B881r

Mortuary & Obituaries:

Mertens, Nova M., Death notices, clippings from Brown County Democrat, 1950-1951. 1951. [51pp.]   p.f. 977.201 Buncat.

Reeve, Helen H., ...Bond Funeral home records, 1922-1978. 1978. 261pp.   977.201 B881re

___, ...Selected records: funeral homes of Columbus, Indiana: Barkes, Inlow & Weaver, 1935-1949, Hathaway-Myers, 1907-1975, Reed-Jewell, 1891-1975. 1978. 164pp.   977.201 B881ree

Miscellaneous:

Hamblen, A.P., A Man, a tree, a mark, supplemented by Petro's tales. 1919. [13pp.]   p.f. 977.201 Buncat. no. 1

Naturalization records, 1860-1889.   miCrofilm

CARROLL COUNTY

Formed 1828 from Delaware (N.P.), Wabash (N.P.)*   County Seat—Delphi

Births:

WPA, Index to birth records, 1882-1920.	977.201 C319u
Moore, Phyllis D., Index to birth records...January 1, 1921-November 1, 1978. 1978. vol. 3	977.201 C319mo

Deaths:

WPA, Index to death records, 1882-1920.	977.201 C319u

Deeds:

Deed indexes, 1829-1900.	microfilm

Marriages:

Marriages, 1828-1855.	microfilm
Marriages, 1828-1847 (THG, vol. 21 #4, Dec. 1981).	977.2 H789
WPA, Index to marriage records, 1850-1920.	977.201 C319u
Carroll Co. Hist. Soc., ...Marriage records, 1828 to 1850. [1969]. 51pp. (and index, 26pp.).	977.201 C319c

Probates:

Probates, 1829-1852; indexes, 1853-1899.	microfilm

Wills:

DAR, Wills...1830-1897. Comp. by Ivy Neff & Meredith Stephenson. 1951. 83pp.	977.201 C319dw

Cemetery & Church:

Carroll Co. Gen. Soc., St. Joseph Catholic cemetery...church death records translated from Latin...names taken also from the burial permits of the sexton...gravestone names and dates....1973. 76pp.	977.201 C319ca
Carroll Co. Hist. Soc., Our ancestors at rest. 1969 [40pp.]. (lists cemeteries, but no names).	977.201 C319w
DAR, Cemetery records....By Mrs. Charles V. McCloskey. 1938-1949. 300pp. (Index, 15pp).	977.201 C319d
___, Cemetery records. Comp. by Ivy J. Neff & Meredith J. Stephenson. 1952. 2 vols.	977.201 C319da
___, Register of St. Mary's Episcopal church, Delphi....Comp. by Meredith J. Stephenson. 1951. 56pp.	977.202 D363d
The History of the Oak Grove church, Jefferson twp...1880-1980. [1980?]. [131pp.].	977.202 M791ho
Ind. Hist. Soc. (L'Anguille Valley Memorial Assoc.), [Cemetery records...]. 9pts.	p.f. 977.201 C319 no. 1
Session book of the associate congregation of Pleasant Run, 1833-1850....3pp.	p.f. 977.201 Cuncat. no. 1

Miscellaneous:

DAR, Index of Revolutionary War patriots, who are ancestors of the members of Charles Carroll Chapter, DAR [Delphi, Indiana]. 1976. [6], 50pp.	973.34 I385dar
Gick, Mrs. Roberta S., ...1845 Tax list. 62pp.	977.201 C319gt
___, Enumeration of white male inhabitants over 21 in...1850. 31pp.	977.201 C319g
U.S. Bureau of the Census, Index to: census of 1840....Comp. by Grace Merritt. 1965. 46pp.	977.201 C319m
WPA, Commissioners' record...1828-1841....2 vols.	Ind. His. Soc. Library
...Tract book 1. Printed by Mrs. Floyd Bixler, Mrs. C. Scott, Mrs. Eugene Gick. 1971. 62pp.	977.201 C319ct

* See footnote 2.

CASS COUNTY

Formed 1829 from Carroll — County Seat—Logansport

Births:
WPA, Index to birth records, 1882-1941.	977.201 C343u

Deaths:
WPA, Index to death records, 1882-1920.	977.201 C343u
Wolfe, Barbara E., ...Index, death records...[1884-1907]. [1977]. 615pp.	977.201 C343wc

Deeds:
Deed indexes, 1830-1897.	microfilm

Marriages:
DAR, ...Marriage records, 1920-1942. 1967. 3 vols. (Also supplement).	977.201 C343d
[Henderson, Laura D.], Early marriage records...[1829-1835]. n.d. [17pp.]	p.f. 977.201 C343 no. 1
Kiesling, Mrs. Walter, Marriage records...1829-1850. 1962. n.p.	977.201 C343k
WPA, Index to marriage records, 1850-1920.	977.201 C343u
Wolfe, Barbara E., Marriage book I...1829-1851. 1970. 30pp.	977.201 C343wm

Probates:
Probates, 1837-1855; indexes, 1850-1898 (books 9, 10, 17-22 missing).	microfilm

Wills:
Early wills...1831-1852 [incomplete?]. [3pp.] (Bound with Early marriage records).	p.f. 977.201 C343 no. 1
Wills, 1831-1895.	microfilm
Wolfe, Barbara, Will book I....[1969?]. 23pp.	977.201 C343w
Wolfe, Barbara E., Will index...book 1-17. 1976. 138pp.	977.201 C343ww
___, Index, estates...1829-1900. 1976. 110pp.	977.201 C343wi

Cemetery & Church:
Ind. Hist. Soc. (L'Anguille Valley Memorial Assoc.), Cemetery records. Cop. by R.B. Whitsett. 1939-44. 10 vols. and 131 pts. (Also 291pp. index). (2 vols. in 977.201 C343f) (Also on miCrofilm).	977.201 C343i
St. Vincent DePaul cemetery, Logansport...annual report of the Board of Trustees, 1939-1940. 1943.	p.f. 977.202 L831 no. 1
Cemetery on Wallace Eikenberry farm, R.R. 5, Logansport....1pp.	p.f. 977.201 Cuncat. no. 1
Wolfe, Barbara E., Cemeteries...(list of location only). 1976. 15pp.	p.f. 977.201 C343wo
[Roll of members and officers of the church, 1859-1941], Spring Creek [Christian] church...1978. 1 vol.	977.201 C343s

Mortuary & Obituaries:
Cass Co. Gen. Soc., Burial record extracts, 1901-1950, Kroeger Funeral home, Logansport....1981. [45], 574pp.	977.202 L831bu
Hofmann, Roberta B., Deaths in Logansport...newspapers: Democratic Pharos Weekly, 1858-1859, 1869-1871, July 31, 1872; Logansport Weekly Journal, 1870-1876. 1981. 105, [2]pp.	977.201 C343zLh
___, ...Some pre-1880 [i.e. 1884] obituaries. [1979?]. [12pp.]	977.201 C343h
Obituaries [1858-59; 1869-71; July 1872] (THG, vols. 19 #4, 20 #4, Dec. 1979, Dec. 1980).	977.2 H789

Miscellaneous:
DAR, Excerpts of the Canal Telegraph, 1834-1835. Comp. by Barbara S. Wolfe. 1970. 8pp.	p.f. 977.201 C343 no. 3

___, ...Tract book 1 and 2. 1968. 228pp.   977.201 C343dt

___, Tax list 1845....1966. 83pp.   p.f. 977.201 C343 no. 2

U.S. Bur. of the Census, 1840 Census....[Cop. by] N. Schreiner. [1960]. [40pp.]   977.201 C343un

Wolfe, Barbara E., Genealogical records. 1971. 166pp.   977.201 C343wg

___, Revolutionary War soldiers....1976. 10pp.   973.34 I385wo

CLARK COUNTY

Formed 1801 from Knox   County Seat—Jeffersonville

Births:

Births, 1882-1893, 1897-1907.	microfilm
WPA, Index to birth records, 1882-1920.	977.201 C593u

Deaths:

WPA, Index to death records, 1882-1920.	977.201 C593u

Deeds:

Deed indexes, 1801-1900.	microfilm

Marriages:

Marriages, 1808-1901.	microfilm
Marriages, 1807-1824 (Indiana Magazine of History, vols. 41, 42, 43, 1945-1947).	p.f. 977.201 Cuncat. no. 10 977.2 I39
WPA, Index to marriage records, 1905-1920.	977.201 C593u
Slevin, Ruth M., Clark county...marriage records, (1825-1897). 1971-73. 4 vols.	977.201 C592s

Probates:

Probates, 1815-1852; indexes, 1852-1892 [incomplete].	microfilm

[handwritten: Probate Order Book. 1835; 1836] *[handwritten: film]*

Wills:

Wills, 1801-33, 1852-55, 1877-95. *[handwritten: 1801-? ; 1817-1833]*	microfilm
Wills, 1801-33 (abstracts IMH, vols. 35, 36, 1939-1940).	p.f. 977.201 Cuncat. no. 9 977.2 I39
Riker, Dorothy, ... Abstracts of wills and executors' records, 1801-1833 and marriage records, 1807-1824. 1969. 57, Xpp.	977.201 C592r

Cemetery:

Atkinson, Mr. & Mrs. Charles O., Smith cemetery, Silver Creek Twp....4pp.	p.f. 977.201 Cuncat. no. 6
Bower, Mrs. Buford E., "Cemetery marker is memorial to Bowyers"....1974. 1pp.	p.f. 977.201 Cuncat. no. 7
Ind. Hist. Soc., [Cemetery records...]. 34pts.	p.f. 977.201 C596 no. 1
Greear, William R., [Cemetery records...]. (pt. 1, Staples cemetery, 1971 [2pp.]).	p.f. 977.201 C596 no. 6
Ind. Junior Hist. Soc., ...Cemetery records. (pt. 1, Old Borden Town, Pleasant Ridge, Mt. Moriah, Mt. Lebanon, Mountain Grove, Ebenezer, Swayback, Bowery, Forest Grave or Willey's Chapel, Johnson family (Borden), McKinley-Packwood, Hosea family). 1971.	p.f. 977.201 C596 no. 7
Van Hook, James M., Cemetery records of soldiers....1947. 9pp.	p.f. 977.201 Cuncat. no. 1
...Cemetery records (Silver Creek; Mt. Zion; Sylvester family; Hale family and Stewart family). [9pp.]	p.f. 977.201 Cuncat. no. 2
Hudson, Roy D., "Barnes community house" cemetery...2 miles east of Nabb....1949. 2pp.	p.f. 977.201 Cuncat. no. 3
Kiser, W.H., List of cemeteries....n.d. 8pp.	p.f. 977.201 C596 no. 3
Noe, Ada M., Salem Methodist Church cemetery. [4pp.]	p.f. 977.201 C596 no. 2
St. Clair, James O., Inscriptions on remaining gravestones in private cemetery known as St. Clair graveyard, Henryville....1954. 4pp.	p.f. 977.201 Cuncat. no. 11

Court:

Alien record, 1845-1852.	microfilm
Appraisal & estates of Jonathan Jennings (1833-1840).	microfilm
Circuit court and Court of common pleas records, 1801-1820, 1824-1831.	microfilm

Commissioners records, 1785-1820, 1817-1828, 1832-1852.	microfilm
Court of quarterly sessions, minute book, 1801-1808.	microfilm
Court order book, 1807-1813.	microfilm

Land:

Clark, William, Official plat book of Clark's Grant...1789-1810. 1925. n.p. (And index, 65pp.)	977.201 C593c
Gibson, Thomas W., Clark's Grant, abstracts for each grant, purchases and sales, up to about 1849. Jeffersonville abstract of lots up to 1849.	microfilm

Schools:

Cook, Claude E., School enumeration...(1884 Monroe Twp.). 1pp.	p.f. 977.201 C596 no. 5
Seminary record [Charlestown], 1830-1851.	microfilm

Voters:

A List of voters of Clark County, Indiana territory, 1802. (From NGSQ, vol. 111 #4, 1915). 1pp.	p.f. 977:201 Cuncat. no. 8
Voters 1802 (IMH, vol. 11, 1915).	977.2 I39
Voters 1809 (THG, Jan-Feb., Mar-April, 1962).	977.2 H789

Miscellaneous:

DAR, ...Historical and genealogical records. Collected by Mrs. Julia D. Waugh. 1929. 39, [12]pp.	977.201 C592da
___, Bible records....1956. 89pp.	977.201 C592db
Estray book, 1802-1818.	microfilm
Estray book, 1801-1817 (THG, vol. 15 #1, Jan-Mar. 1975).	977.2 H789
McCoy, W.H., The pioneer families of Clark County, 1885. 1967. [10]pp.	p.f. 977.201 C596 no. 4
Memorial to the U.S. Congress...from militia serving on the expedition to Tippecanoe, Sept. 11, 1811...seeking compensation for loss of provisions and property. 3pp.	p.f. 977.201 Cuncat. no. 5
Negro slaves, 1805-1810 (THG, vol. 17 #3, Sept. 1977). (Also p.f. 977.2 Runcat. no. 1).	977.2 H789

CLAY COUNTY

Formed 1825 from Owen, Putnam, Vigo, Sullivan   County Seat—Brazil

Births:

WPA, Index to birth records, 1881-1920	977.201 C622u

Deaths:

WPA, Index to death records, 1882-1920.	977.201 C622u
Finley, Pearl, Several...death records prior to 1882. n.d. n.p.	p.f. 977.201 C622 no. 2

Deeds:

Deed indexes, 1829-1902.	microfilm

Marriages:

Marriage affidavits prior to 1852 [incomplete].	microfilm
(Also IMH, vol. 56, 1960)	977.2 I39
(Also)	p.f. 977.201 Cuncat. no. 2
WPA, Index to marriage records, 1860-1920.	977.201 C622u
WPA, Index to supplemental record, marriage transcript, 1880-1920.	977.201 C622u
Selby, Robert E. & Phyllis J., ...Marriage records, 1851-1869. 1981. 78pp.	977.201 C622se

Probates:

Index to probate order books, 1-22. n.d.	microfilm

Cemetery:

Buck, Morris L., ...Cemetery records (Owens, Pell, Calcutta), 1970. n.p.	977.201 C622b
DAR, Cemeteries....Comp. by Margreta H. Jackson & Hope Swearingen Ray. 1975. 139pp.	977.201 C622j
Tarvin, Ann, ...Cemeteries. [1979/1980]. 286pp.	977.201 C622t
Finley, Dorathea P., First burials and burial places....n.d. n.p.	p.f. 977.201 C622 no. 3
[Orman cemetery, Bowling Green...]. 1965. 1pp.	p.f. 977.201 Cuncat. no. 3
Shultz, Charles R., [List of cemeteries...]. 1pp.	p.f. 977.201 Cuncat. no. 4
...Cemeteries, Snoddy and Zenor cemeteries. Cop. by Mrs. Jean Evans. 2pp.	p.f. 977.201 Cuncat. no. 5
DAR, Indiana cemetery records in Clay county....4pp. (Girton, Zenor, Williams cemeteries).	p.f. 977.201 Cuncat. no. 7
Hixon cemetery, Perry twp....1pp. (From Clay County Researcher, vol. 2, 1981).	p.f. 977.201 Cuncat. no. 8

Miscellaneous:

The Clay County Researcher. vols. 1-2. 1980-1.	p.f. 977.201 Cuncat. no. 6
Finley, Pearl, Landowners tract book no. 1, 1810-1855. 1955. n.p.	p.f. 977.201 C622 no. 1
Posson, Cornelius F., Soldiers of the War of the Revolution....1929. 7pp.	p.f. 977.201 Cuncat. no. 1
Riker, Dorothy, Heads of families...1830. (From IMH, vol. 56).	p.f. 977.201 Cuncat. no. 2 pt. 2

CLINTON COUNTY

Formed 1830 from Tippecanoe County Seat—Frankfort

Births:

WPA, Index to birth records, 1882-1920.	977.201 C641u

Deaths:

WPA, Index to death records, 1882-1920.	977.201 C641u

Deeds:

Deed indexes, 1829-1901.	microfilm

Marriages:

Marriages, 1830-1860.	microfilm
Marriages, 1830-1844 (THG, vol. 20, #3, Sept. 1980).	977.2 H789
DAR, Copy of marriage licenses issued...1830-1847...cop. by Mrs. Ada K. Phipps. 1932. 152pp.	q977.201 C641c
Clinton county first marriage records, 1830-1844, Gem City Genealogical Shoppe. [1968]. 39pp.	977.201 C641gm
WPA, Index to marriage records, 1852-1905.	977.201 C641u
WPA, Index to supplemental record, marriage transcript, 1882-1904.	977.201 C641u
WPA, Index to supplemental record, marriage applications, 1905-1920.	977.201 C641u
Grove, Helen E., ...Marriage records, 1830-1852. 1980. 39, 13, 41. [19]pp.	977.201 C641gr

Probates:

Probates, 1831-1853; indexes, 1853?-1900?	microfilm

Wills:

Wills, 1833-1904.	microfilm
Slevin, Ruth M., ...Will records, 1830-1904, bks. 1-4, [197-]. 237pp.	977.201 C641s
Bohm, Joan, Index to first will book...1830-1857. 1973. 11, [16]pp.	p.f. 977.201 C641 no. 5

Cemetery:

Merritt, Grace H., [Cemetery records...]. 3pts. (Rossville, Pleasant View, Mennonite cemeteries)	p.f. 977.201 C641 no. 1
DAR, [Cemetery records...]. 2pts. (Kirklin, McIntire cemeteries).	p.f. 977.201 C641 no. 2
Grove, Mrs. Richard, [Cemetery records...]. 16pts.	p.f. 977.201 C641 no. 3
Geetingsville cemetery and church records....4pts.	p.f. 977.201 C641 no. 4
Merrick, C.S., comp., [Middlefork Baptist Church, Middlefork, Indiana], Copy of the minutes of the organization meeting of...Baptists...1849. 1941. 1pp.	p.f. 977.201 Cuncat. no. 1
Goldsbarry, Mrs. A.W., Cemetery west of Luke Coats' Farm....1pp.	p.f. 977.201 Cuncat. no. 2
Bolt cemetery....1961. 4pp. (THG, no. 6, 1961)	p.f. 977.201 Cuncat. no. 3
...Cemeteries, Gem City Genealogical Shoppe. n.d. 2 vols. in 1. (Also 1980 ed., 2 vols. with index).	977.201 C641g
Rossville Jr. Hi History Club, Cemetery report [Clinton and Carroll counties]. 1968. n.p.	977.201 C641r
Fair Haven North and Fair Haven South (located approx. 1 1/2 mi. south of Mulberry...). 1975. [59]pp.	q977.201 C641f
Merrick, Donas, Middleford cemetery, Warren twp....1980. 9pp.	p.f. 977.201 Cuncat. no. 5
Slipher, Donald P., A record of the tombstones found in the old South cemetery on June 1, 1938 [Frankfort]. [1955?] n.p.	977.202 F829s

Census:

Grove, Helen, Index for 1840 census....n.d. [11], 32pp.	977.201 C641uc Index
U.S. Bur. of the Census, Census of 1840..., comp. by Grace H. Merritt. 1957. 41pp.	977.201 C641m
WPA, Index to supplemental record, federal census, 1880. (Lists names, sex, color, age).	977.201 C641u

Land:

Grove, Helen, ...Duplicate first tract book with index, 1828-1844. 1980. 139pp.	977.201 C641gd
Tract book 1, 1826-1853.	microfilm

Miscellaneous:

Bibliography of genealogical works in the Frankfort Community Public Library [and] the Clinton County Historical Society. 1980. 11pp.	p.f. 977.201 Cuncat. no. 4
Elsie Bates' Scrapbook of deaths in the Mulberry area, 1923-1980. 98pp.	q977.202 M954ed
Laura Landis' Scrapbook of Mulberry marriages, 1929-1949. 3 vols.	q977.202 M954em
Elsie Bates' Scrapbook of weddings, storms...in the Mulberry area, 1930's to 1970's. 54pp.	q977.202 M954ew

CRAWFORD COUNTY

Formed 1818 from Harrison, Orange, Perry   County Seat—English

Deeds:

Deed indexes, 1819-1878.	microfilm

Marriages:

Marriages, 1818-1835 (THG, vol. 10 #1-2, Jan.-Feb., Mar.-Apr., 1970).	977.2 H789
Marriages, 1818-1900.	microfilm
Noblitt, Ivan E., An Index of...marriages...1818-1955.	microfilm
Slevin, Ruth M., ...Marriages, 1881-1896: books E & F, 1972. 47, 47pp.	977.201 C899sl

Probates:

Probates, 1818-1851; indexes, 1851-1903.	microfilm

Wills:

Wills, 1818-1899.	microfilm
Slevin, Ruth M., ...Will records: books 1-2. 1974. 71pp.	977.201 C899s

Others

Enlow, Opal Jean, ...Cemeteries (Patoka and Sterling townships). 1975. 1 vol.	977.201 C899e
Gilliatt, Katherine W., Eastridge cemetery...Patoka township. [1951]. 2pp.	p.f. 977.201 C899 no. 2
[Incomplete listing of stones found in an old unmarked cemetery...Union twp... west of Sulfer]. 1pp.	p.f. 977.201 Cuncat. no. 1
Ind. Hist. Soc., Old Leavenworth cemetery. 1947. 1pp.	p.f. 977.201 C899 no. 1
Neighborhood Youth Corps., Marengo cemetery....1970. 33pp.	977.201 C899n
Cook, Claud E., [School enumerations...]. pt. 1 [Whiskey Run township, 1884 & 1885]. [2pp.]	p.f. 977.201 C899 no. 3
Leistner, Doris, ...1850 census. 1980. 168pp.	977.201 C899Le
Naturalizations, [1822-1896]. (THG, vol. 22 #1, Mar. 1982)	977.2 H789

DAVIESS COUNTY*

Formed 1817 from Knox   County Seat—Washington

Births:

WPA, Index to birth records, 1882-1920.   977.201 D256u

Deaths:

WPA, Index to death records, 1882-1920.   977.201 D256u

Marriages:

Bogner, Stella, [Cemetery and marriage records...]. (Marriages, 1817-1850). n.d.
    2 vols.   977.201 D256bo

Bogner, Stella M., Marriage records...1817-1850. 1974. [155pp.]   977.201 D256boa

Marriages, 1817-1840 (THG, vol. 5 #2-3, Mar.-Apr., May-June, 1965).   977.2 H789

WPA, Index to marriage records, 1850-1920.   977.201 D256u

Probates:

Abstract of probate records, 1817-1850; 1850-1866, comp. by Mrs. Stella Bogner.
    1933. 2 vols. in 1.   977.201 D256b

Cemetery:

Bogner, Stella M., ...Cemeteries. 1 vol.   977.201 D256bob

DAR, Cemetery records...Harrison township....1977. [7pp.] (Baldwin, Brown,
    Glendale, East Union cemeteries).   977.201 D256d

___, Old City cemetery, Washington....n.d. 17pp.   p.f. 977.202 W317 no. 3

Arvin, Charles S., ...Cemetery inscriptions. 1. Helvestine cemetery, Reeve twp.; 2.
    [Name unknown], cemetery, Reeve twp. 1962. [4pp.]   p.f. 977.201 Duncat. no. 3

Haffey, Mary, Verified list of persons buried in the old Catholic cemetery and the old
    City cemetery, Washington, Indiana. [1936]. 60pp.   977.202 W317h

Ind. Hist. Soc., [Cemetery records...]. [23pp.] (East Union, Oak Grove).   p.f. 977.201 D256 no. 1

Barkley, Grace, [Cemetery records...]. [4pp.] (Ketchem cemetery).   p.f. 977.201 D256 no. 2

Ingalls, Mrs. Robert, [Cemetery records...]. [3pp.]. (Odon, Walnut Hills, Sims).   p.f. 977.201 D256 no. 3

Baker, Natalie M., St. Mary's cemetery...registered July, 1972....n.d. 23pp.   p.f. 977.201 D256 no. 4

List of cemeteries...(The Forks, vol. 1, 1975). [2pp.]   p.f. 977.201 Duncat. no. 5

Ferguson (Chandler) cemetery...(The Forks, vol. 3, 1976). [5pp.]   p.f. 977.201 Duncat. no. 6

Jones, Ramona, Kilgore cemetery markers....1958. [4pp.]   p.f. 977.201 Duncat. no. 2

CHURCH:

Bethany Christian Church, Montgomery, Indiana, 150th anniversary services,
    September 30, 1979....[1979]. 19pp.   977.202 M788be

Bogner, Stella M., ...History of Westminster Presbyterian Church, Washington,
    Indiana, 1814-1964. n.d. 10, 96pp.   977.202 W317b

___, [History of Westminster Presbyterian Church, Washington, Indiana]. [1942].
    4pp.   p.f. 977.202 W317 no. 1

McLoughlin, A.L., A Souvenir of the centennial of the parish of St. Simon,
    Washington, Indiana. [1937]. 32pp.   p.f. 977.202 W317 no. 2

Miscellaneous:

Bogner, Stella, Vanished towns....18pp.   p.f. 977.201 Duncat. no. 1

The Forks. Daviess county Genealogical Society, vol. 1 #1, Apr/June 1974-   977.201 D257

Purdue, Eleanor, Gleanings from the 1880 census....n.d. 9pp.   p.f. 977.201 Duncat. no. 4

WPA, Commissioners' record...1820-1832....   Ind. Hist. Soc. Library

* 1820 Census of this county is missing

DEARBORN COUNTY

Formed 1803 from Clark   County Seat—Lawrenceburg

Births:

Births, 1882-1906.   microfilm

Deaths:

Deaths, 1882-1900.   microfilm

Deeds:

Deeds, 1826-1830 (some earlier re-recorded deeds because of destruction of earlier volumes).   microfilm

Deeds, 1821-1878.   miCrofilm

Marriages:

Marriages, 1806-1815 (IMH, vol. 41, 1945).   977.2 I39

Marriages, 1826-1934.   miCrofilm

Marriages, 1826-1900.   microfilm

Marriages, 1826-1833 and J.P., 1806-1815 (THG, vol. 14 #4, Oct.-Dec. 1974).   977.2 H789

Slevin, Ruth M., ...Marriages, 1854-1899. 1975-76. 2 vols.   977.201 D285s

Marriage applications, 1826-1877, 1880-1923.   miCrofilm

Marriage affidavits, 1868-1882, 1886-88, 1894-1905.   miCrofilm

Probates:

Probates, 1826-1830.   microfilm

Probates, 1826-1906, 1908-1914.   miCrofilm

Probate order books, 1826-1918.   miCrofilm

Wills:

Wills, 1824-1900.   microfilm

Wills, 1826-1919.   miCrofilm

McHenry, Chris, Early...wills...from...books I and II (including Ohio co. before 1845) and perpetuated testimony books CC. 1976. 51pp.   977.201 D285m

Cemetery & Church:

DAR, Cambridge, East Fork, and West Fork cemetery records....[14pp.]   p.f. 977.201 Duncat. no. 8

Horstman, Helen, Three Dearborn county...cemeteries: German Lutheran, Buchanan Farm, and Bedunnah. 1974. [4pp.]   p.f. 977.201 Duncat. no. 9

McHenry, Chris, Alden, Five Points, Huber-Briggs, St. John's Lutheran, Stephen's Lutheran (Busse Church), and St. Paul's Lutheran Church cemetery records.... 1978. 11pp.   p.f. 977.201 Duncat. no. 10

...Cemeteries (Bainum private, unnamed, cemetery on Sand Run road), (Hoosier J. of Ancestry, vol. 6). [2pp.]   p.f. 977.201 Duncat. no. 11

List of members belonging to the Second Church of Christ in Manchester, when and how received, when dismissed, excluded, and deaths—commencing Sept. 16th 1819. [6pp.]   p.f. 977.202 Muncat. no. 1

Cemetery records (from Lawrenceburg Public Library)   miCrofilm

DAR, Colechapel cemetery; Rand cemetery. 2 pts. 1963.   977.201 D285d

...Cemetery records. Lawrenceburg Public Lib. [1978]. 1 vol.   977.201 D285dea

McHenry, Chris, ...Cemeteries, a preliminary inventory. 1977. 16pp.   977.201 D285de

———, Cemetery lists, Dearborn and Ohio counties....1977. 45pp.   977.201 D285mch

One hundred thirty five years of God's blessings, 1843-1978: St. John's Lutheran Church, Farmers Retreat, Indiana. 1978. 67pp.   977.202 F234o

DAR, [Cemetery records...]. 7pts.	p.f. 977.201 D285 no. 5
DAR, ...Universalist Church membership, 1868-1927. 1975. 6, [6]pp.	p.f. 977.201 D285da
Evans, C.M., Ebenezer Baptist cemetery, Aurora....1964. 7pp.	p.f. 977.201 D285 no. 2
First Presbyterian Church, Aurora, Indiana...register of deaths [1879-1906]. [6pp.]	p.f. 977.202 Auncat. no. 1
Ind. Hist. Soc., [Cemetery records...]. pt.1, Miller cemetery, Lawrenceburg, Ind. [1950]. [2pp.]	p.f. 977.201 D285 no. 1
Ind. Junior Hist. Soc., ...Cemetery records. pt.1, St. Leon cemetery.	p.f. 977.201 D285 no. 4
Smith, Marian, [Cemetery records...]. [9pp.]	p.f. 977.201 D285 no. 3
Persons buried in Old Newton cemetery, Lawrenceburg....1940. 3pp. (pt.1); [Burials in Old Newton cemetery...]. [3pp.] (pt.2); Cemetery records from what is known as the Old cemetery at Lawrenceburg....1939. 3pp. (pt.3).	p.f. 977.201 Duncat. no. 1
Murphy, Thelma M., Mt. Tabor Methodist churchyard, Aurora....1pp.	p.f. 977.201 Duncat. no. 2
Ind. Jun. Hist. Soc., Longnecker cemetery, Harrison township....1970. [6pp.]	p.f. 977.201 Duncat. no. 3
Platt, Chester, Platt, Hogan Hill, M.E. (Manchester), Universalist cemeteries....3pp.	p.f. 977.201 Duncat. no. 4
Tombstone readings—Watts family cemetery....3pp.	p.f. 977.201 Duncat. no. 5
Angevine, Erma, Angevine tombstones at Homestead near Yorkville....1pp.	p.f. 977.201 Duncat. no. 6
Plat of the Old Lawrenceburg cemetery...1940. 1 sheet, 1940. Plan showing details of relocation and reinternment of the Old Lawrenceburg cem. in the Greendale cem. near Nowlin Ave. 1 sheet. [1940].	977.201 D285L

Courts:

Circuit court order book, 1824-1829.	microfilm
Commissioners records, 1845-1851.	microfilm
Index to estates, 1826-1913.	microfilm

Miscellaneous:

Naturalizations (THG, vol. 19 #1, Mar. 1979).	977.2 H789
Naturalizations, 1838-1890.	miCrofilm
Bockhurst, Diane, Some...obituaries. 1972.	977.201 D285b
Condensed obituaries from a scrapbook owned by Clarence Platt of Moores Hill...[1879-1964]. [8pp.]	p.f. 977.201 Duncat. no. 7
Darlington, Jane E., ...Commercial license fee book: 21 October 1839 to December 1853. [1982?]. n.p.	977.201 D285dac
___, List of delinquent taxpayers...for the year 1842. [1981?]. [21pp.]	977.201 D285dar
Family records (from Lawrenceburg Public Library). (Includes birth and death records; church records).	miCrofilm
McHenry, Chris, Climbing the Family Tree, Sept. 1975-Aug. 12, 1976. (Photocopy of a weekly...column...from the Dearborn County Register and Ohio County News and Recorder). 1976. [40]pp.	977.201 D285mc
___, ...Obituaries, 1820-1860. c1983. 41pp.	977.201 D285md
Surveyors books, 1799-1805.	microfilm
Voters 1809; 1812 (THG, 1961; 1969).	977.2 H789

DECATUR COUNTY

Formed 1822 from Delaware (N.P., unorganized)   County Seat—Greensburg

Deaths:

DAR, ...Death records [1882-1899]. 1958; 1963. 2 vols.	977.201 D291da

Deeds:

Deed indexes, 1822-1901.	microfilm

Marriages:

Marriages, 1822-1905.	microfilm
Marriages, 1822-1829; 1829-1837 (THG, vol. 9 #3-4, May-June, July-Aug. 1969).	977.2 H789
General index to Marriages—Males...[December 22, 1822 to February 27, 1848]. [1977?]. [8pp.]	977.201 D291g
Ridlen, Colleen A., ...Early marriage records, 1822-1839. 1977. 41pp.	977.201 D291r
Slevin, Ruth M., ...Marriage records, 1852-1878....n.d. 96, 95pp.	977.201 D291s
Slevin, Ruth M., ...Marriage records, 1878-1905. n.d. 108, 108pp.	977.201 D291sl

Probates:

Probates, 1830-1852; indexes, 1853-1900.	microfilm

Wills:

Wills, 1822-1906.	microfilm
Holmes, Maurice, Will records...1822-1906. 1976. 428pp.	977.201 D291ho

Cemetery:

DAR, Bible records and tombstone inscriptions, comp. by Mrs. C.E. Loucks. [1950]. 97pp.	977.201 D291dab
DAR, Cemetery inscriptions....1960; 1969; 1974; 1972. 4 vols. (vol. 1—Fugit and Clinton twp.; vol. 2—Adams twp.; vol. 3—Saltcreek twp.; vol 4—Washington twp.).	977.201 D291dac
___, Cemetery records....5pts. (Roy Meiers Farm, Center Grove, David Mobley Farm, Nauvoo, Pumphrey). [24pp.]	p.f. 977.201 D291 no. 3
McKee, Jennie S., Old Rossburg cemetery and New Rossburg cemetery....1970. v.p.	p.f. 977.201 D291 no. 4
Talkington, Edgar, Mt. Olivett cemetery, Jackson township....6pp.	p.f. 977.201 Duncat. no. 1
Murphy, Thelma, Cemetery on State Road 421....2pp.	p.f. 977.201 Duncat. no. 2
Sandcreek Hist. Club, [Cemetery records] copied by the Sandcreek Hist. Club. [no. 1, A few private cemeteries in Decatur and Jennings counties....no. 2, Records of Westport City Cemetery...]. [7pp.]	p.f. 977.201 Duncat. no. 3
Hoyt, Mrs. Leo, [...Cemetery records. 4 pts.] (Cemetery near Rossburg; Cem 1/2 mile e. of Waynesburg; Hooker; abandoned cem. 3 miles n. of Greensburg).	p.f. 977.201 Duncat. no. 4
[Inscriptions of Sand Creek, Layton, Wood, and Jackson cemeteries located north of Greensburg...]. [3pp.]	p.f. 977.201 Duncat. no. 5
Kirby, Emmett, [Report of the Rossburg, Ross, and New Pennington cemeteries, Salt Creek township...]. 2pp. (only a few names listed).	p.f. 977.201 Duncat. no. 6
DAR, Old Pumphrey cemetery located in Decatur county....1978. 2pp.	p.f. 977.201 Duncat. no. 7
Ind. Junior Hist. Soc., ...Cemeteries. [1981]. 38pp.	977.201 D291dc
Ind. Hist. Soc., [Cemetery records...]. pt. 1 (Eggleston, Sand Creek), [incomplete listings]. 1pp.	p.f. 977.201 D291 no. 1
Church of Jesus Christ of Latter Day Saints, [Cemetery records...]. (Swails cemetery). 1pp.	p.f. 977.201 D291 no. 2

Ind. Junior Hist. Soc., ...Cemetery records (Shiloh, Pearce, Downeyville cemeteries and cemetery at Road no. 421). 1976. [12pp.]   p.f. 977.201 D291i

Thie, Joseph A., Enochsburg and St. John's Church....1976. 149pp.   977.202 E59t

Miscellaneous:

DAR, Enrollment of soldiers, their widows and orphans, of the armies of the United States, residing in the state of Indiana...Decatur county...1894. 1953. 60pp.   977.201 D291d

Holmes, Maurice, Early landowners....1975. 38, 50pp.   977.201 D291h

___, Court records...1822-1848. 1980. 469pp.   977.201 D291hc

McKee, Harley S., Record of children or babies delivered by Harley S. McKee, M.D. n.d. 348pp.   q977.201 D291m

Records of births and deaths of people born in and around St. Paul...to 1964. n.d. 1 vol.   977.202 S149r

Naturalizations, 1867-1874 (THG, vol. 21 #4, Dec. 1981).   977.2 H789

DE KALB COUNTY

Formed 1835; organized 1837 from Allen, LaGrange　　　　　　　　　　　　County Seat—Auburn

Births:

Harter, Fayne E., Birth records...1921-1944. 1972. 2 vols.	977.201 D328h
WPA, Index to birth records, 1882-1920.	977.201 D328u

Deaths:

WPA, Index to death records, 1882-1920.	977.201 D328u

Deeds:

Deed indexes, 1837-1901.	microfilm

Marriages:

Carey, Dr. Willis, ...Marriages [1837-1862, incomplete?]. [2]pp.	p.f. 977.201 Duncat. no. 2
Marriages, 1837-1899.	microfilm
Marriages, 1837-1857 (THG, vol. 11 #4, Oct.-Dec. 1971).	977.2 H789
WPA, Index to marriage records, 1882-1920.	977.201 D328u

Probates:

Probates, 1847-1856; indexes, 1859-1899.	microfilm

Wills:

Wills, 1852-1910.	microfilm

Miscellaneous:

Carey, Dr. Willis, [...Cemetery records]. [pt. 1] White City cemetery, Spencerville; [pt. 2] St. Joseph cemetery.	p.f. 977.201 Duncat. no. 1
___, Eastside cemetery, Spencerville, Indiana. [12pp.]	p.f. 977.201 Duncat. no. 3
Ind. Junior Hist. Soc., [...Cemetery records]. 1970. 32 pts.	p.f. 977.201 D328 no. 1
Newhard, Malinda E.E., Cemetery inscriptions....1972-1978. 3 vols.	977.201 D328n
Corunna, Ind., Board of Health records, 1909-1919. 2 vols. [pt. 1] Births. [pt. 2] deaths.	977.202 C831c
DAR, Bible records..., presented by Mrs. Douglas Vose. 1980. [23]pp.	977.201 D328bi
Tract book [1833-1856].	microfilm
WPA, Index to supplemental records, registered voters, 1920.	977.201 D328u

DELAWARE COUNTY*

Formed 1827 from Randolph   County Seat—Muncie

Births:
WPA, Index to birth records, 1882-1920.   977.201 D343u

Deaths:
WPA, Index to death records, 1882-1920.   977.201 D343u

Deeds:
Brown, Immogene B., Land records of Indiana. 1965-1972. 5 vols. (Vol. 2, Delaware County).   977.2 B878L

Deed indexes, 1829-1902.   microfilm

Marriages:
DAR, Early history of Delaware county...marriage records, 1827-1840; wills, 1830-1860. Cop...[by] Lelia L. Hill. n.d. 46pp.   977.201 D343d

Marriages, 1827-1837, 1838-1841 (THG, vol. 6 #2-3, Mar.-Apr., May-June 1966).   977.2 H789

DAR, ...Marriage records...[1827-1860]. Comp. by Mary W. Young. 1966-1975. 4 vols. (vol. 1 includes wills, 1830-1852; vol. 2 by A. Petro).   977.201 D343dm

WPA, Index to marriage records, 1827-1920.   977.201 D343u

WPA, Index to supplemental record, marriage applications, 1837-1893.   977.201 D343u

WPA, Index to supplemental record, marriage transcript, 1882-1911.   977.201 D343u

Probates:
Probates, 1830-1849; indexes, 1852-1931.   microfilm

Wills:
Wills, 1860-1901.   microfilm
(see also DAR under "Marriages" for wills 1830-1860 and 1830-1852).

DAR, ...Will records—book 2, abstracts...1852-1870. 1974. [184pp.]   977.201 D343dd

DAR, ...Will records—book 3, abstracts...[1869-1879]. 1975. 139, 4pp.   977.201 D343dda

Wills, 1831-1845 (THG, vol. 7 #3, May-June 1967).   977.2 H789

Young, Mrs. Gerald S., ...Wills, 1831-1845. 2pp. (THG, vol. 7).   p.f. 977.201 Duncat. no. 4

Cemetery:
DAR, Cemetery records....1956-1962. 4 vols.   977.201 D343dc

DAR, Cemetery records, Salem township....Cop. by Mrs. Kenneth J. Petro. 1978. 95pp.   977.201 D343pet

DAR, Cemetery records, Harrison and Perry townships...Cop. by Mrs. Kenneth J. Petro. [1977?]. 88pp.   977.201 D343p

DAR, Cemetery records, Monroe township....1978. 124pp. (Cop. by Mrs. Kenneth J. Petro.)   977.201 D343pe

DAR, Carmichael and Rees cemeteries, Muncie.... 3, 13 pp.   p.f. 977.201 D343 no. 12

Bowles, Helen, [List of cemeteries...]. 1948. 2pp. (missing 1982).   p.f. 977.201 Duncat. no. 1

Eaton cemetery...newspaper clipping (not complete). 1pp. (missing 1982).   p.f. 977.201 Duncat. no. 2

Wierbach, Eugene S., The Old Wilson cemetery on White River. [1941]. 2pp. (From IMH)   p.f. 977.201 Duncat. no. 3

Buckles, Ginn, Leaird, and Roderick cemeteries....[18pp.]   p.f. 977.201 Duncat. no. 5

Petro, Mrs. Kenneth J., Cemetery records, Niles township....1979. 61pp.   977.201 D343pen

DAR, Revolutionary War soldiers buried in Delaware...19—. 16pp.   p.f. 973.34 I385dap

---

* Not the Delaware County created from the New Purchase, see Footnote 2.

Colvin, Kathryn R., Cemetery west of...Wheeling on the Wheeling Pike....1971. 6pp.	p.f. 977.201 D343 no. 9
[Ind. Hist. Soc.], [Cemetery records...]. 1941. 10 pts.	p.f. 977.201 D343 no. 1
DAR, Cemetery record....4 pts. (Julian, Strong, Yorktown, Elizabethtown cemeteries).	p.f. 977.201 D343 no. 2
Heavilin, George E., Buckles cemetery....[1951]. 4pp.	p.f. 977.201 D343 no. 3
Beeson, Cecil, Sr., [Cemetery records...]. 4 pts. (Elizabethtown, Mt. Zion, Ginn, Roderick cemeteries).	p.f. 977.201 D343 no. 4
Church of Jesus Christ of Latter Day Saints, [Cemetery records...]. 14 pts.	p.f. 977.201 D343 no. 6
Maynard, Urbane V., Prairie Grove cemetery, history and tombstone inscriptions...Washington township....1965. 6pp.	p.f. 977.201 D343 no. 7
Beech Grove cemetery survey, prepared by Muncie Central Sesquicentennial Hist. Soc. [1970]. 2 vols.	977.201 D343de
Hamm, Thomas D., Records of Fairview, Rees cemeteries of Delaware county...and Cherry Grove Friends, New Liberty, Snow Hill, Cabin Creek A.M.E., Union Chapel, White River Christian, and Bethel A.M.E. of Randolph county, Indiana. [1977]. [214pp.]	977.201 D343h

Miscellaneous:

Ball State Univ. Hist. class, ...Naturalizations [to 1853]. 1972. 12pp.	p.f. 977.201 D343 no. 11
DAR, ...Declarations of intentions and applications for citizenship. 1975. [94, 4pp.]	977.201 D343di
___, Naturalization service petitions....1971. 27pp.	p.f. 977.201 D343 no. 10
Petro, Mrs. Kenneth J., Early land records, tract book....1981. 67pp.	977.201 D343peL
Young, Mary W., Records from the session record, First Presbyterian church, Muncie....1838-1867. 1963. 28, [5]pp.	977.202 M963r

DUBOIS COUNTY

Formed 1818 from Pike   County Seat—Jasper

Births:

Births, 1882-1906.	microfilm

Deaths:

Deaths, 1882-1901.	microfilm

Deeds:

Deed indexes, 1839-1900 [also earlier re-recorded deeds because of destruction of records].	microfilm

Marriages:

Davidson, Marie A., Marriages....Book A, 1839-1848. 1970. 20pp.	977.201 D815m
Doane, Lillian, ...Marriage licenses: index to marriage record books 3-4-5, January 1873 to June 1895. 1979. 132pp.	977.201 D815do
Index to...marriage records, book no. 1, 1848-1861. 1950. 34pp. [Index only to microfilm book 1].	p.f. 977.201 Duncat. no. 1
Marriages, 1839-1902.	microfilm
Marriage applications, 1882-1901.	microfilm
Marriages, Aug. 1839-Aug. 1848 (THG, vol. 16 #4, Dec. 1976).	977.2 H789
Slevin, Ruth M., ...Marriages, 1839-1872. 1970. 69, 70pp.	977.201 D815s

Wills:

Doane, Lillian, ...Wills, November 1840 to May 7, 1924. [19—]. 20pp.	977.201 D815du
Wills, 1841-1902.	microfilm
Wills, 1841-1851 (THG, vol. 15 #4, Oct.-Dec. 1975).	977.2 H789

Cemetery:

Baertich, Frank, ...Cemeteries. [1972?]. v.p. (Jasper City cemetery; Birdseye; M.E. Church?, Jackson twp.; Shiloh cemetery; Mt. Vernon cemetery).	p.f. 977.201 D815 no. 3
DAR, Cemetery records...(Evangelical St. Paul, Sherritt, Mt. Vernon, Old Holland Methodist and Mt. Zion). 1975. 19pp.	p.f. 977.201 D815d
___, Niblack, Dillin, Anderson cemeteries....1974. 2pp.	p.f. 977.201 D815 no. 4
Fierst, John J., Anderson, Armstrong and Main cemeteries....1975. [3]pp.	p.f. 977.201 D815 no. 5
___, ...Cemeteries, including Bethel Cemetery, Dugan..., St. Joseph..., Cavender..., Armstrong..., Dillin..., Hope....1975. 1 vol.	p.f. 977.201 D815 no. 6
Murphy, Thelma, ...Cemeteries (Adam Sendelweck, Elmer Freyberger Farm, and Hope cemetery). 1pp.	p.f. 977.201 Duncat. no. 2
Kellems cemetery....[3pp.]	p.f. 977.201 Duncat. no. 3
Clapp, Elmo F., Cemetery on the Maurice Gelhausen farm....1pp.	p.f. 977.201 Duncat. no. 4
McElroy, Kathryn D., Armstrong cemetery....1pp.	p.f. 977.201 Duncat. no. 5
Clapp, Pauline, Wininger cemetery....1976. 6pp.	p.f. 977.201 Duncat. no. 6
___, Weaver cemetery....1977. 1pp.	p.f. 977.201 Duncat. no. 7
___, Two...cemeteries: Robison and Cuzco. n.d. 21pp.	p.f. 977.201 Duncat. no. 8
Meredith, Mildred. Cemeteries. [1979?]. 63, 4, [4]pp.	977.2 M559c
Persinger, Patricia, Hobb's cemetery at Hillsboro, west of Ireland....[1965]. 5,[2]pp.	p.f. 977.201 D815 no. 1

Church:

DAR, Baptism record, 1869-1917, Salem United Church of Christ (Evangelical Lutheran) Huntingburg, Ind....[1978?]. 143, [37]pp.	977.202 H948d

Rudolph, Rose S., A History of Lemmon's Presbyterian Church, 1860-1960, Boone township....22, [2]pp.   977.201 D815r

St. Joseph's Catholic Church of Jasper, Indiana (baptisms, marriages, deaths).   microfilm

Miscellaneous:

Dillard, Fred, Dubois county, Indiana. 4pts. (Dubois county displaced persons; Dubois county families; Sinclair cemetery, Dillard family).   p.f. 977.201 D815 no. 2

Index for the Jasper Weekly Courier, March 19, 1858—June 19, 1896, ed. by Clement Doane and indexed by Lillian Doane. [1978]. 171pp.; index, 30pp. (v.p.) [name and topic indexes].   977.202 J38i and 977.202 J38in

Index to estates #1.   microfilm

Naturalizations, 1853-1906.   microfilm

Naturalizations, 1852-1869 (THG, vol. 16 #4, Dec. 1976).   977.2 H789

Weber, John H., Settlers of Bretzville....[1966]. 35pp.   977.202 B845w

ELKHART COUNTY

Formed 1830 from Cass, Allen   County Seat—Goshen

Births:

WPA, Index to birth records, 1882-1920.	977.201 E43u
WPA, Index to birth records, city of Elkhart, 1882-1920; city of Goshen, 1882-1920; city of Nappanee, 1907-1920.	977.201 E43u

Deaths:

WPA, Index to death records, 1882-1920.	977.201 E43u
WPA, Index to death records, city of Elkhart, 1882-1920; city of Goshen, 1882-1920; city of Nappanee, 1904-1920.	977.201 E43u

Deeds:

Deed indexes, 1831-1898.	microfilm

Marriages:

DAR, Marriage records...1850-1853....1974. [38]pp.	977.201 E43daa
DAR, Marriage records...1830 through 1849. 1973. [109pp.]	977.201 E43da
Howorth, M.C., The Protestant Episcopal Church in the U.S. Northern Ind. Diocese, Goshen..., St. James Parish register. 1969. 59pp.	977.202 G676h
Marriages, 1831-1858.	microfilm
Marriages, 1830-1849 (THG, vol. 10 #6, Nov.-Dec. 1970; vol. 11 #1, Jan.-Mar. 1971).	977.2 H789
Slevin, Ruth M., ...Marriage records, 1830-1849. 1971. [10], 27pp.	977.201 E43sle
WPA, Index to marriage records, 1850-1920.	977.201 E43u

Probates:

Probates, 1830-1852; indexes, 1852-1900.	microfilm

Wills:

Wills, 1845-1891, 1893-1900.	microfilm
Slevin, Ruth M., ...Will records, 1845-1881. 1971. 156pp.	977.201 E43sl

Cemetery & Church:

DAR, Tombstone records...Comp. by Reah McGaffey. 1971. 104pp.	977.201 E43d
Ind. Hist. Soc., [Cemetery records...]. 2pts. (Stutsman, Jackson cemeteries).	p.f. 977.201 E43 no. 1
Goshen, Indiana, Cemetery records (1900 and prior years). 2pts. ([1] Oak Ridge cemetery; [2] Violett cemetery).	.p.f. 977.202 G676 no. 1
List of cemeteries....(From Michiana Searcher, vol. 3, 1971). [4pp.]	p.f. 977.201 Euncat. no.1
Giesinger cemetery....(From Michiana Searcher, vol. 3, 1971). 1pp.	p.f. 977.201 Euncat. no. 2
Middleton memorial....(From Michiana S., vol. 3, 1971). 1pp.	p.f. 977.201 Euncat. no. 3
Dutch Lutheran Southwest cemetery. (From MS., vol. 10, 1978). 5pp.	p.f. 977.201 Euncat. no. 4
Primitive Baptist cemetery. (From M.S., vol. 10, 1978). 4pp.	p.f. 977.201 Euncat. no. 5
Mishler, Iverson E., Historical sketch of Whitehead cemetery. (From M.S., vol. 10, 1978). 3pp.	p.f. 977.201 Euncat. no. 6
[Inscriptions from] Alwine cemetery. (From M.S., vol. 10, 1978). 12pp.	p.f. 977.201 Euncat. no. 7
[Inscriptions from] Inbody cemetery....(From M.S., vol. 10, 1978). 8pp.	p.f. 977.201 Euncat. no. 8
Troup, Linda, Vistula cemetery, Vistula...Indiana. (From M.S. vol. 10, 1978). [12pp.]	p.f. 977.202 Vuncat. no. 1
McGaffey, Reah Jane, Vital statistics record of Trinity Methodist Episcopal Church of Elkhart...1862 to 1900. 1972. 105pp.	977.202 E43e

Miscellaneous:

Michiana Searcher, Elkhart County Genealogical Society....Vol. 1 #1, March 1969-	977.201 E43s
Michiana Roots: queries excerpted from the genealogy column...South Bend Tribune....1973-1976. 3 vols.	977.2 M624
Collins, Carolyn, Michiana Roots...1980. vol. 2.	977.2 M624c
Elkhart County Genealogical Society Newsheet. (scattered issues in 1967-8).	977.201 E43n
Pickrell, Martha M., Index to the 1880 federal census of the City of Elkhart. 1979. 31pp.	p.f. 977.202 Euncat. no. 1
Obituaries, administrative notices and other news items abstracted from early South Bend newspapers, November 1831 through December 1854 (THG, vol. 18 #1, Mar. 1978).	977.2 H789
Tract book, 1830-1854.	microfilm

FAYETTE COUNTY

Formed 1819 from Franklin, Wayne　　　　　　　　　　　　　　　　County Seat—Connersville

Births:

Births, 1893-1899.	microfilm
Births, Connersville, 1883-1904.	microfilm

Deaths:

Deaths, 1883-1907.	microfilm
Deaths, 1829-1849 (THG, vol. 19 #1, Mar. 1979).	977.2 H789

Deeds:

Deed indexes, 1816-1903.	microfilm

Marriages:

DAR, Marriage records...[1819-1822].	p.f. 977.201 F284 no. 4
Fayette...marriages, 1819-1822; 1823-1826; 1825-1830. (From IMH, vol. 52, 1956). 3pts.	p.f. 977.201 Funcat. no. 3
Marriages, 1819-1901.	microfilm
Slevin, Ruth M., ...Marriages, 1870-1905. [197-?]. 78, 78pp.	977.201 F284s

Probates:

Probates, 1829-1838; indexes, 1852-1911. *Prob. Court Estate, Inv. + Sale 1819-20 —*　　microfilm / *film*

Wills:

Wills, 1819-1900.　　　　　　　　　　　　　　　　　　　　　　　　　　　　microfilm
Wills — by Ruth Slevin 1819-1895 + some early intestate Records —　　977.801 F284z

Cemetery:

D.A.C., Old cemeteries....[1964]. 227pp.; also 100pp. index; also Additions.... 1976. [4pp.]	977.201 284n / 977.20F284n *Sup.*
DAR, [Cemetery records...]. 6pts.	p.f. 977.201 F284 no. 3
John Conner Junior Hist. Soc., ...Cemetery survey, 1978-1980, Connersville High School. [1980?]. 168pp.	977.201 F284fc
[Ind. Junior Hist. Soc., ...Cemetery records]. (Orange cemetery). 1pp.	p.f. 977.201 F284 no. 6
Elliott, Maize and Mary Neff, [Records] notes taken, Connersville (Ind.)—City cemetery. 1956-62. 6pts.	p.f. 977.202 C752 no. 1
Mayhill, R.T., ...Cemetery, Harrison township, located 4 3/4 miles south of Bentonville. 1pp.	p.f. 977.201 Funcat. no. 4 pt. 2
Waterloo cemetery. (From Illiana Geneal., vol. 7, 1971). 1pp.	p.f. 977.201 Funcat. no. 5
[Miscellaneous...permits for burial, removal, and interments]. 2pp.	p.f. 977.201 Funcat. no. 6
Lick Creek cemetery...Harrison township. 8pp.	p.f. 977.201 Funcat. no. 7
Gordon, Robert T., Funeral invitations of Connersville....1973. [14pp.]	p.f. 977.201 Funcat. no. 8
Stevens, C.P., Stevens graveyard....[3pp.]	p.f. 977.201 Funcat no. 1
Quinlan, Elsie, The Mt. Garrison cemetery. 3pp.	p.f. 977.201 Funcat. no. 2
Mayhill, R.T., [Location of some Fayette and Wayne county cemetery records] clipping from Eastern Indiana Farmer, Jan. 9, 1962. 1pp.	p.f. 977.201 Funcat. no. 4 pt.1

Taxes:

Assessor's book...Jackson township...1878, 1879, 1880. (Original handwritten record book).	977.201 Funcat. no. 1
Taxpayers, 1829 (THG, vol. 11 #4, Oct.-Dec. 1971).	977.2 H789
Darlington, Jane E., ...1842 tax book. [1982]. n.p.	977.201 F284d

Miscellaneous:

DAR, [Marriages and deaths from Mrs. Kelsey's scrapbook, Fayette, Wayne and Rush counties]. 1938. [6]pp.	p.f. 977.201 F284 no. 1
___, [Miscellaneous collection of records copied from memory books and diaries]. [5pts.]	p.f. 977.201 F284 no. 5
Enumeration of white and colored males over 21 years of age...1877. 5pts. (Columbia; Jackson; Jennings; Orange; Posey twps.).	977.201 Funcat. no. 2
Holmes, Maurice, Court records...1819-1849. 1978. 328pp.	977.201 F284ho
___, Early landowners....1976. 17, 67pp.	977.201 F284h
Manuscripts of historic Connersville, Indiana [includes records of Trinity Episcopal Church and First Presbyterian Church].	microfilm
Scrapbook of Althea Thomas, 1927-1935, Fairview area. (obituaries primarily).	microfilm

FLOYD COUNTY

Formed 1819 from Clark, Harrison   County Seat—New Albany

Births:

Births, 1882-1907.	microfilm
WPA, index to birth records, 1882-1920.	977.201 F645u

Deaths:

WPA, Index to death records, 1882-1920.	977.201 F645u

Deeds:

Deeds, 1818-1829; indexes, 1803 [?]-1904.	microfilm

Marriages:

DAR, First marriage book...1819-1845. 1964, 1972. 2 vols.	977.201 F645dm
Marriages, 1819-1853; 1885-1891.	microfilm
Slevin, Ruth M., ...Marriages, 1837-1845. [197-.] 27, 27pp.	977.201 F645s
WPA, Index to marriage records, 1845-1920.	977.201 F645u
WPA, Index to supplemental records, marriage transcript, 1880-1905.	977.201 F645u

Probates:

Probates, 1830-1846; indexes, 1868-1872.	microfilm
Probate index, 1830-1837 (THG, vol. 4 #5. Sept.-Oct. 1964; vol. 5 #1-2, Jan.-Feb., Mar.-Apr. 1965).	977.2 H789

[handwritten: Probate Book L + Index 1862-1864   film]

Wills:

DAR, [Wills and court order records...]. Sept. 28, 1892-Jan. 6, 1893. [1958]. 16pp.	977.201 F645d
DAR, Will book A, 1819-1830 and probate court records, 1830-1837....1964. 121pp.	977.201 F645dw
DAR, Will and bond record "B", Mar. 1853-Sept. 1864....Abstracted by Mrs. M. Arthur Payne. 1973. [134pp.]	977.201 F645dau
Wills, 1819-1829, 1852-1900.	microfilm
Abstracts of...wills, book A, 1818-1829. (From THG, vol. 4 #5-6, Sept.-Oct., Nov.-Dec. 1964)	p.f. 977.201 Funcat. no. 4
Index to intestate records, will book A, 1819-1829 (THG, vol. 5 #1, Jan.-Feb. 1965)	977.2 H789

Cemetery & Church:

DAR, Bible and cemetery records. Comp. by Mrs. Elizabeth S. Payne. 1967, 1970. 2 vols.	977.201 F645dbc
___, [Floyd county cemetery records]. 3pts. (Bert Collins' farm; A.F. Dant farm; Schrader cemetery).	p.f. 977.201 F645 no. 1
___, 950 tombstone inscriptions from cemeteries in Floyd, Clark and Harrison counties....Comp. by Mrs. M. Arthur Payne. 1963. 110pp.	977.201 F645n
___, Cemetery records....1953. 64pp.	p.f. 977.201 F645 no. 3
Stoner, Frederica C., Old "Scott" grave yard, New Albany....1952. 5pp.	p.f. 977.201 F645 no. 4
Ind. Junior Hist. Soc., ...Cemetery records. [1], Schwarz, Knierieman, Mt. Eden, Johnsons Chapel, Dow.	p.f. 977.201 F645 no. 5
Summers, Catherine, Gunn family plot....1972. 1pp.	p.f. 977.201 F645 no. 6
Dearing, Michael L., Census of St. Mary Catholic cemetery, Navilleton....1979. 23pp.	p.f. 977.201 Funcat. no. 2
Inscriptions from the Monahon, Fisher, and Hessing cemeteries of Georgetown township....[9pp.]	p.f. 977.201 Funcat. no. 3

Carr, M.W., History of catholicity in New Albany and Jeffersonville, and Floyd and Clark counties.... 1890. 71pp.   p.f. 977.201 Funcat. no. 5

Family:

DAR, Ancestral papers. Comp. by Mrs. Elizabeth S. Payne. 1967. 143pp.   977.201 F645da

___, Bible records and family records. Comp. by Mrs. M. Arthur Payne. 1961. 219pp.   977.201 F645db

___, Genealogical records for Piankeshaw Chapter. (Contains wills, probates, tombstone records). 2pts.   p.f. 977.201 F645 no. 2

Mouser, Mrs. Sylvan L., [...Genealogy notebook, 1937-1941]. 230pp.   p.f. 977.201 Funcat. no. 1

Miscellaneous:

DAR, Abstracts of entries of government lands....Cop. by Mrs. Elizabeth S. Payne. 1965. 146pp.   977.201 F645dL

Payne, Elizabeth S., Index to applications for citizenship.... 1973. 22pp.   977.201 F645p

WPA, Commissioners' record... 1818-1824....   Ind. Hist. Soc. Library

FOUNTAIN COUNTY

Formed 1826 from Montgomery, Parke   County Seat—Covington

Births:

WPA, Index to birth records, 1887-1920.	977.201 F771u

Deaths:

WPA, Index to death records, 1882-1920.	977.201 F771u

Marriages:

Luke, Miriam, ...Marriage records—Book 1-2, 1826-1848 and letters of administration, 1832-1846. n.d. [32], 62pp.	977.201 F771Lm
DAR, [...Records]. 1928, 1938. 3 vols. (vol. 2, marriages, 1826-1848).	977.201 F771d
WPA, Index to marriage records, 1848-1920.	977.201 F771u
WPA, Index to supplemental record, marriage transcript, 1880-1905.	977.201 F771u

Wills:

Luke, Miriam, ...Abstracts of first book of wills (1827-1851) and original land records. [1968]. 70pp.	977.201 F771L
Wills, 1827-1848, 1852-1899.	microfilm

Cemetery:

Bounell, Mrs. E.G., Tombstone inscriptions, Cain township....1937. 36pp.	977.201 F771b
DAR, Cemetery records of Van Buren township....[1960]. 83pp.	977.201 F771dc
———, [Fountain County, Indiana records]. 1928, 1938. 3 vols. [vol. 1, History and genealogies....[164]pp.; vol. 2, Marriages, 1826-1848. [119]pp.; vol. 3, pt. 1, Cemetery records for Davis, Logan, Richardson, Shawnee twps. [159]pp.; vol. 3, pt.2, Record of burials in Troy, Wabash and Fulton twps., prior to 1875....[89]pp.]	
Centennial cemetery, Millcreek township....1974. [1], 36, [8]pp.	977.201 F771c
DAR, A History of centennial church and the old cemetery and founders, Redenbaugh and Myers. By Iona H. Male and Retha H. Featherstone. 1970. 233pp.	977.201 F771dm
Grimes, W. Oscar, Nolan cemetery....1961. [1], 1pp. McCormick, Ruth G., Harveysburg cemetery....1975. 24, [7]pp.	977.201 F771g
Hallett, Katherine, Bonebrake cemetery, Van Buren township....1977. 51, [11]pp.	977.201 F771h
Church of Jesus Christ of Latter Day Saints, Cemetery records...Union cemetery. 1962. 29pp.	p.f. 977.201 Funcat. no. 4
Hardin, Rebecca S., Information regarding "Crazy Corner" Progressive Friends cemetery....[7pp.]	p.f. 977.201 Funcat. no. 5
[Ind. Hist. Soc.], [Cemetery records].... 12pts.	p.f. 977.201 F771 no. 1
———, [Church records...]. [Church of Christ, Cold Spring]. 9, 28pp.	p.f. 977.201 F771 no. 2
DAR, Scotts Prairie cemetery. 1953. [4]pp.	p.f. 977.201 F771 no. 3
Livengood, George H., Zackmire cemetery...Jackson twp....1961. 9pp.	p.f. 977.201 F771 no. 5
Barkley, Grace, [Cemetery records...]. [1] Davis cemetery, Wabash township [2] Hibbs cemetery, Wabash township. 1963. [3pp.]	p.f. 977.201 F771 no. 6
Cox, Carroll O., [Cemetery records...]. [1], Riverside cemetery, Attica. [1966]. 2pp.	p.f. 977.201 F771 no. 7
Ringold, Dorothy V., Babb cemetery, Veedersburg....1972. 1pp.	p.f. 977.201 F771 no. 8
Ind. Junior Hist. Soc., ...Cemetery records in Cain, Jackson, Millcreek, Van Buren, and Richland townships. 1969. [34pp.]	p.f. 977.201 Funcat. no. 1
Beulah, Raymond Wilson farm, unnamed...cemeteries....(From Illiana Geneal., vols. 2, 4, 5, 12). [4pp.]	p.f. 977.201 Funcat. no. 2

Hallett, Katherine, Old town cemetery of Hillsboro...Cain township. 1976. 25pp. p.f. 977.202 H655h

Livengood, George H., Phanuel Lutheran church, Wallace, Indiana, a listing of the graves in the old section of the Lutheran cemetery. 1959. 29, [8]pp. p.f. 977.202 W187L

Grimes, W.O., A Record of the new addition of Wallace Lutheran cemetery (up to 1968). (Phanuel). [1969]. v.p. p.f. 977.202 W187La

Miscellaneous:

DAR, Bible records. 1954. [21pp.] p.f. 977.201 F771 no. 4

Dillon, Mrs. Clark, Deaths...1889-1898. (...From the old Fisher Funeral home at Veedersburg, printed in Illiana Geneal., vol. 13, 1977). [5pp.] p.f. 977.201 Funcat. no. 3

Luke, Miriam, ...Court records: also, some former residences of early Fountain county families from original land patents and bounty land warrants. 1979. v.p. 977.201 F771Lu

———, Revolutionary soldiers...[1978?]. [8pp.] 973.34 I385Lu

WPA, Index to supplemental record, registered voters, 1920. 977.201 F771u

FRANKLIN COUNTY

Formed 1811 from Clark, Dearborn, Jefferson   County Seat—Brookville

Births:

Births, 1882-1907.	microfilm
WPA, Index to birth records, 1882-1920.	977.201 F831u

Deaths:

WPA, Index to death records, 1882-1920.	977.201 F831u

Deeds:

Deed indexes, 1811-1902.	microfilm

Marriages:

DAR, Marriage records...1811 to 1852. Cop. by Mrs. Roscoe C. O'Byrne. 1944. [186]pp.	977.201 F831dm
Marriages, 1811-1890.	microfilm
O'Byrne, Mrs. Estella, [Marriage records...1811-1820]. n.p. 1927. 3pts.	p.f. 977.201 F834 no. 2
WPA, Index to marriage records, 1850-1920.	977.201 F831u
WPA, Index to marriage transcript record, 1882-1920.	977.201 F831u
Marriages, 1811-Mar. 1824 (THG, vol. 13 #3, July-Sept. 1973).	977.2 H789

Probates:

Probates, 1811-1854. *[handwritten: Probate order Book 1 T 27, 34]* *[handwritten: Lots of Probate material. see Vol 34 p #3]*   microfilm

Wills:

Slevin, Ruth M., ...Will records, 1813-1936. [19—]. 3 vols. (Surname index by Maurice Holmes. 1978).	977.201 F831sL
Wills, 1814-1831; 1852-1900.	microfilm

[handwritten: Will settlement 1837-54]   *[handwritten: film]*

Cemetery:

DAR, [Cemetery, Bible and church records...]. Comp. by Mrs. Roscoe C. O'Byrne. 1942. [36pts.] 100pp.	977.201 F831d
Eldon, Howard, Old Quick burial ground, Brookville township....1967. 2pp.	p.f. 977.201 Funcat. no. 8
...Cemetery records, Fairfield township. (High school term papers).	p.f. 977.201 Funcat. no. 9
...Cemetery records (unnamed cemeteries). (High school term papers). 2pts.	p.f. 977.201 Funcat. no. 6
Ind. Hist. Soc., [Cemetery records...]. [pt. 1] McKindrie Missionary Baptist Church. 1942. 1pp.	p.f. 977.201 F834 no. 1
DAR, Cemetery records....7 pts.	p.f. 977.201 F834 no. 3
Eldon, Howard I., Cemetery records....[1] Eldon cemetery; [2] Holliday cemetery. [2pp.]	p.f. 977.201 E834 no. 5
Ind. Junior Hist. Soc., [...Cemetery records]. 1970. 12 pts.	p.f. 977.201 F834 no. 6
Vandenbosch, Mrs. Joseph, List of deaths and burials of Saint Anne's Hamburg.... [1974]. [7pp.]	p.f. 977.201 F834 no. 7
Newman, John J., et al, ...Cemetery records. 11 pts.	p.f. 977.201 F834 no. 8
...Cemetery records. High school term papers. 9 pts. [#2 missing 1982].	p.f. 977.201 F834 no. 9
Portteus, George W., et al, Names in stone, a record of the Wesley Chapel cemetery near Mt. Carmel, Indiana. [1981?]. 12pp.	977.201 F831cn
Davis, Virgil C., Big Cedar Baptist church records and cemetery inscriptions...n.d. 101pp.	977.201 F831da

Church:

The Admission, baptismal, and marriage records of Harmony Presbyterian Church, established May 26, 1837 in Bath township....Cop. by Virgil E. Davis. 1951. [24pp.]	p.f. 977.201 Funcat. no. 5 pt.2
Data copied from the original record book of the old Franklin Church. 18pp.	p.f. 977.201 Funcat. no. 4
Harmony Presbyterian Church records...with listing of early members and a calendar of 1906. 21pp.	p.f. 977.201 Funcat. no. 5 pt.1
Records of the Mt. Carmel Presbyterian Church, Mt. Carmel...1835-1866. [224], 12pp.	977.202 M928m
DAR, Presbyterian church history, Mt. Carmel...1824-1950. Cop. from booklet prepared by Mrs. John A. Craig from record and session books of Church. 1958. 19pp.	977.202 M928p

Court:

Apprentice record, 1831-1853.	microfilm
Commissioners record, 1847-1852.	microfilm
Court of common pleas and circuit court records, 1811-1836.	microfilm
Estates, 1811-1820.	microfilm
Issue docket, 1811.	microfilm
Naturalizations, 1826-1929.	microfilm
Naturalizations, Sept. 1826-Mar. 1839 (THG, vol. 18 #4, Dec. 1978).	977.2 H789

Family:

Genealogical notes from Indiana American, Franklin Repository, Brookville Inquirer, 1827-1839. 36, [14]pp.	977.201 F831g
Genealogical notes from Indiana American, 1840-1849. 64, [18]pp.	977.201 F831ga
Genealogical notes from Indiana American and the Franklin Democrat, 1850-1859. 94, [18]pp.	977.201 F831gb
Genealogical notes from the Franklin Democrat, 1860-1869. 68, [13]pp.	977.201 F831gc
Genealogical notes from Franklin Democrat, Brookville American, 1870-1879. 2 vols.	977.201 F831gd
Genealogical notes from Franklin Democrat and Brookville American, 1880-1889. 2 vols.	977.201 F831ge
Genealogical notes from Franklin Democrat and Brookville American, 1890-1899. 1 vol.	977.201 F831gf
Genealogical notes [from Brookville Democrat, 1901?-1905]. 42, 7pp.	977.201 F831gg
Holmes, Maurice, ...Genealogy items. 1974. 93pp.	977.201 F831h
Genealogical notes, From scrapbook of Mrs. Phebe Davis. 8pp.	p.f. 977.201 Funcat. no. 3

Mortuary & Obituaries:

Holmes, Maurice, Mortuary records: Thorpe and Williams Mortuary, Metamora, Indiana for the years 1878-1932. 1974. 61pp.	977.202 M587h
[Obituaries of pioneer residents...], newspaper clippings....[4pp.]	p.f. 977.201 Funcat. no. 2

Taxes:

Assessment records, 1833.	microfilm
Darlington, Jane E., "A List of the taxable property in the township of Bath...subject to taxation according to the different revenue lists taken for the year 1822...." [1981?] [9pp.]	977.201 F831dar 1981
O'Byrne, Mrs. Roscoe C., ...Tax lists [1812-1849]. 1966/1968. 3 vols.	977.201 F831o

...Tax list, 1819. n.p.   q977.201 F831t

Taxpayers 1811 (THG, vol. 11 #3, July-Sept. 1971)   977.2 H789

Miscellaneous:

DAR, ...Tract book [1804-1821]. 1952. 7, 30pp.   p.f. 977.201 F834 no. 4

Early settlers...as shown by signatures on petitions for pardon, Centerville, May 14, 1825. 5pp.   p.f. 977.201 Funcat. no. 1

Estray book, 1811-1814.   microfilm

Register of negroes and mulattoes....[1852]. 17pp.   p.f. 977.201 Funcat. no. 7

Register of negroes, 1853-1856.   microfilm
    (also in THG, vol. 17 #2, June 1977).   977.2 H789

Stock brands, 1811-1839.   microfilm

Newman, John J., Index to...1840 federal census....1965. n.p.   977.201 F831n

Stewart, Alta Mae, Peoria Academy. [14]pp.   977.201 F831s

FULTON COUNTY

Formed 1835; organized 1836 from Cass, St. Joseph   County Seat—Rochester

Deaths:

WPA, Index to death records, 1882-1920.	977.201 F974u

Deeds:

Deeds, 1836-1839; indexes, 1836-1897.	microfilm

Marriages:

Marriages, 1836-1905.	microfilm
Marriages, 1836-July 1845 (THG, no. 5, Sept.-Oct. 1963)	977.2 H789
Tombaugh, Jean, ...Marriage record, 1921-1965. 1969. 418pp.	977.201 F974tm
WPA, Index to marriage records, 1850-1920....1962. 449pp.	977.201 F974un 1962

Probates:

Probates, 1842-1851; indexes, 1851-1907.	microfilm

Wills:

Tombaugh, Jean, ...Abstracts of wills, 1838-1899. 1967. 301pp.	977.201 F974tw

Cemetery & Church:

[Ind. Hist. Soc., Cemetery records...]. 3 pts. (Hizer, Fletcher's Lake Presbyterian cemetery, Old South Mudlake German Baptist Brethren...).	p.f. 977.201 F974 no. 1
Bright, Velma, ...Cemetery inscriptions, Henry township, plus a 1933 roll call of the Akron American Legion post. Indexed & typed by Jean C. Tombaugh. 1974. 343pp.	977.201 F974b
Tombaugh, Jean C., ...Cemetery inscriptions (with genealogical notes). 1976-1981. 4 vols.	977.201 F974tc
Taylor, Marcia K., ...(Poor) farm cemetery record, Rochester, Indiana. 1973. [3]pp.	p.f. 977.201 F974 no. 3
White, Fletcher W., [Information about Olive Bethel Church...]. [3pp.]	p.f. 977.201 Funcat. no. 1

Court:

Tombaugh, Jean C., Indiana commissioners record "A" (Apr. 1836-Mar. 1845). 1974. 440pp.	977.201 F974tf
———, ...Judgment docket A, 1836-1850. 1974. 78pp.	977.201 F974to
———, ...Wayne township, justice of peace docket, 1877-1882; 1882-1898; 1894-1921. 1967, 1970. 3 vols.	977.201 F974t

Miscellaneous:

Estates, 1865-1883.	microfilm
Tract book, 1832-1874.	microfilm
Ind. State Library, ...1840 census. 1970. 5pp.	p.f. 977.201 F974 no. 2
Tombaugh, Jean C., ...Newspapers abstracted. The Rochester Sentinel, Jan. 4, 1862-Dec. 20, 1862. 1975. 100pp.	977.201 F974tn
———, ...School enumeration record, 1896. 1970. 249pp.	977.201 F974ts
———, Register book of the...poor farm (1871-1965). 1966. 131pp.	977.201 F974f
Fulton Co. Hist. Soc., Fulton County Folks. 1974/1981. 2 vols.	977.201 F974
Van Duyne, Fred K., A History of the Mt. Zion community. 1972. 65pp.	977.202 M928v

GIBSON COUNTY

Formed 1813 from Knox   County Seat—Princeton

Births:

Births, 1882-1907.   microfilm

WPA, Index to birth records, 1882-1920.   977.201 G448u

Deaths:

WPA, Index to death records, 1880-1920.   977.201 G448u

Deeds:

Deeds, 1813-1833.   microfilm

Marriages:

DAR, Early marriage records...[1813-1859]...some of Knox Co. and Pike co.
    Comp. by Mrs. George Shawhan. [1967]. n.p.   977.201 G448d

Chandler, Ruth A., Indiana early Gibson county marriages [1807-1868]. [1970?].
    133pp.   977.201 G448c

...Marriage records, 1813-1822, 1823-1832 (From THG, vol. 9 #5-6, Sept.-Oct.,
    Nov.-Dec. 1969). 14pp.   p.f. 977.201 Guncat. no. 2
                                                                                                                                           977.2 H789

Marriages, 1813-1869, 1875-1890.   microfilm

WPA, Index to marriage records, 1850-1920.   977.201 G448u

WPA, Index to supplemental record, marriage transcript, 1880-1920.   977.201 G488u

Probates:

Probates, 1817-1830.   microfilm

Wills:

Wills, 1813-1834.   microfilm

Cemetery & Church:

Cox, Carroll O., ...Cemetery records (Archer, Clark, Fitzgerald, Maple Hill, Mauck,
    Maumee, Odd Fellows-Hazleton, Odd Fellows-Princeton, Old Schoolhouse,
    Phillips, Presbyterian, Patoka, Shiloh, Warnock). 1967. v.p.   p.f. 977.201 G448 no. 1

Stone, Jane L., Gudgel graveyard....1972. 1pp.   p.f. 977.201 G448 no. 2

[Woods, Robert M.], Marsh creek cemetery....4pp.   p.f. 977.201 G448 no. 3

[Ind. Hist. Soc.], ...Cemetery records. Comp. by Ella C. Wheatley. 1942. 109pp.
    (Oakland City Baptist Church, Montgomery cemetery).   977.201 G448i

Plat map of Warnock cemetery....   p.f. 977.201 Guncat. no. 3

Jacobus, Grace B., Soldiers and patriots of the American Revolutionary War buried in
    Gibson....1978. 46pp.   973.34 I385j

Turman, Robert E., Cemetery records of southern Indiana (Tombstone data copied
    from 17 old cemeteries in Posey, Gibson, and Vanderburgh county in the vicinity
    of Owensville, Cynthiana, and Poseyville, Ind.). 20pp.   p.f. 977.201 G448t

———, ...(same as above but edited and with additional genealogical data 1977 by
    Madge Yeager Olson. 1977. 36pp.).   977.201 G448t 1977

Cox, Gloria M., Big Creek Baptist Church...minute book. 1976. [4]pp.   p.f. 977.201 G448co

Miscellaneous:

Court of common pleas and circuit court records, 1813-1839.   microfilm

Cunningham, Leland S., Early Hazleton, Indiana. 1980. 73pp.   977.202 H431c

Dunn, Caroline, Notes on material concerning Seminary township...in minutes of
    trustees of Vincennes University....1953. [2pp.]   p.f. 977.201 Guncat. no. 1

Smith, William W., Newspaper abstracts of Owensville and Gibson
 county...1872-1915....Ed. and with index by Michael L. Cook. 1978. 160pp.   977.201 G448n

Tax lists, 1819, 1826.   microfilm

GRANT COUNTY

Formed 1831 from Madison, Delaware, CassCounty Seat—Marion

Deeds:

Deed indexes, 1831-1899.microfilm
    (By townships, scattered dates)

Marriages:

DAR, [Records of...]. 1943-1957. 9 vols. (vols. 1-2, Marriages, 1831-1886).977.201 G761d

Marriages, 1831-1898.microfilm

Marriages, 1831-1853 (THG, vol. 14 #2, Apr.-June 1974).977.2 H789

Slevin, Ruth M., ...Marriage records, 1831-1882. 1974. 151, 152pp.977.201 G761s

Probates:

Probates, 1831-1853; indexes, 1858-1871, 1875-1898.microfilm

Wills:

DAR, [Records of...]. 1943-1957. 9 vols. (vol 5, Wills, 1839-1889).977.201 G761d

Miscellaneous:

DAR, [Records of Grant county, Indiana]. 1943-1957. 9 vols. [Vol. 1, pt.1, marriage records, 1831-1864, 66pp.; vol. 1, pt.2, marriage records, 1865-1886, 49pp.; newspaper items from the Marion Chronicle, 1867-1886, 55pp.; vol. 2, pts. 1-2, cemetery records, 257, 167pp.; vol. 3, methodists and methodism, 200pp.; vol. 4, pts.1-3, Civil War diaries and letters, 266, 323, 210pp.; vol. 5, wills, 1839-1889, 115pp.; vol. 6, newpspaer items (obituaries, 1867-1925), 128pp.; vol. 7, old letters and papers, 208pp.; vol. 8, family records, 228pp.; vol. 9, miscellaneous data, 140pp.]977.201 G761d

Tract book 1825-1857.microfilm

Ellis, Ellwood O., Early friends...(1825-1913). 1961. 26pp. (Published originally in the Centennial History of Grant County, Indiana, 1812-1912. 1914).977.201 G761e

Hodge, Robert A., An Index to the marriage and death notices in the Marion Chronicle, 1867-1882 (A newspaper of Marion, Grant county, Indiana). 1981. 126pp.977.202 M341ho

[Ind. Hist. Soc.], Cemetery records....5pts.p.f. 977.201 G761 no. 1

Kendall, Mrs. John W., ...Soldiers of the War of 1812 who are buried in Grant County. 1944. 1pp.p.f. 977.201 Guncat. no. 1

Grant Co. Junior Hist. Soc., A Century of development....1937. 52pp.p.f. 977.201 Guncat. no. 2

"Lest we forget". Reminiscences of the pioneers....1921. n.p.p.f. 977.201 Guncat. no. 3

Sketches of early pioneers, article from the Fairmount News, Aug. 11, 1903. 4pp.p.f. 977.201 Guncat. no. 4

"Exhibit K" book. "Contains names of parties entitled to land and discriptions... partition of the reservation of Me-shin-go-me-sia, a Miami Indian approved June 1, 1872".p.f. 977.201 Guncat. no. 5

GREENE COUNTY

Formed 1821 from Daviess, Sullivan County Seat—Bloomfield

Births:

WPA, Index to birth records, 1885-1920.	977.201 G812u
WPA, Index to supplemental records, births recorded out of county, 1882-1920 (Sullivan, Clay, Monroe counties).	977.201 G812u

Deaths:

WPA, Index to death records, 1893-1920.	977.201 G812u
Ind. Junior Hist. Soc., Some...death records, 1894-1910. 1972. n.p.	p.f. 977.201 G812 no. 9

Deeds:

Deed indexes, 1822-1902.	microfilm

Marriages:

Marriages, 1821-1827, 1832-1854.	microfilm
Marriages, 1821-1827 (THG, vol. 4 #2, Mar.-Apr. 1964).	977.2 H789
WPA, Index to marriage records, 1821-1920.	977.201 G812u
WPA, Index to supplemental record, marriage transcript, 1882-1893.	977.201 G812u
WPA, Index to supplemental record, marriage applications, 1905-1911.	977.201 G812u

Probates:

Probates, 1823-1843, 1848-1852; indexes, 1852-1900?	microfilm

Wills:

Wills, 1839-1904.	microfilm
...Will records, 1825-1904, books 1-5. [1975?]. 177pp. (also 1981 edition, 210pp.).	977.201 G812gr

Cemetery & Church:

DAR, [Cemetery records...]. 9pts.	p.f. 977.201 G812 no. 3
Hunter, Mardenna J., Cemetery records....2pts. (Old Slinkard, Bynum).	p.f. 977.201 G812 no. 2
Ind. Hist. Soc., [Cemetery records...]. 1946. 2 pts. (Chambers, Hicks Church).	p.f. 977.201 G812 no. 1
Royal, Mrs. Dennis, Simpson Chapel cemetery....[16pp.]	977.201 G812ro
Hudson, Mrs. Merle, Owensburg cemetery, Jackson twp....[1964]. 3, 6pp.	p.f. 977.201 G812 no. 4
Ingalls, Mrs. Robert, [Cemeteries...]. 1pp. (L.W. Creager farm, Edington Springs, Old Owensburg).	p.f. 977.201 G812 no. 5
Hull, Evelyn J., Names from the Hays cemetery near Worthington....n.d. [5pp.]	p.f. 977.201 G812 no. 6
Dalby, Barbara M., A Few cemetery listings near Worthington....1970? 17pp.	p.f. 977.201 G812 no. 7
Ind. Junior Hist. Soc., ...Cemetery records. 1971-1973. 3 pts.	p.f. 977.201 G812 no. 8
Kelley, Phyllis, Carmichael cemetery, section 24, Center township....1974. 25pp.	p.f. 977.201 G812 no. 10
Bland, H.J., [Lebanon cemetery...correspondence from H.J. Bland, Jasonville...]. 1pp.	p.f. 977.201 Guncat. no. 1
Williams, Mrs. Thomas H., Baker and Thompson family cemetery inscriptions.... 2pp. (missing 1982)	p.f. 977.201 Guncat. no. 2
Cline, Sam, Waggoner cemetery, Grant township....4pp.	p.f. 977.201 Guncat. no. 3
[Inscriptions of stones on the old George W. Morgan farm near old Marco....] (From Illiana Geneal., vol. 5, 1969). 1pp.	p.f. 977.201 Guncat. no. 4
Unnamed cemetery...(From Illiana Geneal., vol. 5, 1969). 1pp.	p.f. 977.201 Guncat. no. 5
Accounts of Dr. James D. English and J.I. Speeker, partners in South Hill cemetery [Worthington...] 1920-1924. [5pp.]	p.f. 977.201 Guncat. no. 6

Meredith, Mildred, Rainbolt cemetery, Center township....1979. 1pp. p.f. 977.201 Guncat. no. 7

Pergal, Mrs. Edna, Bohley cemetery, Grant township....1980. [7pp.] p.f. 977.201 Guncat. no. 8

Dalby, Mrs. Barbara M., Sander's cemetery....(From Geneal. Ref. Builders, vol. 5, 1971). 3pp. p.f. 977.201 Guncat. no. 9

Peruch, Patricia A., Edwards cemetery, rural Solsberry....1968. (From Geneal. Research News, vol. 7, 1969). 2pp. p.f. 977.201 Guncat. no. 10

Flynn cemetery near Hobbieville....[11pp.] p.f. 977.201 Guncat. no. 11

Meredith, Mildred S., Alphabetical index to Van Slyke cemetery, located at Bloomfield....1979. 6pp. p.f. 977.201 Guncat. no. 12

Scott, Mrs. Bedonna B., Morris Chapel cemetery. 9pp. p.f. 977.201 Guncat. no. 13

Old Moss cemetery (also known as Humphreys cemetery). 3pp. p.f. 977.201 Guncat. no. 14

Meredith, Mildred, Cemeteries....[1979?]. 63, 4, [4]pp. 977.2 M559c

Cogswell, Edith B., A History of the Hicks Presbyterian Church...1854-1951. 1945, rev. 1978. 91pp. 977.201 G812c

Miscellaneous:

Darlington, Jane E., ...Delinquent tax list 1843 (with 1842), received April 22, 1844. [1982?]. [23pp.] 977.201 G812dar

HAMILTON COUNTY

Formed 1823 from Delaware (N.P., unorganized), Marion   County Seat—Noblesville

Births:

WPA, Index to birth records, 1882-1920.	977.201 H222u

Deaths:

WPA, Index to death records, 1882-1920.	977.201 H222u

Deeds:

Deed indexes, 1825-1901.	microfilm

Marriages:

Gibbs, Patricia, Abstracts of...marriage records, 1833-1843. 1978. [42pp.]	977.201 H222g
———, Abstracts from book A...marriage records, 1843-1850. 1979. [42pp.]	977.201 H222ga
[Index to] ...marriage record, book A, June 1843-April 1851. [22pp.]	p.f. 977.201 Huncat. no. 18
Marriages, 1835-1850.	microfilm
Slevin, Ruth M., ...Marriage records, 1837-1845. 24pp.	p.f. 977.201 H217 no. 2
WPA, Index to marriage records, 1850-1879, 1880-1899, 1900-1920. 3pts.	977.201 H222u
WPA, Index to supplemental record, marriage transcript, 1880-1905.	977.201 H222u

Probates:

Probate order books, 1824-1852.	microfilm

Wills:

Wills and estates, 1823-1901.	microfilm
Bevelhimer, Susan, Abstracts of the will records...1824-1901. 1981. 223pp.	977.201 H222bev
Ingmire, Frances T., ...Will record, book A, 1823-1838. 1980. 143pp.	977.201 H222in

Cemetery & Church:

Brooks, Dr. Earl, ...Cemetery records [Fall Creek twp.]. [1951]. [53pp.]	977.201 H222b
Cemetery map...: A Bicentennial project of Marion-Adams Genealogical and Historical Society and the Hamilton County Historical Society. 1976. map.	f977.201 H222c
Correll, James L., Arcadia Brethren cemetery....1979. 3 vols.	q977.202 A668c
Evans, Nellie E., Crown View cemetery, Sheridan, Indiana. 1970. 82pp.	977.202 S552e
[Ind. Hist. Soc., Cemetery records...]. 1939. 5 pts. (Unnamed, Pleasant Grove, Carmel, Old Friends, Anti-Slavery Friends).	p.f. 977.201 H217 no. 1
Hoyt, Mrs. Leo, Cemetery records....[1] White Chapel Methodist Church. 1961. 3pp.	p.f. 977.201 H217 no. 3
Eck, Irene, ...Cemetery records. [pt.1] Zimmer cemetery; Mount Pleasant cemetery; Teeter's Woods; Bethlehem cemetery.	p.f. 977.201 H217 no. 4
Ind. Junior Hist. Soc., ...Cemetery records. [1] Arcadia and Arcadia Lutheran. 1969 [8pp.]	p.f. 977.201 H217 no. 5
Miller, Suzanne, Cemetery—known as Cox cemetery. 1974. 2pp.	p.f. 977.201 H217 no. 6
Dawson, E.H., [...Cemetery records]. 2pts. (White Chapel cemetery, West Grove Quaker Church cemetery).	p.f. 977.201 Huncat. no. 2
Murphy, Thelma M., Pleasant Grove Methodist churchyard....1pp.	p.f. 977.201 Huncat. no. 3
———, Cemetery west of Little Eagle Creek, Washington township....2pp.	p.f. 977.201 Huncat. no. 4
Hoyt, Mrs. Leo, Farley cemetery, 106th street, Indianapolis (Hamilton county)....6pp.	p.f. 977.201 Huncat. no. 5
———, Unnamed cemetery...1/10 mile west and 1/10 mile north of White Chapel Methodist Church cemetery on E. 116th Street. 1pp.	p.f. 977.201 Huncat. no. 6

———, Pleasant Grove Methodist Church cemetery, Delaware township...at 106th Street and College. 2pp.   p.f. 977.201 Huncat. no. 7

McDonnell, Mrs. Robert C., Inscriptions from the Stern cemetery, Wayne township....2pp.   p.f. 977.201 Huncat. no. 8

Helms Burial ground, Fallcreek township....1pp.   p.f. 977.201 Huncat. no. 9

Fisher, Robert V., Hair cemetery, Wayne township....[not complete]. 2pp.   p.f. 977.201 Huncat. no. 10

Jarrett, Aloise R., A Complete census of the old Colip cemetery about one-half mile from Strawtown....[3pp.]   p.f. 977.201 Huncat. no. 11

Ind. Junior Hist. Soc., Aroma Methodist Church cemetery, White River township....1970. 4pp.   p.f. 977.201 Huncat. no. 12

———, Carey cemetery, White River township....1970. 4pp.   p.f. 977.201 Huncat. no. 13

———, Crown Hill cemetery, southwest of Arcadia, Jackson township....1970. 4pp.   p.f. 977.201 Huncat. no. 14

———, McCarty cemetery, southwest of Atlanta, Jackson township....1970. 3pp.   p.f. 977.201 Huncat. no. 15

Inscriptions on tombstones at Cicero cemetery, Cicero....1pp.   p.f. 977.201 Huncat. no. 16

Eck, Irene, Zimmer cemetery, Noblesville township....[12pp.]   p.f. 977.201 Huncat. no. 17

Evans, Nellie E., Quaker records and cemetery, 1969, 59, [2]pp.   977.201 H222e

———, Hamilton...cemeteries....vol. 2   977.201 H222ev

Imler, Margaret P., Tombstone inscriptions....[1975-1976]. [30pp.]   p.f. 977.201 H222im

Noblesville Daily Ledger, Seek history of cemeteries in the county, Jan., 1949. clipping. 1pp.   p.f. 977.201 Huncat. no. 1

Pleasant Ridge or Ridge cemetery....(From Illiana Geneal., vol. 6, 1970). [6pp.]   p.f. 977.201 Huncat. no. 21

Stover, Barbara T., Calvary cemetery, Calvary Poplar Grove Church....3pp.   p.f. 977.201 Huncat. no. 22

Roberts Chapel, Kauffman, McCarty, Arcadia and East Union cemeteries...: Ridge cemetery in Tipton county: and Hills cemetery in Clinton county (From "Pictorial History Atlas and Plat Book of Tipton County".). 2pp.   p.f. 977.201 Huncat. no. 25

Essex, Wanda H., Interments in Eagle Creek cemetery...1914 thru 1981. [32pp.]   p.f. 977.201 Huncat. no. 23

Usher, Roddy, Cemetery at Geist Reservoir [Hamilton or Marion counties?, Indiana]. [6pp.]   p.f. 977.201 Huncat. no. 24

2nd Fall Creek Regular Baptist Church records. Cop. by W. Heiss. 1954. [21pp.] (Ollo, Ind.)   p.f. 977.202 046 no. 1

Hinkle Creek Friends [1836-1936].   microfilm

Family:

Bishop, Reginald, "Roberts Heritage Rich", [Roberts Settlement...]. 1976. 1pp.   p.f. 977.201 Huncat. no. 19

Barker, Myrtie, "Families trace roots to migrant orphans" from "My Window" column, Indianapolis News, January 4/5?, 1977.   p.f. 977.201 Huncat. no. 20

Hamilton Co. Hist. Soc., ...Ancestors and their descendants. 16 vols. and index by applicant.   977.201 Huncat.

Miscellaneous:

Conner Prairie Pioneer Settlement Manuscript Collection.   microfilm

Index to estates #1-2 [1840-1937].   microfilm

Ind. State Library, Index to 1840 census....1971. 29pp.   977.201 H222i

Ingmire, Frances T., ...Naturalization certificates, 1855-1905. 1980. 209pp.   977.201 H222ing

Woodard, Marion C., Names in...death notices: An index to the Noblesville Ledger, September 11, 1874 to March 20, 1881. 1978. 2, 52pp.   977.201 H222w

HANCOCK COUNTY

Formed 1827; organized 1828 from Madison   County Seat—Greenfield

Births:

Delayed births prior to 1941 [partial].	miCrofilm
WPA, Index to birth records, 1882-1920.	977.201 H235u

Deaths:

WPA, Index to death records, 1882-1920.	977.201 H235u

Deeds:

Deed indexes, 1827-1905.	microfilm
Deeds, 1828-1887; indexes, 1828-1886.	miCrofilm

Marriages:

Marriages, Apr. 1828-Jan. 1841 (THG, vol. 8 #5-6, Sept.-Oct., Nov.-Dec. 1968).	977.2 H789
Marriages, 1828-1921.	miCrofilm
Marriage applications, 1891-1899, 1904-1921.	miCrofilm
Ridlen, Colleen A., ...Early marriage returns, 1828-1847. 1976. 41pp.	977.201 H235r
WPA, Index to marriage records, 1836-1920 [some earlier marriages to 1828].	977.201 H235u
WPA, Index to marriage transcripts (supplemental record), 1882-1905.	977.201 H235u
WPA, Index to marriage applications (supplemental record), 1905-1920.	977.201 H235u

Probates:

Probates, 1828-1853.	microfilm

Wills:

Holmes, Maurice, Will records...1876-1908. 1977. 220pp.	977.201 H235how
Wills, 1846-1902.	microfilm

Cemetery & Church:

DAR, Mount Carmel cemetery, Center township....1949. [5pp.]	p.f. 977.201 H235 no. 1
Hancock Co. Hist. Soc., Philadelphia cemetery, Sugar Creek township....1974. 84pp.	977.201 H235h
Ind. Junior Hist. Soc., ...Cemetery records. 1976. [57pp.]	977.201 H235i
———, [Greenfield Park cemetery...]. 1978. [20pp.]	p.f. 977.201 H235in
Montrose, Beverly, Pope cemetery, located on farm 1 mile north and 1/2 mile west of Mohawk, Buck Creek twp....1976. 1pp.	p.f. 977.201 H235mo
Shoemaker, Irene E., Photographic records of tombstones of early Indiana settlers, Hancock, Henry and Wayne counties. 57pp.	977.201 H235s
Methodist Episcopal Church, Records of McCordsville charge, Muncie district. [1968?]. n.p. (3 sections).	977.202 M131r
Harper, John E., Cemetery records....[pt.1] Shiloh cemetery, Blue River twp. [1951]. (Also a 1965 ed. cop. by Julia Jones and Beverly Montrose).	p.f. 977.201 H235 no. 3
Heiss, Willard C., [Cemetery records...]. 5pts. (Baptist, Pleasant Hill M.E., Green twp. cem., Olvey-Jackson, Hayes).	p.f. 977.201 H235 no. 4
Ind. Junior Hist. Soc., Cemetery records....[1] Mount Comfort cemetery. [1957]. 8pp.	p.f. 977.201 H235 no. 5
Hoyt, Mrs. Leo, Cemetery records....7 pts.	p.f. 977.201 H235 no. 6
Church of Jesus Christ of Latter Day Saints. [Cemetery records...]. (Little Sugar Creek cemetery). 13pp.	p.f. 977.201 H235 no. 7
Hancock Co. Hist. Soc., Cemetery records....19 pts.	p.f. 977.201 H235 no. 8

Sample, Harriet L., Gilliam Chapel cemetery, McCordsville, Ind. n.d. [3pp.] p.f. 977.201 H235 no. 9

Brown, Immogene B., ...Cemetery records. 3 pts. (Cooper, Harlan, Willow Branch). p.f. 977.201 H235 no. 10

Davis, Rick, Simmons cemetery, Fortville....1971. [5pp.] p.f. 977.201 H235 no. 11

Roney, Amy, Cemetery records....[1] Service men buried in Hancock county; [2] Six Mile cemetery. p.f. 977.201 H235 no. 12

Inscriptions from Simmons cemetery....[6pp.] p.f. 977.201 Huncat. no. 1

Low, Julia, Westland cemetery, Blue River township....1965. [6pp.] p.f. 977.201 Huncat. no. 2

Road map of Fortville...and vicinity...(location of cemeteries in this area). p.f. 977.201 Funcat. no. 1

Miscellaneous:

Condo, Harold, Funeral accounts, Wilkinson, Indiana...(1901-1905; 1908-1912). 2pts. p.f. 977.201 H235 no. 2

Holmes, Maurice, Early landowners....1974. 31, 31pp. 977.201 H235ho

———, Court records...1828 to 1859. 1976. [1], 301pp. 977.201 H235hol

Index to estates [1873-1913]. microfilm

Indentures, 1843-1876. miCrofilm

Naturalizations, 1854-1906. miCrofilm

Montrose, Beverly, List of names on 1840 tax duplicate list....[36pp.] 977.201 H235m

HARRISON COUNTY

Formed 1808 from Knox, Clark   County Seat—Corydon

Births:

Births, 1882-1907.	microfilm
WPA, Index to birth records, 1882-1920.	977.201 H323u

Deaths:

DAR, ...Death returns, 1882-1899. Comp. by Mrs. Albert E. Craydan. 1971. 125, [20pp.].	977.201 H323da

Deeds:

DAR, Deed records A and B...[1809]....1954. 10pp.	p.f. 977.201 H318 no. 2
Deeds, 1809-1829; indexes, 1809-1901 (grantees only, 1843-1854).	microfilm
County land abstract books [1808-1900].	microfilm
Land purchases, 1807-1810 (THG, vol. 11 #2, Apr.-June 1971).	977.2 H789

Marriages:

Beanblossom, Walter S., Marriage affidavits and certificates...1809-18 [65]. 1973. 169, 8pp. (also 66pp. index).	977.201 H323bem
Bruch, Margaret, Marriage register...1809-1817; 1817-1832. 1947/1954. 2 vols. [vol. 2 copied by DAR].	977.201 H323h
Lindsay, Kenneth G., Early marriages in Indiana-Harrison county, 1809-1817. 1977.	977.201 H323L
Marriages, 1809-1817 (THG, vol. 14 #1, Mar. 1974).	977.2 H789
Marriages, 1809-1892.	microfilm
Marriage affidavits, 1866-1875.	microfilm
Slevin, Ruth M., ...Marriages, 1832-1849. 1970? 52, 51pp.	977.201 H323s
WPA, Index to marriage records, 1850-1920.	977.201 H323u
WPA, Index to marriage transcript (supplemental record), 1882-1920.	977.201 H323u

Probates:

Probates, 1814-1852; indexes, 1852-1900.	microfilm

Prob Court Record 1817-29   *film*

Wills:

Abstracts of early wills...1821-1827, 1827-1832 (IMH, vol. 37, 1941). [6pp.]	p.f. 977.201 Huncat. no. 9
Wills, 1809-1832 (THG, vol. 6 #5-6; vol. 7 #1, Sept.-Oct., Nov.-Dec. 1966, Jan.-Feb. 1967).	977.2 H789
DAR, Wills...from books A, B, D [1809-incomplete?]. 1954. 25pp.	p.f. 977.201 H318 no. 3
Wills, 1809-1900.	microfilm

Cemetery:

Cox, Carroll O., Cemetery records....(Bethel, Mt. Zion, Highland Christian, Mauckport).	p.f. 977.201 H318 no. 5
Benson, Amelia, German Reform cemetery, R.R. 3, Corydon, Indiana (located two miles south of Crandall, Ind.). 1967. [6pp.]	p.f. 977.201 H318 no. 6
Griffin, Frederick P., Cemetery records....4 pts.	p.f. 977.201 H318 no. 7
———, ...Cemeteries. [1974?]. 1 vol. (and 18pp. contents index to books 1-3. 1974).	977.201 H323g
Ind. Junior Hist. Soc., ...Cemetery records. [1] Pfrimmers Chapel cemetery. 1971. [3pp.]	p.f. 977.201 H318 no. 9
Fisher, Eugene H., Webster township....Name of cemetery: Smith's Camp Ground....1937. 2pp.	p.f. 977.201 H318 no. 10
Ind. State Lib..., Incomplete index to...cemeteries. 1975/78. 165pp.	977.201 H323i

Neighborhood Youth Corps., ...Cemeteries. 1970. 513pp.	977.201 H323n
———, ...Cemeteries; also three cemeteries, Crawford county. 1971. 271pp.	977.201 H323n 1971
Ryan, Rhonda, Index to...cemeteries (by 1971 N.Y.C.). 1977. 84pp.	977.201 H323r
Summers, Catherine, ...Cemetery records. n.d.	977.201 H323su
DAR, Genealogical records taken from the office of the cemetery custodian (Corydon, Ind.). 1951-54. 3 pts.	977.202 C833c
Griffin, Frederick P., Cedar Hill cemetery...Corydon, Indiana....Rev. to Jan. 1, 1973. [1974?]. 2 vols.	977.202 C833g
[Ind. Hist. Soc. Cemetery records...]. 77 pts. (pt. 66 missing 1982).	p.f. 977.201 H318 no. 1
Four...cemeteries: Charley family, old Conrad, old Goshen, and Silver Lake. [1939-1943.] (From IMH, vols. 35, 36, 39). 11pp.	p.f. 977.201 Huncat. no. 7
Clapp, Pauline, Inscriptions in "Minton" cemetery, west of New Albany....1978. 1pp.	p.f. 977.201 Huncat. no. 8
Gray cemetery....(From Clay Co. Researcher, vol. 2, 1981). 1pp.	p.f. 977.201 Huncat. no. 10
Wilson, James E., Little Flock cemetery, Taylor township....1954. [2pp.]	p.f. 977.201 Huncat. no. 3
Martin, Mrs. Roy, Strong family cemetery...with map showing location. 3pp.	p.f. 977.201 Huncat. no. 4
Ind. State Board of Health, Burial permits...[1899-1904]. 24pp. (missing 1982).	p.f. 977.201 Huncat. no. 5

Church:

Bickel, George, The History of St. Peter's Evangelical Lutheran Church, Corydon, 1852-1952. 7pp.	p.f. 977.201 Huncat. no. 1
[History of] the Corydon Presbyterian Church, Corydon, Indiana. 1pp.	p.f. 977.202 Cuncat. no. 1
Simler, Donnie, History of Wesley Chapel Church...Washington twp....[1962?]. [12pp.]	p.f. 977.201 H318 no. 4

Court:

Circuit court order book, 1817-1820, 1820-1825 (only pages containing applications for Rev. War pensions filmed from this book).	microfilm
Commissioners records, 1844-1853.	microfilm
Court of common pleas and circuit court records, 1809-1819.	microfilm
Beanblossom, Walter S., Naturalization papers...1973. 1 vol. (v.p.).	977.201 H323ben

Family:

Beanblossom, Walter S., South Harrison ancestors (based on a talk given at a meeting of the Harrison County Historical Society on Sept. 25th, 1972). 11p.	p.f. 977.201 H323bes
Deatrick, B.A, Some Harrison...families. Comp. by Walter S. Beanblossom from material collected by B.A. Deatrick. n.d. 8 vols.	977.201 H323d
Genealogy files of Harrison county...families from the historical collection of Frederick Porter Griffin.	microfilm

Military:

Funk, Arville L., Revolutionary War soldiers of Harrison....1975. 37pp.	973.34 I385f
Militia election list, October 18, 1817, [Corydon...]. (From Tipton Papers 109). [4pp.]	p.f. 977.202 Cuncat. no. 2
Petition of sundry inhabitants of Harrison...terr. who served as mounted riflemen in the expedition on the Wabash...Dec. 3, 1812....5pp.	p.f. 977.201 Huncat. no. 2
Wiseman, Rita, Enrollment of the late soldiers, their widows and orphans of the late armies of the United States residing in Harrison...for the year 1886. 1970/71. 54pp.	977.201 H323ha

Miscellaneous:

1810 Census...(Harrison and Exeter townships). (From THG, vol. 16 '2, June 1976). [30pp.]	p.f. 977.201 Huncat. no. 6
Darlington, Jane E., ...Duplicate tax list for 1844. [1981?]. [49pp.]	977.201 H323dar
Estray book, 1809-1817.	microfilm
Funk, Arville L., Historical almanac....1974. 81pp.	977.201 H323f
Cook, Claude E., School enumerations...Blue River township....12pp.	p.f. 977.201 H318 no. 8
Seminary record, 1827-1851.	microfilm
Tract book, 1807-1841.	microfilm
Voters,1809 (THG, Nov.-Dec. 1961)	977.2 H789
McClure Working Men's Institute, 1855-1858.	microfilm

HENDRICKS COUNTY

Formed 1824 from Delaware (N.P., unorganized), Putnam   County Seat—Danville

Births:

Delayed births prior to 1941.	miCrofilm
WPA, Index to birth records, 1882-1920.	977.201 H498u

Deaths:

WPA, Index to death records, 1882-1920.	977.201 H498u

Deeds:

Deed indexes, 1823-1907, except grantees, 1880-1907.	microfilm
Deeds, 1825-1856, 1864-68, 1874-1886; indexes, 1826-1889.	miCrofilm

Marriages:

Marriages, 1824-1925.	miCrofilm
Marriage record book 1 1/2, 1831-1837. 140pp.	q977.201 H498h
Marriage record book, 1824-1837. 2 vols.	977.201 H498he
Marriage applications, 1905-1922.	miCrofilm
Marriage affidavits, 1866-1879.	miCrofilm
Ridlen, Colleen A., ...Early marriage records, 1824-1841. 1980. 42pp.	977.201 H498ri
WPA, Index to marriage records, 1823-1920.	977.201 H498u
WPA, Index to supplemental record, marriage transcripts, 1880-1920.	977.201 H498u

Probates:

Probates, 1825-1871; indexes, 1871-ca1900.	microfilm
Probates, 1826-1905; probate order book, 1825-1918.	miCrofilm

Wills:

Wills, 1822-1906.	microfilm
Wills, 1822-1926.	miCrofilm
Wills, 1822-1846 (THG, vol. 13 #4, Oct.-Dec. 1973).	977.2 H789

Cemetery:

Burials in Brownsburg cemetery....1981.	977.201 H498b
Center Valley cem. association, Liberty twp...minute book. [1980]. 147pp. (also 12pp. index).	977.201 H498c
Cooper, Ernest L., Christy cemetery records...(Center township). 1981. 28pp.	977.201 H498co
[Ind. Hist. Soc., Cemetery records...Washington township. Comp. by H. Dale Sommers]. 1940. [60pp.]	977.201 H498i
McDonald, Nina Jo., Tincher cemetery, Springtown, Indiana....1962. [6pp.]	p.f. 977.201 H498m
Mill Creek Friends burying ground, Center township....1944. n.p.	977.201 H498
Cox, Grace..., Danville South cemetery inscriptions, with locations of stones (to November 1977). 1981. 347, 66pp.	977.202 D197dan
Spangler, Mrs. H.C., Eel River township [cemetery records]. [4pp.]	p.f. 977.201 H498 no. 1
Scott, Geraldine Jones, Abner's Creek cemetery. 1938. [5pp.]	p.f. 977.201 H498 no. 2
[Leak, Roscoe R., Old cemetery dates, mostly to 1875 in Union township...]. 9pp.	p.f. 977.201 H498 no. 3
Herr, Ben, Cemetery records....[1] Johnson cemetery, Brown twp. [1956]. 1pp.	p.f. 977.201 H498 no. 4
Hoyt, Mrs. Leo, Cemetery records....5 pts.	p.f. 977.201 H498 no. 5
Pritchard, Ruth M., Cemetery records....11 pts. (pt. 10 missing 1982).	p.f. 977.201 H498 no. 6
Church of Jesus Christ of Latter Day Saints, Cemetery records....3 pts.	p.f. 977.201 H398 no. 8

Myers, Hortense, Headstone inscriptions, old Shiloh burying ground....1964. 1pp.	p.f. 977.201 H498 no. 9
Heiss, Willard C., Friends burying ground....3 pts.	p.f. 977.201 H498 no. 10
Bryant, Elizabeth, Cemetery records....5 pts.	p.f. 977.201 H498 no. 11
Hendricks Co. Hist. Soc., ...Cemetery records. 1969. [1] Davis, Hardwick, Hoadley, Miles, Ransey, Roberts, Springtown Methodist Episcopal Church; [2] Bailey farm north of Lizton, Cundiff, Groover, Griffith, Leach, Montgomery Chapel (M.E.), Pritchett, Veiley, Lizton K of P.	p.f. 977.201 H498 no. 12
Ind. Junior Hist. Soc., ...Cemetery records. [1] McCormack, Moravian, North Salem Baptist, Robbins, Scherer, Vannice, West Branch Friends, Sam McCown farm, Friendship Baptist, McClain; [2] Walker cemetery, Brownsburg.	p.f. 977.201 H498 no. 13
Pritchard, Mrs. Amo, ...Cemetery records. no. 1 Old cemetery west of Center Valley....no. 2 Sketch of east end of Friendship cem. at Center Valley....	p.f. 977.201 Huncat. no. 1-2
Murphy, Thelma, [Irons cemetery....]. 1pp.	p.f. 977.201 Huncat. no. 3
Hoyt, Mrs. Leo C., Sugar Grove cemetery....19pp.	p.f. 977.201 Huncat. no. 4
Merritt, Grace, H., Merritt cemetery, Washington township....1pp.	p.f. 977.201 Huncat. no. 5
Higgins cemetery, Marion twp....1pp.	p.f. 977.201 Huncat. no. 6
Robbins cemetery—Maynard Noland farm and Vannice cemetery—Robert McGown family farm, Marion township....4pp.	p.f. 977.201 Huncat. no. 7
[Inscriptions from the] Spring Friends cemetery near Amo....[5pp.]	p.f. 977.201 Huncat. no. 8
Leak, Roscoe R., Eight...cemeteries: Vieley, Cundiff, Bailey farm, Griffith, Groover, Pritchett, Leach, Montgomery Chapel. (From IMH, vol. 36, 1940). 11pp.	p.f. 977.201 Huncat. no. 9
White Lick cemetery...Washington twp....2pp.	p.f. 977.201 Huncat. no. 10
Collins, Judy, Bethesda, Johnson graveyard, and Salem cemeteries....[17pp.]	p.f. 977.201 Huncat. no. 11

Miscellaneous:

DAR, ...Genealogy records. 1936. 75pp.	977.201 H498da
The History of Hendricks county, 1914-1976: A compilation of historical material and biographical profiles, written by the people of Hendricks county. Ed. by John R. McDowell. 1976. 640pp.	977.201 H498hi
Hosier, Scott F., Abstract of public record....1971. 15, 6pp. (Record of indentures, apprentices and poor children, book 1).	977.201 H498ho
Ind. State Lib..., Index to 1840 census....1972. 17pp.	977.201 H498in
Kocker, Florence, et al., ...1830 Census. 1977. [20pp.]	977.201 H498un
Indentures [1837-1849].	microfilm
Lamb, Ursula, List of the extant physicians' applications for license, physicians'...filed with the clerk...July 23, 1885, November 2, 1911. 1982. 22pp.	977.201 H498L
Naturalizations, Intentions, 1852-1906.	miCrofilm
Naturalizations, Final oath, 1856-1906.	miCrofilm
Pritchard, Ruth M., ...Voting records, 1826-1832. 1971. 177pp.	977.201 H498un
Stock marks, 1824-1841.	microfilm
Tract book, [1821-1851].	microfilm

HENRY COUNTY

Formed 1822 from Delaware (N.P., unorganized)   County Seat—New Castle

Births:

WPA, Index to birth records, 1882-1920.   977.201 H525u

Deaths:

WPA, Index to death records, 1882-1920.   977.201 H525u

Deeds:

Deed indexes, 1824-1905.   microfilm

Mayhill, R. Thomas, Land entry atlas...1821-1849. 1974. [41]pp.   f977.201 H525ma

Marriages:

Marriages, 1823-1838 (THG, vol. 5 #4-5, Jul.-Aug., Sept.-Oct. 1965).   977.2 H789

Marriages, 1823-1851.   microfilm

Ridlen, Colleen A., ...Early marriage records, 1823-1839. 1979. 43pp.   977.201 H525ri

WPA, Index to marriage records, 1850-1920.   977.201 H525u

Probates:

Probates, 1828-1852.   microfilm

Wills:

Wills, 1822-1901.   microfilm

Cemetery:

Hamm, Thomas D., ed., Early cemetery records, Liberty township....1973. 72pp.   977.201 H525h

———, ed., Cemetery records, Henry and Jefferson townships....1976. 128pp.   977.201 H525ha

———, Cemetery records, Dudley township....1977. 114pp.   977.201 H525ham

Ind. Hist. Soc., [Cemetery records...]. [pt.1] Chicago Corner cemetery. 2pp.   p.f. 977.201 H521 no. 1

Church of Jesus Christ of Latter Day Saints, Cemetery records....5pts.   p.f. 977.201 H521 no. 2

Ind. Junior Hist. Soc., ...Cemetery records. 1973. 11 pts.   p.f. 977.201 H521 no. 3

———, ...Cemetery epitaphs and inscriptions. [1973]. 39pp.   p.f. 977.201 H521 no. 4

Ratcliff, Richard P., Cemetery records, Spiceland township...(1824-1974), comprising the following three cemeteries: Old Friends cemetery, Spiceland; Circle Grove cemetery, Spiceland; Dunreith cemetery, Dunreith....1974. 100pp.   p.f. 977.201 H521 no. 5

Irvin, Mildred L., "Old cemetery on north edge of city an interest place." An article about a cemetery in Knightstown...1951. 1pp.   p.f. 977.201 Huncat. no. 2

Stewart, Ray, [...Cemeteries located on the John Herr farm, Dudley township, and the west side of Wilbur Wright Road, Liberty township]. [2pp.]   p.f. 977.201 Huncat. no. 3

Wierbach, Eugene S., East Lebanon cemetery....(From IMH, vol. 36, 1940). 1pp.   p.f. 977.201 Huncat. no. 4

Hamblen, Evelyn, Needmore cemetery inscriptions....1974. [4pp.]   p.f. 977.201 Huncat. no. 5

Hamm, Thomas D., Messick cemetery, Blue River township....1974. 5pp.   p.f. 977.201 Huncat. no. 6

Woodlawn cemetery—Springport Christian Church, Springport....(From A History of Springport, Indiana, the church and community, 1879-1979). [5pp.]   p.f. 977.201 Huncat. no. 7

Mayhill, R. Thomas, Combined edition, Wayne, Greensboro and Harrison township...cemetery records. 1968. 90, 60pp.   977.201 H525m

Church:

Jeffers, Phebe, Quaker records, Indiana Yearly Meeting. 2 pts. (Spiceland M.M. births; Duck Creek M.M. marriages).   p.f. 977.201 Huncat. no. 1

Ratcliff, Richard P., The Quakers of Spiceland...: A History of Spiceland Friends meeting, 1828-1968. 1968. 78pp.   p.f. 977.202 S754r

Miscellaneous:

Caldwell, Mary, Bible records of Henry County Historical Society. 1972. 31pp.	977.201 H525c
Enumeration of white and colored males...1913. 89pp. (also 1931. 99pp.).	977.201 H525e
Index to estates [1822-?].	microfilm
Henry Co. Hist. Soc., Applications for...pioneer certificates: descendants of Henry county pioneers who resided in the county in 1850 or before....1975. 6 vols.	977.201 H525he
Record of the first sale of lots in Knightstown, Indiana, September 10th, 1825 (From The Banner, April 20, 1961). 1pp.	p.f. 977.202 Kuncat. no. 1

HOWARD COUNTY

Formed 1844 from Carroll, Cass, Miami, Grant, Hamilton County Seat—Kokomo
Named changed from Richardville to Howard in 1846.

Births:

WPA, Index to birth records, 1875-1920.	977.201 H853u

Deaths:

WPA, Index to death records, 1875-1920.	977.201 H853u

Deeds:

Deed indexes, 1846-1902.	microfilm

Marriages:

WPA, Index to marriage records, 1844-1920.	977.201 H853u
WPA, Index to supplemental record, marriage applications, 1882-1899.	977.201 H853u

Wills:

Wills, 1868-1905.	microfilm
DAR, Abstracts of wills and administration accounts...1844-1870. Comp. by Mr. and Mrs. E.C. Crider. 1942. 68pp.	977.201 H853d

Cemetery:

Gorman, Mr. and Mrs. James L., Cemetery inscriptions of Eastern Howard county....[1969]. 405pp.	977.201 H853g
Van Hart, Barbara, Coleman cemetery....1975. 1pp.	p.f. 977.201 H853v
Ind. Hist. Soc., [Cemetery records...]. 4 pts. (Oak Mound, Poplar Grove Friends, Rush Settlement, Bassett).	p.f. 977.201 H853 no. 1
Church of Jesus Christ of Latter Day Saints, [Cemetery records...]. 3 pts. (North Union, Randolph, Clay township).	p.f. 977.201 H853 no. 2
Stetler, Ethel M., A History of the Barnett cemetery, located in the southeast section of Ervin township....[1965]. 16pp.	p.f. 977.201 H853 no. 3
Larland, Betty Jane, Small cemetery...western Howard county....n.d. [2pp.]	p.f. 977.201 H853 no. 4
Haworth, C.V., New London pioneer cemetery records...New London, Indiana and Pleasant Hill cemetery records. 1964. 8pp.	p.f. 977.201 H853 no. 5
Freeland, Owen, Cataloging of [1] Pete's Run cemetery; [2] Price cemetery, Ervin twp.	p.f. 977.201 H853 no. 6
[Few miscellaneous...cemetery records. 4pp.]	p.f. 977.201 Huncat no. 1
Names of persons buried in the "Upper Kokomo Church" cemetery...Taylor township....2pp. (and Pleasant Hill cemetery).	p.f. 977.201 Huncat. no. 2
Lewis, Lincoln R., Pre-Civil War markers moved to make way for cemetery's renovation [New London Friends cemetery...]. (clipping). 1974. 1pp.	p.f. 977.201 Huncat. no. 3

Miscellaneous:

Kastle, Richard, ...Index to book A...land deeds, April 15, 1844 to April 23, 1847. [1982?]. [19pp.]	977.201 H853h
Index of estates and guardianships, 1844-1909.	microfilm
WPA, Index to federal census, 1880. (lists names, sex, color, ages).	977.201 H853u
Tract book, 1842-1853.	microfilm
Kingman Bros., Combination atlas map....1976. 99pp. [i.e. 111]. (reprint of 1877 ed).	f977.201 H853k 1976

HUNTINGTON COUNTY

Formed 1832; organized 1834 from Grant, Allen　　　　　　　　　　　County Seat—Huntington

Births:

WPA, Index to birth records, 1875-1920.	977.201 H953u

Deaths:

WPA, Index to death records, 1882-1920.	977.201 H953u

Deeds:

Deed indexes, 1834-1899.	microfilm

Marriages:

Marriages, 1837-1900.	microfilm
Marriages, 1837-1852 (THG, vol. 15 #4, Oct.-Dec. 1975)	977.2 H789
Slevin, Ruth M., ...Marriage records, 1837-1883. 1970. 125, 125pp.	977.201 H953sL
Slevin, Ruth M., ...Marriage records, 1883-1900. 1970. 97, 100pp.	977.201 H953sLe
WPA, Index to supplemental record, marriage transcript, 1882-1920.	977.201 H953u

Probates:

Probates, 1842-1850; indexes, 1858-1873.	microfilm

Wills:

DAR, Wills, 1841-1900. 2 vols.	977.201 H953w

Cemetery:

DAR, Old cemeteries....1961-62. 51pp.	977.201 H953d
Ind. Junior Hist. Soc., Cemetery located on the Carr property approx. 1/2 mile south of Indiana 218...Wayne township....1970. 1pp.	p.f. 977.201 Huncat no. 2
———, ...Cemetery records. [11pp.]	p.f. 977.201 Huncat. no. 3
Miller, Virginia, Some cemeteries....1977. [39], 200pp.	977.201 H953m
Shultz, Lawrence W., Lancaster cemetery (1837-1967)...: plots and alphabetical index of lot owners and burials with data taken from the monuments and cemetery records. 1967. 72pp.	977.201 H953s

Church:

Holloway, Emma G., Maple Grove Monthly meeting, Indiana Yearly meeting....2pp.	p.f. 977.201 Huncat no. 1
Ind. Hist. Soc., Church records. 2 pts. (Center Christian Church, Salamonite Church of the Brethren).	p.f. 977.201 H953 no. 1
Sts. Peter and Paul Roman Catholic Church, Huntington, Indiana baptismal record, March 1857-June 1876. 1976. 145, 20pp.	977.201 H953st

Miscellaneous:

Shelley, Agnes H., Looking back....A collection of historical incidents and happenings in the lives of the farm people in Polk township....1979. 56pp.	977.202 M815s
DAR, [Revolutionary ancestors of the members of the DAR, Samuel Huntington Chapter, Huntington, Indiana]. 1960. [168pp.]	p.f. 977.202 Huncat. no. 1
Huntington Public Library Obituary file. 1978.	microfilm
Tract book, 1830-1853.	microfilm

JACKSON COUNTY

Formed 1816 from Clark, Jefferson, Washington   County Seat—Brownstown

Births:

WPA, Index to birth records, 1882-1920.	977.201 J14u
Delayed births prior to 1941.	miCrofilm

Deaths:

WPA, Index to death records, 1882-1920.	977.201 J14u

Deeds:

Brown, Immogene B., Land records of Indiana. 1965-1972 5 vols. (Vol. 5, Jackson County).	977.2 B878L
Deed indexes, 1815-1900.	microfilm
Deeds, 1837-68, 1878-1886; indexes, 1816-58, 1874-1888.	miCrofilm

Marriages:

Marriages, 1816-1922.	miCrofilm
Marriages, 1816-1836 (THG, vol. 13 #2, June 1973).	977.2 H789
Marriages, 1816-1821, 1830-1902.	microfilm
Marriages, 1817-1850, see DAR listing under "Miscellaneous".	
Slevin, Ruth M., ...Marriage records, May 1849-April 1856, book C. [197-]. 32, 32pp.	977.201 J14s
WPA, Index to marriage records, 1850-1920.	977.201 J14u
...Marriage records [1816-1817]. Cop. by Dorothy Riker. 1940. 1pp.	p.f. 977.201 Juncat. no. 1

Probates:

Probates, 1847-1873; indexes, 1873-1877, 1889-1902.	microfilm
Probates, 1817-1851, see DAR listing under "Miscellaneous".	
Probate order books, 1829-1865	miCrofilm

Wills:

Wills, 1818-1837, 1844-1928.	miCrofilm
Wills, 1853-1909.	microfilm
Wills, 1817-1829 (IMH, vol. 34, 1938).	977.2 I39
Abstract of early wills...[1817-1829]. (From IMH, vol. 34).	p.f. 977.201 Juncat. no. 6

Cemetery:

Tatlock, Donald L., Cemeteries in Grassy Fork township....[1979?]-1980. 2 vols.	977.201 J14t
Heuss, Lois I.H., Driftwood cemetery, Driftwood township....[1977?]. 44pp.	977.201 J14h
D.A.C., Indiana miscellaneous records, Jackson and Jennings counties obituary and cemetery records. 1981/2. 19, 31, 45pp.	977.201 J14i
Jackson Co. Hist. Soc., 1978 Recording of Brownstown cemetery: established 1818, location one block east of Sugar Street....[1978?]. [13pp.]	977.202 B885j
Ind. Hist. Soc., Cemetery records...]. 5 pts. (Collins, Pioneer, Cem 3 1/2 mi n. of Seymour, Old German Reformed, New Hope).	p.f. 977.201 J14 no. 1
DAR, ...Cemetery records. 2 pts. (Chestnut Ridge, Russell Chapel).	p.f. 977.201 J14 no. 2
Hoyt, Mrs. Leo, Cemetery records....[1] Reddington cemetery. [1961].	p.f. 977.201 J14 no. 3
Hudson, Roy D., Uniontown cemetery records (partial) and Lexington cemetery records (additional)....1949. 2pp.	p.f. 977.201 Juncat. no. 2
Gilliatt, Mrs., New Hope cemetery, Vernon twp....2pp.	p.f. 977.201 Juncat. no. 3
Beldon, Roy H., The Pioneer cemetery, Grassy Fork township....4pp.	p.f. 977.201 Juncat. no. 4

———, The Pioneer cemetery of Grassy Fork township....[1944]. 3pp. (From IMH,
vol. 40, 1944).   p.f. 977.201 Juncat. no. 5

The Pioneer cemetery of Grassy Fork township, early Jackson county...landmark.
1981. [12pp.] (And additional information updating Grassy Fork....2pp.). 2pts.   p.f. 977.201 Juncat. no. 7

"Table of contents" for Jackson County History, by Ed. Boley. 2pp.   p.f. 977.201 Juncat. no. 8

Tatlock, D.L., Grassy Fork township...cemeteries. 1980. 4pp.   p.f. 977.201 Juncat. no. 9

Pioneer section, Driftwood cemetery, Vallonia....1pp. (From OCCGS Quarterly,
vol. 15, 1978).   p.f. 977.201 Juncat. no. 10

Miscellaneous:

DAR, Historical and genealogical records....1952. 237pp. (Includes Bible records,
cemetery records, marriages, 1817-1850, and probate court records, 1817-1851).   977.201 J14d

Apprentice record, 1884-1889.   miCrofilm

Swampland records, 1852-1880.   miCrofilm

Partition record, 1855-1857, 1873-1928.   miCrofilm

General index to estates, 1877-1881.   miCrofilm

Negro register, 1853-1854.   miCrofilm

Naturalizations, 1852-1906.   miCrofilm

JASPER COUNTY

Formed 1835; organized 1838 from White, Warren — County Seat—Rensselaer

Births:

Jasper Co. Health Dept., Index to birth records, 1921-1977. 1980. 432pp.	977.201 J39i
WPA, Index to birth records, 1882-1920.	977.201 J39u

Deaths:

Banet, Charles H., Index to death records...1921-1977....1979. 199pp.	977.201 J39b
WPA, Index to death records, 1882-1920.	977.201 J39u

Deeds:

Deeds, 1838-1864; indexes, 1838-1897.	microfilm

Marriages:

Marriages, 1865-1900.	microfilm
WPA, Index to marriage records, 1850-1920.	977.201 J39u
WPA, Index to supplemental record, marriage applications, 1905-1911.	977.201 J39u

Probates:

Probate indexes, 1865-1907.	microfilm

Wills:

Wills, 1864-1899.	microfilm

Miscellaneous:

Tract book thru 1845 (THG, vol. 4 #4-5, July-Aug., Sept.-Oct. 1964).	977.2 H789
Ferguson, Edna L., S. Barkley Methodist cemetery....1pp.	p.f. 977.201 Juncat. no. 1
DAR, Jasper county, Indiana. 1944-1960. 5 vols. (Vol. 1 pts. 1-2, Family Bible records. [150]pp.; vol. 2, Church records, Presbyterian Church of Rensselaer, 1847-1892. [57]pp. vol. 3, Cemetery records. 445pp.; vol. 4, Tract book, 1838-1870. 227pp.; vol. 5, Discharge papers of Civil War soldiers, 1865-1905. 462pp.).	977.201 J39d
WPA, Index to supplemental record, federal census, 1880. (Lists name, sex, color, age).	977.201 J39u
Paulus, Margaret B., Revised list of soldiers buried in Jasper county....1963. 28pp.	p.f. 977.201 J39
DAR, Genalogical records....1929. 40, [6]pp.	977.201 J39dg
Howe, Zera E.H., Pioneer churches & cemeteries of Gillam township....1979. 127pp.	977.201 J39h

JAY COUNTY

Formed 1835; organized 1836 from Delaware, Randolph   County Seat—Portland

Births

WPA, Index to birth records, 1882-1920.	977.201 J42u

Deaths:

WPA, Index to death records, 1882-1920.	977.201 J42u

Deeds:

Glentzer, Peggy, ...Original land purchases. [1974?]. 22pp.	977.201 J42g

Marriages:

D.A.C., Marriage records...1844-1853. [1958]. 70pp.	977.201 J42j
DAR, Marriage records...1837-1844, 1854-1865, 1866-1883, 1884-1886, 1887-1889, 1890-1892. [1953?-1975]. 6 vols. (Vol. 1 also includes estate records, 1838-1847 and church records, 1852-1885).	977.201 J42d
WPA, Index to marriage records, 1850-1920.	977.201 J42u
WPA, Index to supplementary record, marriage applications, 1880-1920.	977.201 J42u
WPA, Index to supplementary record, marriage transcripts, 1882-1920.	977.201 J42u

Cemetery & Church:

DAR, Bible records...church record of St. Paul's Congregation German Reformed church....1954-62. 2 vols.	977.201 J42da
———, Partial list of tombstone inscriptions from cemeteries....[1955?-1957]. 2 vols.	977.201 J42dp
[Cemetery records...], East Jay Junior High School History Club and others. 1979. [33pp.]	977.201 J42c
Heavilen, George E., [Cemetery records...]. [pt.1] Gillead cem., Balbec, Indiana. 1942. [2pp.]	p.f. 977.201 Juncat. no. 1
Ind. Junior Hist. Soc., Whitaker or Winters cemetery, Knox township....1969. [16pp.]	p.f. 977.201 Juncat. no. 2
———, ...Cemetery records, Zoar cemetery. 1976. 4pp.	p.f. 977.201 Juncat. no. 3
Ind. Hist. Soc., [Cemetery records...]. [pt.1] Kunce cemetery. 1945. [3pp.]	p.f. 977.201 J42 no. 1
Ind. Junior Hist. Soc., East Jay Junior High School, Old Salamonia cemetery....1978. [10pp.]	977.201 J42i
———, ...Cemetery records; (West Grove, Conservation Club, Bloomfield, Liber, Jaqua cemeteries). [1979]. [6pp.]	q977.201 J42in

Miscellaneous:

D.A.C., Miscellaneous records, discharges of Civil War soldiers....1969/1970. 72pp.	977.201 J42dd
DAR, Records of a midwife, 1862-1900, "Aunt Mariah Mendenhall". 1960. 35, 8pp.	q977.201 J42m
Beeson, Cecil, Pennville, Indiana, scrapbook and index. [1978]. [40pp.]	977.202 P415b
McFarland, Helen A., Tract book of entry...1832-1854. 1955-56. 129pp.	977.201 J42t
[Papers relating to the history and people of Jay county...]. (Dunkirk Public Lib.). 1975.	microfilm
WPA, Commissioners' record...1836-1850....	Ind. Hist. Soc. Library

JEFFERSON COUNTY

Formed 1811 from Dearborn, Clark   County Seat—Madison

Births:

Births, 1882-1907.	microfilm
Delayed births prior to 1941; 1941-1970.	miCrofilm

Deeds:

Deeds, 1812-1886; indexes, 1812-1886.	miCrofilm
Deeds, 1811-1830; indexes, 1812-1900.	microfilm

Marriages:

Marriages, 1811-1831 (THG, vol. 13 #4, Oct.-Dec. 1973).	977.2 H789
Hill, Mary, ...Marriage records [1811-1831]. 27pp.	p.f. 977.201 J45 no. 1
Marriages, 1811-1873, see DAR listing under "Miscellaneous".	
Marriages, 1811-1853; indexes to males, 1853-73; 1873-1900.	microfilm
Marriages, 1811-1922.	miCrofilm
Ritchie, Betty M., ...Marriage records, 1811-1831; 1820 heads of households listed. [19—]. 56pp.	977.201 J45r
Slevin, Ruth M., ...Marriage records, 1811-1873. [197-]. 230, 230pp.	977.201 J45s

Probates:

Probates, 1837-1852; indexes, 1852-1869.	microfilm
Probates, 1837-1880; indexes, 1829-1940.	miCrofilm
Probate order book, 1811-1918.	miCrofilm

Wills:

DAR, Early wills and administrations..., [1811-1867]. 1945. 78pp.	977.201 J45d 1945
DAR, ...Wills and administrations, 1811-1852. 1937. 53pp.	977.201 J45d
Wills and administration of estates, 1811-1832, 1852-1891.	microfilm
Wills, 1853-1924.	miCrofilm

Cemetery:

Cemetery records; Children's Home records.	miCrofilm
Cowen, Carl C., Hanover cemetery inscriptions, South Hanover.... Also...information copied from the undertakers record of the cemetery....1963. 47, [1]pp.	977.201 J45c
Cull, Betty, Cemetery of two tales [Wirt Baptist Church cemetery...]. (Article from the Indianapolis Star Magazine, Dec. 26, 1976).	p.f. 977.201 Juncat. no. 2
Danner, Mrs. Effa M., The Caledonia Church and cemetery [on Jefferson-Switzerland county lines, Indiana]. [1945]. 2pp. (From IMH, vol. 41, 1945).	p.f. 977.201 Juncat. no. 3
Gilliatt, Katherine W., Underwood cemetery...Madison township. [1951]. 1pp.	p.f. 977.201 J45 no. 9
Sutherland, Ruth, [Cemetery records...]. 1936. [pt.1] Greenbrier graveyard, Hanover...; [2] Carmel cemetery, Hanover township.	p.f. 977.201 J45 no. 2
DAR, [Cemetery records]. 2 pts.	p.f. 977.201 J45 no. 3
Cemeteries in Jennings and Jefferson counties...; a few outside county and state. 1982. 63pp.	977.201 J45ci

Census:

U.S. Bureau of the Census, A Part of the 1850 census....Cop. for DAR by Mary Hill. 57pp.	977.201 J45u

———, 1870 Census....Cop. for DAR by Mrs. Anna L. Peddie and Mary Hill. 1958. 2 vols.	977.201 J45un
1870 Census records.	miCrofilm

Church:

Anderson, John M., Records of the Carmel Congregation of the Associate Presbyterian Church, near Hanover....1975. 25, 25pp.	977.201 J45an

Court:

Circuit court records, 1811-1819.	microfilm
Civil order book, 1812-1818.	microfilm
Commissioners records, 1817-1822, 1847-1854.	microfilm
WPA, Commissioners' record...1817-1822....	Ind. Hist. Soc. Library

Family:

D.A.C., Bible records. 1974. 2pp.	p.f. 977.201 J42 no. 2
DAR, Biographies of residents....1957. 49pp.	977.201 J45db
———, Family records, 1945-1954. 7 pts.	977.201 J45df
———, Family records of Blanche Ross Matthews, Madison....1951. 41pp.	p.f. 977.201 J45 no. 8
———, Pioneer women....1945. 13pp.	p.f. 977.201 J45 no. 5
———, Bible and family records of...families. n.d. 25pp.	p.f. 977.201 J45 no. 6
Family records (from Jefferson County Library)	miCrofilm

Mortuary:

DAR, Vail's undertaker records, Madison...(1840-1890). 1948-54. 3 vols. (1840-1936 on film also)	977.202 M182v
Records of the Vail Funeral home, 1840-1936. Madison....1979.	microfilm

Naturalization:

DAR, List of aliens who applied for citizenship...list of indentures of apprentices....1957. 52pp.	977.201 J45dL
Naturalizations, 1853-1904.	miCrofilm

Miscellaneous:

Apprentice record, 1847-1882.	miCrofilm
DAR, [Jefferson county...records]. (A list of persons due taxes to William Vawter for the year 1815; a list of taxable property not listed for the year 1816; list of stores and taverns...1816; list of the names of the voters at the Madison polls, in Madison twp....1826; poll book of election held at Madison...1828; poll book...for the township of Milton...1819 and 1828; voters names, Lexington township...1818; poll book of election...Graham township...1828; poll of an election in Shelby township 1828; Republican township election...1817 and 1828). [31pp.]	p.f. 977.201 J45 no. 4
———, [Jefferson county records]. 1929-1952. 5 vols. (Vol. 1, Cemetery records. 518pp.; vol. 2, Marriage records, 1811-1873, and "bride index". 302pp.; vol. 3, Items from early newspapers...1817-1886. 452pp.; vol. 4, Genealogical records. 65pp.; vol. 5, Additional items from...newspapers, 1870-1887. 82pp.).	977.201 J45da
———, Miscellanous records....[1952]. 41pp.	p.f. 977.201 J45 no. 10
———, Newspaper items from the Madison Courier, Madison, Indiana [1874-1879]. 3 pts.	977.201 J45dn
Jefferson Co. (Ind.) Hist. Soc., Historical Society collection in Jefferson County, Indiana, Historical Society. 1954-57. 3 vols.	p.f. 977.201 J45 no. 7
Hill, Mary, [Names of voters at polls...1817-1828]. 9 pts.	p.f. 977.201 Juncat. no. 1

License record, 1816-1837. microfilm
    (licenses for taverns, stores, ferries, etc.)

Madison-Jefferson County Public Library Historical Collection. microfilm

Tax list, 1827. microfilm

Treasurer's book, 1812. microfilm

Record notebook of Joseph G. Officer who taught in the schools of Smyrna and
    Lancaster townships...from 1888-1922....84pp.   p.f. 977.201 Juncat. no. 4

Register of negroes, 1853-1860. miCrofilm

The Jefferson County special. *The Hoosier Journal of Ancestry.* 1981- vol. 1   977.201 J45j

JENNINGS COUNTY

Formed 1817 from Jefferson, Jackson — County Seat—Vernon

Births:

Births, 1882-1907.	microfilm

Deaths:

Deaths, 1882-1913.	microfilm

Deeds:

Deeds, 1817-1833.	microfilm

Marriages:

Marriages, 1818-1837 (THG, vol. 18 #3, Sept. 1978).	977.2 H789
Marriages, 1850-1872, 1879-1923.	miCrofilm
Marriage records—from marriages books 1 [and 2, 1818-1833...]. [10pp.] (From The Hoosier Journal of Ancestry, 1969).	p.f. 977.201 Juncat. no. 4
Marriages, 1818-1887.	microfilm
Marriage returns, 1881-1888.	microfilm
D.A.C., Marriage records...books I and II, 1818-1837. Cop. by Mary L. Osterman. 1960. 26, [7]pp.	977.201 J54dm
Ridlen, Colleen A., ...Early marriage records, 1818-1840. 1979. 42pp.	977.201 J54ri
Slevin, Ruth M., ...Marriages, 1837-1866, books 3-6. 1970? 76, 76pp.	977.201 J54s

Probates:

Probates, 1830-1836.	microfilm

Wills:

Will and probate records, 1818-1829.	microfilm
Holmes, Maurice, Will records...1822-1913. 1977. 313pp.	977.201 J54how

Cemetery & Church:

D.A.C., ...Dodd's burial records. [1891-1941, 1943-1954]. 63pp. (and index). Cop. by William H. Coons. (also includes old Bogey farm cem., east of Old Paris).	
———, Cemetery records...; Graham Presbyterian—Green—Scipio (or Amick)—Queensville—Family cemetery, Queensville. [1977?]. [48pp.]	977.201 J54c
———, Cemetery records...Center and Creek townships. [1976?]. 37pp.	977.201 J54dc
———, ...Cemeteries. [1970-1971]. 2 vols. (and index by D. Benedict. 1975. 40pp.)	977.201 J54dd
DAR, Dodd's burial records, Paris Crossing....1 vol.	977.201 J54do
———, Cemetery records....1958. 17pp.	977.201 J54d
Jennings County Cemetery and family records.	miCrofilm
Horstman, Joe, ...Edwards cemetery, Vernon township. [1977]. 3pp.	p.f. 977.201 J54hor
———, ...Cemetery records, Spencer township. [1977?]. [3pp.] (Buena Vista cem.).	p.f. 977.201 J54hos
Cemeteries in Jennings and Jefferson counties...; a few outside county and state. 1982. 63pp.	977.201 J45ci
[Ind. Hist. Soc.], Records of cemeteries....1941- 12 pts.	p.f. 977.201 J54 no. 1
DAR, Cemetery records....[1] A family cemetery [Prather?]. 1pp.	p.f. 977.201 J54 no. 2
Ind. Junior Hist. Soc., ...Cemetery records. 1973-. 21pts.	p.f. 977.201 J54 no. 3
D.A.C., St. Mary's cemetery, North Vernon....[1974?]. [36pp.]	p.f. 977.201 J54 no. 4
———, Hillcrest cemetery, North Vernon....[1974?]. 59pp.	p.f. 977.201 J54 no. 5
Hoyt, Mrs. Leo, Scipio catholic cemetery....1953. 9, [1]pp.	p.f. 977.201 Juncat. no. 1

Church, R.L., Prather family cemetery....(not complete). 5pp.   p.f. 977.201 Juncat. no. 3

Horstman, Helen, ...Cemetery records: Grove burying ground, Dixon-Cave or Paris, and Wilson? cemeteries. [12pp.]   p.f. 977.201 Juncat. no. 5

Vaught, Mary Ann, ...[Cemetery] records. 1977. [1pp.] (Tull? cem., Lovett township)   p.f. 977.201 J54v

Records of the Graham Baptist Church, formerly the Liberty Baptist Church [1829-1898]....   microfilm

Court:

Circuit court order book, 1817-1822.   microfilm

Commissioners records, 1824-1846.   microfilm

Holmes, Maurice, Court records...1818-1850. 1978. 211pp.   977.201 J54hoc

Naturalization record...1850-1856. Cop. from original by Genealogy Division, ISL. 1971. 18pp.   977.201 J54

Mortuary & Obituaries:

DAR, Funeral home records, cemetery, and miscelleneous family records of Jennings county...and cemetery and family records of Dearborn county....1977. 136pp.   977.201 J54da

D.A.C., Obituaries...1885-1890; and, undertaker's record...1901-1907. 1981. 67, [5], 19pp. (Obituaries taken from Plain Dealer, North Vernon, Ind. Funeral records taken from the Dove Funeral Home, formerly H.H. Dowd & Co., North Vernon, Ind.).   977.201 J54ob

Miscellaneous:

Borden, William W., Jennings and Ripley county maps showing residences in each township in 1875. 1875. n.p.   977.201 J54b

Judge John Carney's scrapbook of Vernon, Indiana. [1918]. 80pp.   q977.202 V541j

Dixon, Williamson W., [Index to account book of W.W. Dixon, a tailor at Old Paris...]. [6pp.]   p.f. 977.201 Juncat. no. 2

Holmes, Maurice, Early landowners....1976. 90pp.   977.201 J54h

———, Miscellaneous records....1976. 71pp.   977.201 J54ho

Ind. State Library..., Index to 1840 census....1972. 14pp.   977.201 J54i

Negro register [1853-1856] (THG, vol. 17 #2, June 1977).   977.2 H789

D.A.C., Indiana miscellaneous records, Jackson and Jennings counties obituary and cemetery records. 1981/2. 19, 31, 45pp.   977.201 J14i

Miscellaneous records and papers relating to Jennings county...history and families.   microfilm

The Jennings county special. *The Hoosier Journal of Ancestry.* 1982- vol. 1.   977.201 J54j

JOHNSON COUNTY

Formed 1823 from Delaware (N.P., unorganized)　　　　　　　　　　　　County Seat—Franklin

Births:

WPA, Index to birth records, 1882-1920.	977.201 J66u
WPA, Index to birth records, 1921-1940, supplement 1941 inc. 1942.	977.201 J66u

Deaths:

WPA, Index to death records, 1882-1920.	977.201 J66u

Deeds:

Deed indexes, 1825-1900.	microfilm

Marriages:

Ridlen, Colleen A., ...Early marriage returns, 1830-1843. 1976. 42pp.	977.201 J66r
Marriages, 1830-1901, see DAR listing under "Miscellaneous".	
WPA, Index to marriage records, 1882-1920.	977.201 J66u
DAR, Marriage records...1901-1913, transcribed by Hollis Hughes....1974. 45, 45pp.	977.201 J66d
DAR, Marriage records...(1913-1926), tr. by Hughes....1975. 66, 66pp.	977.201 J66da

Probates:

Probates, 1823-1831, see DAR, listing under "Miscellaneous".	
Probate order books, 1831-1852; indexes, 1853-1900.	microfilm

Wills:

Wills, 1827-1845 (THG, vol. 13 #3, July-Sept. 1973).	977.2 H789
Wills, 1827-1907.	microfilm
Holmes, Maurice, Will records...1827-1907. 1975. 311pp.	977.201 J66hol

Cemetery:

Tearman, Gertrude, Edna, & Goldie, Nineveh cemetery records, Nineveh...June 1968-Feb. 10, 1971. 1971. 100pp. (Copy of the Old Nineveh cemetery record, comp. by Ruth Hougham bound in).	977.201 J66te
Ind. Hist. Soc., [Cemetery records...]. [pt.1] Hopewell cemetery. [1955]. [31pp.]	p.f. 977.201 J66 no. 1
Mertens, Nova, Bethlehem cemetery records....1952. 19, 2pp.	p.f. 977.201 J66 no. 4
Hoyt, Mrs. Leo, [Cemetery records...]. 6pts.	p.f. 977.201 J66 no. 7
Holmes, Maurice, Grave marker inscriptions in the Smiley Mills neighborhood cemetery, Needham township....1969. 10pp.	p.f. 977.201 J66 no. 8
DAR, [Cemeteries...]. [1] Cemetery on farm of Bennett Utterbeck, Union township. 1973. 1pp.	p.f. 977.201 J66 no. 9
Greenlawn cemetery [Franklin, Indiana] proceedings of meetings of citizens, January 14, 1845. 4pp.	p.f. 977.201 Juncat. no. 5
Murphy, Thelma M., Cemetery located at junctions of State Roads 44 and 135....1pp.	p.f. 977.201 Juncat. no. 6
Morlan, Mrs. W.M., McColgin cemetery, Union township....1pp.	p.f. 977.201 Juncat. no. 7
Vandercook, Dorothy I., Cemetery records of Old Kansas or Nineveh, Indiana. 3pp.	p.f. 977.201 Juncat. no. 9
Sellers, Charlotte, "Rest Haven stones yield Edinburg past". (From the Republic Columbus, Indiana, Dec. 6, 1975), [3pp.]	p.f. 977.201 Juncat. no. 10
Mertens, Nova May, Old Bethlehem Church and cemetery. [1953]. (From IMH, vol. 49, 1953). 14pp.	p.f. 977.201 Juncat. no. 11
Cemetery, Tremont estates. 1pp.	p.f. 977.201 Juncat. no. 12

Lowe cemetery....5pp.   p.f. 977.201 Juncat. no. 14

Jewell, Virgil A., [Johnson County]. 3 vols. (1) Cemetery inscriptions, Greenwood quadrangle. 1969; (2) Cemetery inscriptions. 1970. 236pp.; (3) Miscellaneous. 1971.   977.201 J66je

Church:

Cleland, P.S., A Quarter century, discourse delivered at Greenwood, Ind., Dec. 18, 1864, the 25th anniversary of his ministry to the Presbyterian church in that place. [1955?]. 19pp.   p.f. 977.202 G816 no. 1

Wishard, William H., History of the Greenwood Presbyterian Church....[1955?]. 8pp.   p.f. 977.202 G816 no. 2

[Curry, George L.], Alphabetical roster of the Presbyterian Church, Greenwood, Indiana. [1955]. 28pp   p.f. 977.202 G816 no. 3

———, Infant baptismal record of the Greenwood Presbyterian Church. [1955]. 5pp.   p.f. 977.202 G816 no. 4

Tranter, Vera R., Hopewell Presbyterian church records. 192, [29]pp. (A miscellaneous collection of records.). n.d.   977.201 J66th

———, [Churches...]. n.d. 192pp.   977.201 J66t

Brown, Robert A., History of the Hopewell Presbyterian church...1831-1915. [1955?]. 67pp.   977.201 J66b

Infant baptismal records of Hopewell Presbyterian Church...from its organization, May 23, 1831-Jan. 9, 1916. [1955?]. [16pp.]   p.f. 977.201 J66 no. 5

Communicants' roll [1831-1917] of the Hopewell Presbyterian Church....[1955?]. (pp. 68-127).   p.f. 977.201 J66 no. 6

Jones, Nelson D., One hundred years of religious development in the Hurricane community, 1837-1937. 18pp.   p.f. 977.201 Juncat. no. 1

Centennial anniversary of the Second Mt. Pleasant Baptist Church...organized July 11, 1835. 1935. 34pp.   p.f. 977.201 Juncat. no. 3

Hayward, Elizabeth, Genealogical abstracts from records of Second Mount Pleasant Baptist Church, constituted in 1835....1972. 25pp.   977.201 J66h

Johnson, Bess S., A Commemorative history of the Tabernacle Christian Church of Franklin, Indiana, for the centennial anniversary of its organization. 1948. 71pp, [9pp.]   977.202 F831f

Young, Livy A., A Background glance at Old Union. [19—]. 99, [2]pp.   977.201 J66y

History:

Averitt, Will F., Eighty years of Bagby School history reviewed....1935. 5pp. (missing 1982)   p.f. 977.201 Juncat. no. 4

Blake, Israel George, Pioneers....[1973?]. 5, 212pp.   977.201 J66bl

Burge, Juanita, Heritage of Peoga, Indiana. [1976?]. 44pp.   977.202 P419bu

Curry, George, In memory to the pioneers to the great west (article in Hopewell Herald, Franklin, Indiana). 2pp.   p.f. 977.202 Funcat. no. 1

DAR, Historical records....1929. 11pp.   p.f. 977.201 Juncat. no. 2

[Hutchison, Ruth, et al], Rest Haven: one hundred fifty years. (Edinburg, Ind.). 1977. 799pp.   977.202 E23re

Johnson, Mrs. Richard M., Pioneer history....Articles appearing in the Franklin Star, Franklin, Indiana, from Nov. 1927-Sept. 1937. 28pp.   977.201 J66jo

...Residents before 1825 as indicated by the early grantor land records. 2pp.   p.f. 977.201 Juncat. no. 8

Mortuary & Obituaries:

Hutchinson, Ruth, et al, Partial record of the Mutz Funeral home, Edinburg....[197-]. 37pp. (This record consists of burials by the Mutz funeral home in cemeteries other than Rest Haven cemetery, Edinburg, Indiana).   977.202 E23p

Ind. Hist. Soc., Deaths, Johnson county... 1846-1868. [6pp.] Comp. by George Curry from Johnson Co. newspapers. 1946. p.f. 977.201 J66 no. 3

Miscellaneous:

DAR, Records of Johnson county. 1931-1952. 5 vols. (Vol. 1, Miscellaneous records, [24]pp.; vol. 2, pts. 1-4, Family Bible records. 236, 306, 376, 354pp.; vol. 3, pts. 1-3, Marriage records, 1830-1901. 48, 95, 187pp.; vol. 4, Cemetery records. 243pp.; vol. 5, First order book [1823-1831]. 58pp.). 977.201 J66j

Holmes, Maurice, court records... 1823-1853. 1982. 322pp. 977.201 J66hc

———, Early landowners.... 1974. 16, 25pp. 977.201 J66ho

Nostalgia news. Johnson County Historical Museum. (scattered issues, 1979-1980). p.f. 977.201 Juncat. no. 13

WPA, Commissioners' record...[and board of justices records]... 1826-1838. 2 vols. Ind. Hist. Soc. Library

KNOX COUNTY

Formed 1790 — County Seat—Vincennes

Boundaries at this time embraced all of the present state of Indiana and parts of Illinois, Ohio, Michigan, and Wisconsin; reduced to approximately its present boundaries by 1817.

Births:

Births, 1886-1907.	microfilm
WPA, Index to birth records, 1882-1920.	977.201 K74u

Deaths:

Coan, M. Jeanne, ...Death records, February 1, 1882-September 30, 1900....[1975?]. 238pp.	977.201 K74c
Coan, M. Jeanne, ...Death records, October 1, 1900-December 31, 1904....[1974-1980]. 170pp.	977.201 K74ca
WPA, Index to death records, 1882-1920.	977.201 K74u

Deeds:

Barekman, June, ...Index to deed record A, 1815-1817. [1967?]. 24pp.	p.f. 977.201 K74 no. 2
Deeds, 1814-1817; indexes, 1814-1829.	microfilm

See also entries under Land.

Marriages:

...Marriages, January 1, 1850-July 1854 (index comp. from microfilm...by Indiana State Library). 1972. 20pp.	977.201 K74
Hribal, M.R. & M.J. Coan, Marriage records...1807-1840. 1964. 134pp.	977.201 K74h
Marriages, 1838-1883.	microfilm
Marriage returns, 1881-1889.	microfilm
Record of certificates of marriage...1807-1832; (marriage licenses, 1807-1839). (photostats of records in County Clerk's office). 3 vols.	977.201 K74rc 977.201 K74r
WPA, Index to marriage records, 1850-1920.	977.201 K74u
WPA, Index to supplemental record, marriage transcript, 1880-1920.	977.201 K74u
Lindsay, Kenneth G., Early marriages...1807-1832. 1977. 60pp.	977.201 K74Li
O'Neel, L.B., ...Marriage licenses and certificates, 1806-1816. 1939. 24pp.	977.201 K74o
Marriages, 1807-Mar. 1832 (THG, vol. 14 #3, July-Sept. 1974).	977.2 H789

Probates:

Probates, 1790-1836.	microfilm
...Probate records, 1790-1836. [197-]. 15, [8]pp.	p.f. 977.201 K74kn
...Probate court records from 1817-1835. (Publication no. 14, Vincennes Historical and Antiquarian Society). 1970. ca900pp.	q977.201 K74kno

Wills:

Wills, 1806-1852. (1829-1835-)	microfilm

Cemetery:

DAR, ...Cemetery records. [1940?]. 153pp.	977.201 K74da
(1953 Suppl. reprinted 1968. 29pp.)	977.201 K74da 1968
(1971-73 edition with new listings. 3 vols).	977.201 K74da 1971
Padgett, Mrs. William, ...A complete survey of cemetery records. 1973-1976. 6 vols. in 7. (Book 1, Palmyra & Washington townships; bk. 2, Palmyra and Washington twps.; bk. 3, Busseron and Widner twps.; bk. 4, Decker, Harrison, Johnson & Vincennes twps.; bk. 5, Catholic cemeteries in the city of Vincennes, Ind.; bks. 6A-6B, city cemeteries in Vincennes, Indiana).	977.201 K74p

Church:

DAR, Early churches....Comp. by Estelle Emison. 1947. 111pp.	977.201 K74dc
Asbury Chapel history and cemetery records, Vincennes...including information on the Neal, Huddle, Mason, Kixmiller, Smith, and Peck families. (Articles from issues of the Knox County Daily News, 1970-1). 31pp.	p.f. 977.202 Vuncat. no. 7
Asbury Chapel history...(From Knox County Daily News, April 22 and 24, 1970). [4pp.]	p.f. 977.201 Kuncat. no. 2
McCormick, Marie W., Asbury Chapel and its people, 1847-1972. 1972. 123pp.	977.201 K74mc
Presbyterian church minutes, 1812-1889.	microfilm
Vincennes, First Presbyterian Church, Photostat copy of...marriages, including a few baptismal records [1810-1884]. 61pp.	977.201 K74v
St. Francis Xavier church, Vincennes...records of the Parish, deaths, baptismal, marriages, etc. [1770-1838].	microfilm
St. Francis Xavier church, Vincennes...registers of baptisms, marriages, etc., 1749-1838.	microfilm
[Notes taken from the St. Francis Xavier Parish records, Vincennes...].	p.f. 977.202 Vuncat. no. 5
St. Francis Xavier Parish records, Vincennes....1936. 6 vols. (Vols. 2-6 also on microfilm). (Vol. 7, Index).	q977.202 V767s
St. Francis Xavier Parish records, Vincennes, Ind., English translation. 1971. (also on microfilm).	977.202 V767sa
St. James, Vincennes, church register. Episcopal.	microfilm
Schultheis, Mrs. Rose, Record of baptisms, 1847-1864, St. John's Catholic Church, transc. by Mary Watson. 1948. 19pp.	977.202 V767r

Court:

Common pleas and circuit court records, 1801-1831.	microfilm
DAR, Marks and brands of domestic animals as registered...1807-1841. Cop. by Helen Kackley. 1951. 46pp.	977.201 K74k
Helpingstine, Jeanne, Declarations of intent, 1852-1951 and naturalization books, 1855-1945....[1981]. 66, 20, 5pp.	977.201 K74he

Family:

DAR, Family history of families from Connecticut, Delaware, New Jersey, Virginia, Kentucky, descendants in and near Vincennes....1949. 109pp.	977.202 V767d
———, Descendants of some early settlers in Knox and Sullivan counties....1951. 103pp.	977.201 K74dd
———, Family Bible records....1945-1950. 4 vols.	977.201 K74df
———, Family records....1956-1960. 5 pts.	977.201 K74dfa
———, ...Book of genealogical research. 1933. 200pp.	977.201 K74d
Beeson, Donna, Guide to the genealogy collection of the Bryon R. Lewis Historical Library. 1977. [60pp.] (also 1980 ed., [85pp.])	16.929 B996g

Land:

Barekman, J. and R. Lent, Knox County, Indiana. (contains early land records, court indexes, etc.). [1966]. 2 vols.	977.201 K74b
Barekman, June B., ...Early land records and court indexes, 1783-1815. 1973. 3 vol. in 1. (Vol. 1, Early land records, court indexes, 1783-1806; vol. 2, Early land records, court indexes, 1807-1815; vol. 3, Index to deed record A, 1815-1817 [and] register of negro slaves and masters, 1805-1807).	977.201 K74b 1973

———, Claims in Vincennes district. Locations entered at Vincennes, under the Act of Congress, the 3rd of March, 1807. (Taken from American State Papers). [1966]. 40pp.   p.f. 977.202 V767 no. 1

———, Some early items concerning Vincennes, ...from the year of 1783 through 1790: Grants of land to the early settlers, and donations of land to the militiamen. [1966?]. 17, 21pp.   p.f. 977.202 V767 no. 2

DAR, Locations entered at Vincennes under Act of Congress, 3rd of March, 1807. 1960. 29pp.   p.f. 977.202 Vuncat. no. 3

Lux, Leonard, "The Vincennes donation lands", Ind. Historical Soc. Publication vol. 15, no. 4. 1949.   I977.2 I385i

Roll of officers and soldiers who were allotted land in Clark's Grant (Indiana) for serving under George Rogers Clark...[pay rolls of Clark's army previous to June 1779].   microfilm

Selected records of the Vincennes, Indiana and Springfield, Illinois land offices.   microfilm

Letter from the Secretary of the Treasury transmitting a report and documents from the commissioner of the general land office, in relation to land claims in the Vincennes land district...1835 and 1838 (23rd Congress, 2nd session, H Doc. no. 198 and 455 of 25th Congress, 2nd session). 2 pts.   p.f. 977.202 Vuncat. no. 6 pts. 1-2

U.S. Bur. of Land Management, Selected records of the Vincennes...and Springfield, Illinois, land offices.   microfilm

Mortuary:

DAR, Mortality records...1816-1884, copied from original records of Gardner and Son. 1946. 122pp.   977.201 K74dm

———, Records of the Gardner Mortuary, Vincennes...1816-1854, 1878-1894. 1969. 169pp.   977.201 K74dm 1969

———, Mortality records (Lemen and McClure Funeral Home, Bicknell. 2 vols.)   977.201 K74L

(McClure and Son, Bruceville. 2 vols.)   977.201 K74m

———, Mortuary records of Donaldson & Richardson, Monroe City, Indiana. 1962. [9pp.]   p.f. 977.201 K74 no. 1

Slaves:

Barekman, June B., Register of negro slaves and masters for 1805-1807....1970. 5pp.   977.201 K74ba

Negro slaves, 1805-1807 (THG, vol. 17 #3, Sept. 1977).   977.2 H789

Town:

Commons record, borough of Vincennes, 1818-1837.   microfilm

Journal of borough trustees, borough of Vincennes, 1820-1836; trustees, proceedings, 1815-1816, borough of Vincennes.   microfilm

Miscellaneous papers (Vincennes), 1784-1815.   microfilm

Ordinances, borough of Vincennes, 1816-1836.   microfilm

Poor Relief record, 1821-1832.   microfilm

Treasurers accounts, borough of Vincennes, 1819-1840.   microfilm

Trustees proceedings, 1815-1816.   microfilm

Miscellaneous:

Ind. State Library..., Index to 1840 census....1972. 16pp.   977.201 K74i

Minutes, Board of Trustees, Vincennes University, 1806-1836.   microfilm

Petition of sundry French inhabitants of the district of Vincennes...February 27, 1806....3pp.   p.f. 977.201 Kuncat. no. 1

Northwest Trail Tracer. (Vol. 1-2, 1980-1981).   p.f. 977.201 Kuncat. no. 3

Vincennes Sun Commercial, "200 years of progress", 1749-1949, historical section,
    Vincennes Sun Commercial...April 24, 1949. 32pp.   p.f. 977.202 Vuncat. no. 1

Turman, Robert E., [Days of old Vincennes; and landed gentry]. (Two newspaper
    clippings from Sullivan, Ind. Union, Sept. 1954).   p.f. 977.202 Vuncat. no. 2

The Old Vincennes Cathedral and its environs. 30pp.   p.f. 977.202 Vuncat. no. 4

Voters, 1809 (THG, May-June 1962).   977.2 H789

KOSCIUSKO COUNTY

Formed 1835; organized 1836 from Cass, Elkhart County Seat—Warsaw

Births:

WPA, Index to birth records, 1882 1920.	977.201 K86u
Delayed births prior to 1941.	miCrofilm

Deaths:

WPA, Index to death records, 1882-1920.	977.201 K86u

Deeds:

Deed indexes, 1834-1900.	microfilm

Marriages:

Marriages, 1836-1841 (THG, vol. 4 #3, May-June 1964).	977.2 H789
Riker, Dorothy, ...Marriages, book 1, 1836-1843; book 2, 1843-1845. 1964. 4, 5pp.	p.f. 977.201 K86 no. 1
DAR, Marriage records...1830-1867. 1968. 157pp.	977.201 K86da
Marriages, 1836-1898.	microfilm
Slevin, Ruth M., ...Marriages, 1846-1891. 1972. 2 vols.	977.201 K86s
Marriages, 1836-1921.	miCrofilm
Marriage consents, 1874-1905.	miCrofilm

Probates:

Probates, 1836-1849; indexes, 1836-1899.	microfilm
Probates, complete record, 1836-1915.	miCrofilm
Probate order book, 1836-1919.	miCrofilm

Wills:

Wills, 1844-1900.	microfilm
Wills, 1844-1921.	miCrofilm
Estates, general index to, 1837-1857, 1880-1887, 1908-1922.	miCrofilm

Miscellaneous:

DAR, Cemetery records of pioneer graves...northern division and southern division. 1941-42. 2 vols.	977.201 K86d
Tract book, 1830-1852.	microfilm
Naturalizations, order book, [1855]-1904.	miCrofilm
Petition and record, [1908-1923].	miCrofilm
Binnie, Lester H., Cemetery records for Jackson township....1971. 78pp.	977.201 K86b
———, Early Brethren families in the Eel River congregation in Kosciusko & Wabash counties. 1974? 195pp.	977.201 K86bi
———, ...Cemetery records. 1977-80. 8 vols.	977.201 K86bk
Our Missing Links. (Scattered issues, vol. 1-5, 1977-1981).	p.f. 977.201 Kuncat. no. 1
Brumbaugh cemetery, Jefferson township....(From Michiana Searcher, vol. 10, 1978). 5pp.	p.f. 977.201 Kuncat. no. 2
Lynch, Jean, Stockmarks...1836-1863....12pp.	p.f. 977.201 Kuncat. no. 3

[Handwritten annotations:] Inv. of Personal Estate & Debts 1877-1883; 1895-9 Indexed. Sales of Personal Property of decedents 1853 Indexed.

LA GRANGE COUNTY

Formed 1832 from Elkhart, Allen   County Seat—LaGrange

Births:

WPA, Index to birth records, 1882-1920.   977.201 L178u

Deaths:

WPA, Index to death records, 1882-1924.   977.201 L178u

Deeds:

Deed indexes; 1832-1900.   microfilm

Marriages:

Marriages, 1832-1880.   microfilm

Marriages, 1832-1846, see DAR listing under "Miscellaneous".

WPA, Index to marriage records, 1880-1920.   977.201 L178u

Marriages, 1832-1850 (THG, vol. 22 #2, June 1982)   977.2 H789

Slevin, Ruth M., ...Marriages, 1832-1880....1972. 85, 85pp.   977.201 L178s

Probates:

Probates, 1832-1852; indexes, 1853-1899.   microfilm

Wills:

Wills, 1842-1900.   microfilm

Slevin, Ruth M., ...Will records, volumes 1 & 2, 1842-1896. 137pp.   977.201 L178sl

Miscellaneous:

DAR, ...Records....Comp. by Grace Libey and Carlie Deal. 1949. 148pp.
    (Includes marriages, 1832-1846, cemetery inscriptions, etc.).   977.201 L178d

WPA, Index to supplemental records, registered voters, 1919-1920.   977.201 L178u

Tract book, 1831-1853.   microfilm

Graybill, Leona M., Tamarack cemetery....1980. 8pp.   p.f. 977.201 Luncat. no. 1

LAKE COUNTY

Formed 1836; organized 1837 from Newton, Porter   County Seat—Crown Point

Births:

WPA, Index to birth records, 1882-1920.	977.201 L192u
WPA, Index to birth records, Lake County and Crown Point, 1921-1941.	977.201 L192u
WPA, Index to birth records; East Chicago, 1882-1920; Gary, 1882-1920; Hammond, 1886-1920; Hobart, 1899-1920; Whiting, 1899-1920.	977.201 L192u

Deaths:

WPA, Index to death records, 1899-1920.	977.201 L192u
WPA, Index to death records; Gary, 1908-1920; Hammond, 1882-1920; Hobart, 1899-1920; Whiting, 1899-1920.	977.201 L192u

Marriages:

WPA, Index to marriage records, 1850-1920.	977.201 L192u
DAR, Marriage records...2 pts. (Pt. 1, Records of the first 100 marriages...after the organization of the county, Feb. 15, 1837; pt. 2, 1843-1850); also [5]pp. of marriages, 1837-1845.	p.f. 977.201 L192 no. 1 pts 1-2; No.2
Janowski, Barbara R., First marriage records...from 1837 to 1850. 1976. 23pp.	977.201 L192j

Cemetery:

Ballantyne, Dorothy D., The Old settlers cemetery....1976. 12pp.	977.202 H681b
D.A.C., Cemetery inscriptions, Lake, Porter and Starke cos....1968. 117pp. (Vol. 2 is "LaPorte and Porter counties." 1973. 130pp.).	977.201 L192c
DAR, Cemetery records....[1954-1959]. 13 pts. (with 170pp. index).	977.201 L192d
———, Cemetery records....2 pts. (St. Edward cem., Thompson cem).	977.201 L192do
———, Lowell cemetery, Cedar Creek township, Lowell, Ind. Comp. by Hattie McNay. [1955?]. 44pp.	977.202 L914d
———, Soldiers burial record...1889-1901. Comp. by Frances H. McBride. 1975. 5pp.	p.f. 977.201 L192 no. 3
Two articles concerning the Holzworth cemetery in Merrillville, and Luther's Grove cemetery in Crown Point....	p.f. 977.201 Luncat. no. 3

Church:

Demmon, Mrs. Floyd, Cedar Lake Baptist Church: Cedar Lake...constituted May 19th, 1839....1975. [15]pp.	p.f. 977.202 C389d
DAR, Baptisms and funeral records, First Methodist church, Crown Point, Ind. Comp. by Frances H. McBride. 32pp. (Baptisms, 1888-1935; funerals, 1891-94, 1924-27).	977.202 C953b
———, Marriage records, Methodist church, Crown Point....(1889-1929). 4 vols.	977.202 C953d
———, Record from sessional records, Presbyterian church, Crown Point....(1844-1934). [1962]. 29, 9pp.	977.202 C953dr

History:

Newspaper clippings, 1857-1869.	microfilm
Ball, Timothy H., The Lake of the Red Cedars; or, will it live? Thirty years in Lake, a record of the firsty thirty years of Baptist labors in the county....1880. 357pp.	977.201 L192b
———, Encyclopedia of genealogy and biography...with a compendium of history, 1834-1904....1974 reprint of 1904 ed. 674pp.	977.201 L192ba
DAR, Index to names in reports of the historical secretary of the Old Settlers' Association of Lake County. Comp. by Frances McBride. 1971. V.P.	977.201 L192da

Historical Association of Lake County, Ind. reports and papers. vol. 12. 1970. (Continues Old Settler and Historical Association...Reports of the Historical Secretary). 977.201 L192h

"Old Time News", reminiscences of Lake county from files of early papers, vol. 1, 1857-1862; vol. 2, 1863-1869. Index, Ind. State Library. 1950. 30pp. 977.201 L192L

Woods, Sam B., The first hundred years of Lake county...as lived and acted by Bartlett Woods and family and Sam B. Woods and family....1938. 418pp. 977.201 L192w

Hammond Hist. Soc., Hammond Daily News, Industrial edition. [1904]. 1966. 48, [6]pp. p.f. 977.202 H225 no. 1

Lake Co. Hist. Soc., Historical facts and legends...1934-1966. [7pp.] p.f. 977.201 Luncat. no. 2

Two articles concerning Lake County...historical memorabilia and a courthouse museum. p.f. 977.201 Luncat. no. 4

Ghrist, John R., "Lowell's...historic neighborhood is eyesore." (Article from the Star-Register, June 21, 1979). p.f. 977.201 Luncat. no. 5

Mortuary & Obituaries:

DAR, Geisen Funeral home records, 1868-1924, Crown Point. Comp. by Frances H. McBride. [1960]. 56, 40pp. 977.201 L192g

———, Linton Funeral home records, Aug. 1907-Dec. 1924. Comp. by Frances H. McBride. 1962. 48, 30pp. 977.201 L192Li

———, Obituaries from Lake County Star; Crown Point, Indiana, 3-6-1908—12-19-1913....Comp. by Frances H. McBride. 1976?. 23, [10pp.] p.f. 977.201 L192m

Miscellaneous:

DAR, Bible records. Comp. by Frances H. McBride. 1961. 60, 10pp. 977.201 L192db

———, ...[Some records of deeds, marriages, wills, organization of churches and a list of cemetery sites]. 1929. 5pp. p.f. 977.201 Luncat. no. 1

Family Bible records....[18pp.] p.f. 977.201 Luncat. no. 6

Ind. State Library..., Index to 1840 census....1972. 3pp. 977.201 L192i

WPA, Index to supplemental record, assessments, 1918, Calumet twp., Aetna, Gary, Griffith, Miller, North twp., E. Chicago, Hammond, Hessville, Highland, Munster, Whiting. 977.201 L192u

WPA, Index to supplemental record, registered voters, 1907, Calumet, Cedar Creek, Center, Eagle Creek, Hanover, Hobart, Ross, St. John, West Creek, Winfield, North townships. 977.201 L192u

WPA, Commissioners' record...1837-1858....6 vols. Ind. Hist. Soc. Library

LA PORTE COUNTY

Formed 1832 from St. Joseph   County Seat—LaPorte

Births:

WPA, Index to birth records, 1882-1920.	977.201 L315u
WPA, Index to birth records, Michigan City, 1882-1920.	977.201 L315u

Deaths:

WPA, Index to death records, 1882-1920.	977.201 L315u
WPA, Index to death records, Michigan City, 1882-1920.	977.201 L315u

Deeds:

Deed indexes, 1831-1897 (grantee only, 1831-1848; grantor only, 1933-1948).	microfilm

Marriages:

Marriages, 1832-1861.	microfilm
WPA, Index to marriage records, 1850-1920.	977.201 L315u
WPA, Index to supplemental records, marriage applications, 1850-1920.	977.201 L315u
DAR, ...Marriage (license) records, book A-B, 1832-1850. 1971/73. 2 vols. (Also 1973 ed. of marriages, 1832-1844 containing complete index & courthouse index from marriage books).	977.201 L315dm
Marriages, July 1832-Oct. 1844 (THG, vol. 18 #2, June 1978).	977.2 H789

Probates:

Probates, 1832-1851; indexes, 1852-1900?.	microfilm

Wills:

Wills, 1844-1899.	microfilm
Rowley, Dorothy, ...Abstracts of wills from book A, [1844-1871]. [1968]. n.p.	977.201 L315rw
Wills, 1844-1871 (THG, vol. 8 #2, 3, 4, 5, 6, Mar.-Apr., May-June, July-Aug., Sept.-Oct., Nov.-Dec. 1968).	977.2 H789

Cemetery:

Markanka, Paul H., Atlas of cemeteries....Information from set of WPA maps, Mr. Gene McDonald & various sextons from Oct. 1971 to March 1974....	f977.201 L315m
D.A.C., Cemetery inscriptions, Lake, Porter and Starke cos...1968. 117pp. (Vol. 2 is "LaPorte and Porter counties". 1973. 130pp).	977.201 L192c
DAR, Cemetery records....[1955-1978]. 4 vols. (Also 149pp. index comp. by ISL)	977.201 L315d
Donoghue, Paul F., Springville cemetery records....[1982?]. 14, [6]pp.	977.201 L315do
Munger, Mrs. Robert C., Veterans of the War of 1812 buried in LaPorte county....Comp. from records of LaPorte County Pioneer Cemetery Commission. 1978. [9pp.]	973.5 I39m
[Ind. Hist. Soc., Cemetery records...]. 1941. 23 pts.	p.f. 977.201 L315 no. 1
Vonesh, Mrs. Frederick T., Coulter cemetery, New Durham township....[1972?]. [2pp.]	p.f. 977.201 L315 no. 3
DAR, Westville cemetery inscriptions. [1974?]. 5pp.	p.f. 977.201 L315 no. 4
The birth of Carmel cemetery....2pp. (missing 1982)	p.f. 977.201 Luncat. no. 3

Church:

Bethel Presbyterian Church, Union Mills, Indiana, church sessional records, 1850-1879. 117pp.	977.202 U585be
Methodist Church, Ladies Aid Society, Union Mills, Ind., 1897-1902. 60pp.	977.202 U585me 1980
Garman, Harry O., Methodist Episcopal church, Rolling Prairie, Ind., Kankakee township....(Church history & records, 1835-1933). 1933. 72, [1], 15pp.	977.201 L315g

St. Johns Church records, Michigan City. miCrofilm

Miscellaneous:

DAR, Bible records. Comp. by Gretchen Tyler. 1970. 52pp.	977.201 L315db
Rowley, Dorothy, Bible records....[1963]. 8pp.	p.f. 977.201 L315 no. 2
Ind. State Library, Index to 1840 census....1972. 13pp.	977.201 L315i
Clerk's ledger, Jan. 2-Nov. 30, 1943.	microfilm
Rowley, Dorothy, ...School enumeration of the children between the ages of 5 and 21 years in the 1840's. [1964?]. 572pp.	977.201 L315r
Historical directory....n.d. 4pp.	p.f. 977.201 Luncat. no. 1
Rural directory....[1907?]. 11pp.	p.f. 977.201 Luncat. no. 2

LAWRENCE COUNTY

Formed 1818 from Orange   County Seat—Bedford

Births:

Births, 1882-1900.	microfilm

Deaths:

Deaths, 1882-1899.	microfilm

Deeds:

Deed indexes, 1819-1904.	microfilm

Marriages:

Marriage applications, 1882-1886.	microfilm
Marriage, 1818-1901.	microfilm
Marriages, Sept. 1818-Aug. 1824 (THG, #1, Jan.-Feb. 1963).	977.2 H789
DAR, Marriage records...[1850-1900]. vols. 5-9.	977.201 L419dm
Franklin, Charles M., ...Marriages, 1818-1834. 1981. [33pp.]	977.201 L419f

Probates:

Probate order books, 1818-1875; indexes, 1875-1901.	microfilm

Wills:

Wills, 1821-1870, 1875-1918.	microfilm
DAR, 1870-1875, wills from files....(Index only). 1970. 6pp.	p.f. 977.201 L419 no. 6

Cemetery:

DAR, Cemetery records from Lawrence, Martin, and Greene cos....1963. 162pp.	977.201 L419d
———, Tombstone inscriptions, Eastern Lawrence county....1966/7. 99pp.	977.201 L419da
———, Bible records....1966-70. 2 vols.	977.201 L419db
District school records...1835-1851....[1968]. 36pp.	977.201 L419
DAR, Cemetery records....[1975]. 128pp.	977.201 L419dau
———, Cemetery records...(Gilgal, Ikerd, Christopher McKnight, and Pinhook cems.). 1976. 174pp.	977.201 L419daw
———, Record of Burton cemetery and Burton Gap cemetery....Cop. by Gertrude B. Brown. 1970. 17pp.	977.201 L419dc
Dillman, Wayne, Mount Olive cemetery record, Williams, Ind. [1980?]. 30, [3]pp.	977.201 L419di
Ind. Junior Hist. Soc., ...Cemetery records. 1976. 4 vols.	977.201 L419i
DAR, Burial records of Green Hill cemetery, Bedford, Indiana. 1967-72. 2 vols.	977.202 B411d
Dusendschon, Lee E., Spice Valley cemetery at Spice Valley Baptist Church....1979. [8pp.]	977.202 M681d
Ind. Junior Hist. Soc., Revolutionary War soldiers buried in Lawrence....1978. 35pp.	973.34 I385Lit
Meredith, Mildred, Cemeteries....[1979?]. 63, 4, [4]pp.	977.2 M559c
DAR, Eli Burton family cemetery, Spice Valley twp....1971. [2pp.]	p.f. 977.201 L419 no. 7
Dillman, Wayne, Williams cemetery, Williams, Indiana. 1973. 41pp.	977.202 W724di
[Ind. Hist. Soc., Cemetery records...]. 1941. 9 pts.	p.f. 977.201 L419 no. 1
Ingalls, Mrs. Robert, Cemetery records....4 pts.	p.f. 977.201 L419 no. 2
Baldwin, Ralph E., Isom family cemetery, Mitchell, Ind., following information copied from headstones by Escoe Isom. 1963. 2pp.	p.f. 977.201 L419 no. 3
DAR, Cemetery records....1963-4. 3 pts. (Quaker, Ross, Zike).	p.f. 977.201 L419 no. 4

Robertson, Lela, D., [Cemetery records...].—Dixon or Proctor cemetery. 15, 9pp.   p.f. 977.201 Luncat. no. 2

Hufford, Mrs. M.E., Inscriptions from Lynn family tombstones in the Hamer cemetery in Spring Mill State Park, three miles east of Mitchell, Indiana. 3pp.   p.f. 977.201 Luncat. no. 3

Wagner, Mrs. Emma F., [...Cemetery records...]. 4 pts. (Mayfield-Ferguson; Bridge Church, Indian Creek township; Carl Moore farm, Perry township; Boone).   p.f. 977.201 Luncat. no. 4

Taylor, Ben F., Graves family cemetery....2pp.   p.f. 977.201 Luncat. no. 5

Brattain, Mrs. Dessie, Old Burton cemetery, Marion township....4pp.   p.f. 977.201 Luncat. no. 6

[Incomplete cemetery records of Connelly, Stampers Creek, Talbott, Liberty, and South Lawrenceport cemeteries...]. 3pp.   p.f. 977.201 Luncat. no. 7

Martin, Mrs. Bernice S., Records of the Dodd, Foster, Elijah Allen, and Granny White cemeteries. (From IMH, vol. 35, 1939). 8pp.   p.f. 977.201 Luncat. no. 8

Edwards, Teresa, Edwards cemetery...Mitchell, Indiana. 1980. 1pp.   p.f. 977.201 Luncat. no. 9

Dusendschon, Lee Edwards, Miller cemetery...Mitchell, Indiana. 1979. 1pp.   p.f. 977.201 Luncat. no. 10

Miscellaneous:

Beldon, Roy H., The Collings story of Pigeon Roost massacre. [1957?]. 20pp.   977.202 P629b

Coleman, Lizzie D., History of the Pigeon Roost massacre. 1904. 36pp.   977.202 P629c

Dixon, Benjamin F., Hoosier cousins; first families of Lawrence, a salute to the sesquicentennial. (Benjamin Franklin Junior historical series, no. 18). 1968. 78pp.   977.201 L419dx

Cook, Claude E., School enumeration....(1882, Bono township). 1pp.   p.f. 977.201 L419 no. 5

Cooper, W.F., Record of deaths in and near Tunnelton [1880-1957]....Cop. by Mr. and Mrs. C.E. Cook. 1967. 17pp.   p.f. 977.202 T926 no. 1

Salter, Mrs. Pearl, Notes on Lawrence county....Copy of excerpts from a letter written by Mrs. Pearl Salter, Nebraska. 1pp.   p.f. 977.201 Luncat. no. 1

Lawrence County—Mitchell Public Library Historical Collection. 1977.   microfilm

MADISON COUNTY

Formed 1823 from Delaware (N.P., unorganized)   County Seat—Anderson

Births:

WPA, Index to birth records, 1882-1920.	977.201 M182u

Deaths:

WPA, Index to death records, 1882-1920.	977.201 M182u

Deeds:

Brown, Mrs. Immogene B., Land records of Indiana. 1965-1972. 5 vols. (Vol. 1, Madison county)	977.2 B878L
Brown, Immogene B., ...Information abstracted from deed records, 1824 thru 1840. 1980. 2 vols.	977.201 M182bro
Deed indexes, 1827-1901.	microfilm
Land entries [1822-1837] (THG, vol. 13 #2, Apr.-June 1973).	977.2 H789
Seulean, Anita R., Abstracts of deeds...deed record 1, September 1826-July 1833. 1976. [136pp.]	977.201 M182s

Marriages:

Alatza, Mildred, ...Marriages, 1853-1858. [1964?]. 5pp.	p.f. 977.201 M182 no. 3
WPA, Index to marriage records, 1880-1920.	977.201 M182u
WPA, Index to supplemental record, marriage transcript, 1880-1920.	977.201 M182u
Marriages, 1853-1858 (THG, vol. 4 #4, July-Aug. 1964).	977.2 H789
Early marriage and death records...abstracted from local newspapers. [1981?]. [76pp.]	977.201 M182e
Van Pelt, Francis, Marriages of Anderson...1918-1930; as recorded in the record book of Francis Van Pelt, J.P. of Anderson, Indiana. n.p.	q977.201 M182v
Van Pelt, Francis, Marriages of Anderson, Indiana, ...1918-1930....	p.f. 977.201 Muncat. no. 2
Sansberry, Charles, Some...marriages, 1866-1868, taken from newspapers. [7pp.]	p.f. 977.201 Muncat. no. 1
D.A.C., Marriage records of Fall Creek Monthly meeting of the religious society of Friends near Pendleton, Indiana. [1974?]. 1 vol.	977.202 P398d

Wills:

Wills, 1879-1901.	microfilm
DAR, Abstracts of wills...will record 1, June 1879-November 1892. Comp. by Anita R. Seulean. 1977. [111pp.]	977.201 M182se

Cemetery:

D.A.C., ...Cemetery records. 1957-59. 570pp. (also with 123pp. index).	977.201 M182d
D.A.C., Cemetery and obituary records of Adams township....1976. [82pp.]	q977.201 M182dau
D.A.C., Burial records of Friends burying grounds of Fall Creek Monthly meeting of Friends near Pendleton, Indiana. Comp. by Frank and Ritha Rogers. 1976. 49pp.	977.202 P398da
[Ind. Hist. Soc., Cemetery records...]. 1940. 2 pts. (Gilmore, Crosley).	p.f. 977.201 M182 no. 1
Heiss, Willard C., [Cemetery records...]. 5 pts. (Bunker-Davis, cem. 1/4 mi NE of Ingalls, Huntsville, unnamed, Menden).	977.201 M182 no. 2
Ind. Junior Hist. Soc., ...Cemetery records. 3 pts.	977.201 M182 no. 4
Davis, Russell, Crosley cemetery, Fall Creek township....1pp.	977.201 Muncat. no. 3
Hidden cemetery, Lapel...[with information about Woodward and Brookside cemeteries...]. [4pp.]	977.201 Muncat. no. 4
German, J.L., Cemetery record. [Unnamed cemetery s. of Orestes]. (From Genealogical Ref. Builders Newsletter, vol 4, 1970). 2pp.	977.201 Muncat. no. 6

[Madison Co. Historical Soc., Cemetery Comm.,]...Cemetery maps. 1969. [48pp.]   977.201 M182m

Mortuary & Obituaries:

Alphabetical index of death notices appearing in the Anderson Daily Bulletin, 1921-1925. Comp. by Russell W. Davis.   microfilm

...Obituaries collected from Anderson newspapers...1968-1971. Comp. by Russell W. Davis.   microfilm

Albright Funeral home records...1891-1911. 1962. 11, 12, 13, 13pp.   977.201 M182a

Early marriage and death records...abstracted from local newspapers. [1981?]. [76pp.]   977.201 M182e

J.C. McCarty Funeral home, [Funeral registers]-1896, Aug. 27-1898, 1916-June 4, 1946. 9 vols.   q977.202 L311j

Miscellaneous:

Brown, Immogene B., ...An index of persons that appeared in an old tax list of the county in 1842. 1981. 97pp.   977.201 M182br

Ind. State Library, Index to 1840 census....1972. 13pp.   977.201 M182i

Whitson, Edna O., A Brief history of Van Buren township....[1950?]. 305, [3pp.] (also 1951 supplement).   977.201 M182w

Madison County Historical Gazette. (Scattered issues, 1975-1981).   p.f. 977.201 Muncat. no. 5

Tax record, ca 1842.   microfilm

County tract book, land grants....129pp.   q977.201 M182c

MARION COUNTY

Formed 1822 from Delaware (N.P., unorganized)　　　　　　　　　　County Seat—Indianapolis

Births:

WPA, Index to birth records, 1882-1920 (except Indianapolis).	977.201 M341un
Woodruff Place [Indianapolis...] birth records, 1911-1932. 4pp.	p.f. 977.202 Iuncat. no. 1

Deaths:

WPA, Index to death records, 1882-1901.	977.201 M341un
Woodruff Place [Indianapolis] death records, Dec. 1911-1932 (THG, vol. 7 #2, 3, Mar.-Apr., May-June 1967).	977.2 H789
Deaths reported in Indianapolis Locomotive, 1845-1860 (THG, vol. 14 #2, 3, Apr.-June, July-Sept. 1974).	977.2 H789

Deeds:

Deeds, 1822-1866.	miCrofilm
Murphy, Thelma, ...Deed book "A", May 2, 1822 thru 1827. 1982. [21]pp.	977.201 M341mid
Murphy, Thelma M., ...Index to deed book "B", 1827-1830. 1982. [30pp.]	977.201 M341mu

Marriages:

Marriages, 1822-1901.	microfilm
DAR, Marriage records...[1822-1860]. 1933-41. 3 vols.	977.201 M341d
WPA, Index to marriage records, 1822-1920.	977.201 M341un
WPA, Index to supplemental record, marriage transcripts, 1882-1906.	977.201 M341un
Ft. Wayne & Allen Co. Public Library, Index to marriage records, 1930....1979. 140, 73pp.	977.201 M341fo
Ridlen, Colleen Alice, ...Early marriage records, 1822-1836. 1978. 44pp.	977.201 M341ri
Marriages, 1822-1830 (THG, vol. 4 #2, 3, Mar.-Apr., May-June 1964).	977.2 H789
Day, Henry. The minister's private record of marriages [Philadelphia and Indianapolis, 1855-1892].	977.2 D273m

Probates:

Probates, 1830-1854; probate order books, 1822-1852. (also see common pleas records for continuation of probates).	microfilm
DAR, Record of the probate court and the court for the settlement of intestate estates...[1822-1832]. Cop. by Mrs. Hugh H. Hanna. 1941. 384pp.	977.201 M341m

Wills:

Wills, 1822-1901.	microfilm
DAR, First wills...[1823-1876]. 1935-1960. 7 vols.	977.201 M341da
...Will index, 1822-1938. [Original compiled by WPA in 1939/40; 1982 ed. cop. and corrected by Nancy Blackwell]. 266pp.	

Cemetery:

Sommers, H. Dale, Interment record and tombstone inscriptions of the Bridgeport Friends Church cemetery. 1941. 50pp. (missing 1982)	977.202 B852s
Crown Hill cemetery, Indianapolis. [1896?]. 217pp. (also 23 microfilm reels of burial records)	977.202 I388c
[Crismore, Mary T.], Crown Hill; the origin, organization and management... together with a list of officers, corporations and lot holders for 1875. 1975. 100pp.	977.202 I388cr
Nicholas, Anna, The story of Crown Hill. [1928]. 346pp.	IPL977.202 I388n

Trounstine, Philip J., "City of the dead: Crown Hill has reflected and made history of Indianapolis for 114 years". (Article from the Indianapolis Star, June 26, 1977...).	p.f. 977.202 Iuncat. no. 6
Greenlawn cemetery, Indianapolis. 4pts. in 1.	977.202 I388
Greenlawn cemetery, Indianapolis..., Grave lot locations. 1 vol.	977.202 I388gr
Moore, J.R.H., Transcript of the gravestones remaining in Greenlawn cemetery.... 1920 (bound in above volume I388in)	977.202 I388m
Garman, Harry O., Part of Green Lawn cemetery gravestone inscriptions; graves moved 1924 to other cemeteries. [1924?]. n.p.	977.202 I388ti
Greenlawn cemetery, Indianapolis...additional records especially list of Confederate dead buried there. (Also "names of Confederate prisoners who died at Camp Morton, Ind. during the war") [50pp.]	p.f. 977.202 Iuncat. no. 5
Chalmers, Hazel H., Bethel M.E. cemetery, located west of High School road on Seerley road...Decatur township....1979. 22pp.	977.201 M341c
DAR, Cemetery records of Marion county and some adjoining counties. 1970. 289pp.	977.201 M341dc
Union Title Co., Indianapolis, ...Cemetery record books of the Union Title Company, Indianapolis. Pts. 1-2. 1927. 84pp.	q977.201 M341u
Plat of the Union cemetery in the city of Indianapolis. 4pp.	f977.202 I388p
[Ind. Hist. Soc., Cemetery records...]. 1939. 46pts.	p.f. 977.201 M341 no. 1
[Ind. Junior Hist. Soc., Cemetery records...]. 2 pts. 1. Menon cemetery, Lawrence twp. [1957]. 2. Burials...in and around Marion county (incomplete). 1957.	p.f. 977.201 M341 no. 3
Hoyt, Mrs. Leo, Cemetery records....21 pts.	p.f. 977.201 M341 no. 4
Apple, Lois M., [...Cemetery records...]. 2 pts. (Mock, McCord).	p.f. 977.201 M341 no. 5
Williamson, Wallace F., An Index to the old section of the Mount Jackson cemetery....1964. [19pp.]	p.f. 977.201 M341 no. 6
Morlan, Mrs. W.M., [Cemetery records...]. [1] Todd cemetery. 1pp.	p.f. 977.201 M341 no. 7
Roper, Kate, Crows Nest cemetery....1975. 4pp.	p.f. 977.201 M341 no. 8
Tombstone inscriptions, Whitesell cemetery (abandoned) Johnson Road at State Road 37, Castleton, Lawrence township. [1974?]. [5pp.]	p.f. 977.202 I39 no. 1
Hendricks, A.W., Piner's cemetery association news. [2pp.]	p.f. 977.201 Muncat. no. 3
Hoyt, Mrs. Leo, ...Cemetery records.	p.f. 977.201 Muncat. no. 5-8, 11-13
Murphy, Thelma M., Kemper farm, Franklin township....1954. 1pp.	p.f. 977.201 Muncat. no. 9
Hoyt, Mrs. Leo, Mundy cemetery on Southport Road....1pp.	p.f. 977.201 Muncat. no. 14
[The Tombstone inscription of Margaret Freeland, wife of James, who died Sept. 8, 1863...]. [2pp.]	p.f. 977.201 Muncat. no. 15
[...Cemetery records, Newby, Bacon, and DeFord cemeteries]. (Newspaper clippings). 4pp.	p.f. 977.201 Muncat. no. 16
...Cemeteries, unnamed (Wayne township). 3pp.	p.f. 977.201 Muncat. no. 17
...Cemeteries: information on deeds, etc. from recorder's office....1pp.	p.f. 977.201 Muncat. no. 18
Salzarulo, Frank, "Erosion threatens graves". Article about the M.E. (Methodist) cemetery, Decatur township.... (From Indianapolis News, Feb. 10, 1976). 1pp.	p.f. 977.201 Muncat. no. 19
McCordsville cemetery. Cop. by Marie Doyle. 1973 [4pp.]	p.f. 977.201 Muncat. no. 20 pt. 1
David, Richard A., McCordsville cemetery addenda. [2pp.]	p.f. 977.201 Muncat. no. 20 pt. 2

DeFord, Kathleen, New information on the DeFord cemetery. [1pp.]   p.f. 977.201 Muncat. no. 22

"Decatur township...keeps up three old cemeteries". (From The Times, Mooresville, Indiana, July 7, 1977). 1pp.   p.f. 977.201 Muncat. no. 23

Long, Scott, Bill's cemetery, Lawrence township....1979. 3pp.   p.f. 977.201 Muncat. no. 24

Ind. Junior Hist. Soc., Burials in cemetery located at U.S. 100 and Moore Road, New Augusta, Indiana, Pleasant Hill cemetery. 32pp.   p.f. 977.201 Muncat. no. 25

West Union cemetery, 30th and Tibbs, Indianapolis....4pp.   p.f. 977.201 Muncat. no. 26

Church:

Friends, Soc. of, Beech Grove Monthly Meeting, Comm. on Education, Minutes, 1870-1874. n.p.   977.201 M341f

Friends, Soc. of, Beech Grove Monthly Meeting, Records, 1863-1881. 2 vols.   977.201 M341fr

Friends, Soc. of, Beech Grove Monthly Meeting, Constitution and minutes, 1882-1892. n.p.   977.201 M341fri

First Lutheran Church, Indianapolis, Archives: vol. 1-2. 1975. 2 vols. in 1 (Vol. 1 from 1837; vol. 2, thru 1891).   977.202 I388f

Marriages [1871-1896] from record of Marietta circuit, Indianapolis district, Southeastern Indiana Conference. ...by S. Tinher pastor, by order of the Quarterly Conference...March 4, 1871 at Marietta. [19pp.]   977.2 Iuncat. no. 17

In the beginning...the story of how the Maywood Methodist Church and the Decatur Bethel Church united to become Aldersgate United Methodist Church, 1827-1973. [1973]. 32pp.   977.202 I388in

Moudy, Vera M.G., History of the New York Street United Methodist Church, Indianapolis...with biographical and genealogical data. 1976. [6], 313pp.   977.202 I388mo

Court:

Circuit court order books, 1822-1834.   microfilm

Common pleas record, 1853-1871 [1880?]; common pleas order books, 1853-1873.   microfilm

Murphy, Thelma M., Index to cases recorded in book A of the...circuit court, 1822. [11pp.]   p.f. 977.201 Muncat. no. 10

Darlington, Jane E., Abstracts of some naturalization papers filed...1832-1903. 1980. [182pp.]   977.201 M341dra

———, Abstracts of naturalizations filed...1904, 1905, 1906. 1980. 43pp.   977.201 M341drab

Naturalizations, 1843-1853 (THG, vol. 20 #3, vol. 21 #1-2, Sept. 1980, Mar.-Apr., May-June 1981).   977.2 H789

List of aliens and exempts from the draft of October 6, 1862...as reported to the auditor by the enrolling commissioners. 1862. 77pp.   p.f. 977.201 M341 no. 2

Darlington, Jane E., Index of personal names in entry docket #1, bastardy....[1978?]. 23pp. (Entry docket #1 covers cases dating from January 1877 to January 1921).   977.201 M341dr

WPA, Commissioners' record...1822-1840....6 vols.   Ind. Hist. Soc. Library

Census:

Ind. Hist. Soc., Names of persons enumerated...1830. 1908. [29pp.]   p.f. 977.201 Muncat. no. 2

U.S. Bureau of the Census, "Names of persons enumerated in Marion county...1830". (Indiana Historical Society Publications, vol. 4, no. 5. 1908).

Ind. State Library, Index to 1840 census....[1971?]. [25pp.]   977.201 M341i

Taylor, Isaac, Our old residents, an alphabetical list, names of all persons, Indianapolis and Marion county, June 1, 1880, aged 65 years or more from the U.S.. census reports of 1880....31pp.   p.f. 977.201 Muncat. no. 1

WPA, Index to supplemental record, federal census, 1880 (includes parts of only Center and Warren townships and lists names, sex, color, ages).   977.201 M341un

Murphy, Thelma, Marion county...natives who were 80 years (or more) when they died in 1950. 1953. 4pp.   p.f. 977.201 Muncat. no. 4

Family:

Brown, Immogene B., Indiana genealogy articles appearing in Indianapolis Sunday Star, 1926-1933. 1976. 399pp.   977.2 B878i

DAR, Bible records, genealogical records, obituaries, wills, deeds, etc. 1971. 105pp.   977.201 M341db

———, Bible records, genealogical records, wills, deeds, notes, charts, etc. 1973. 118pp.   977.201 M341dba

———, Bible records, genealogical records, family histories. 1976. 209pp.   977.201 M341dbi

———, Bible records, genealogical records, cemetery records, and other records. 1977. 135pp.   977.201 M341dbr

———, Genealogical records. Pt. 1, Bible records, genealogical records, obituaries. Pt. 2, Wills, deeds, etc. 1970. 226pp.   977.201 M341dg

Church of Jesus Christ of Latter-Day Saints..., Index of surnames of genealogical pedigrees. 1966. 26, 4pp.   977.202 I38ch

Jackson, Mrs. Robert, Cemetery and genealogy records [Indianapolis]. 3pp.   p.f. 977.202 Iuncat. no. 2

Willard Heiss, Betty McCay, Pearl Brenton, and Vicki Scott have written genealogical columns in Indianapolis newspapers. These columns and some indexes are available in the Indiana State Library.

Maps:

L.M. Brown Abstract Company, Abstract of title for property in S W 1/4, Sec. 3, T16N, R4E, Indianapolis....1965. 67pp.   p.f. 977.202 Iuncat. no. 8

[Map of S W 1/4, Sec. 3, T16N, R4E...]. map   p.f. 977.202 Iuncat. no. 8 pt. 2

Map of Indianapolis, published by Luther R. Martin, real estate broker, Indianapolis....1870.   p.f. 977.202 Iuncat. no. 4

[Map of Franklin township...1889]. (Reprinted from the atlas of Indianapolis and Marion County...by Griffing, Gordon, and Co., Philadelphia).   p.f. 977.201 Muncat. no. 21

Taxes:

1829 tax assessment (THG, vol. 20 #2, June 1980)   977.2 H789

Browning, Eliza G., Lockerbie's assessment list of Indianapolis, 1835. (From Ind. Hist. Soc. Publications, vol. 4, 1909). [19pp.]   p.f. 977.202 Iuncat. no. 9

Darlington, Jane E., ...List of delinquent tax returns for 1842. 1982. 54pp.   977.201 M341md

Miscellaneous:

Coffin, Elizabeth B., Indianapolis...newspaper index for The Locomotive and the Indiana State Guard, August 16, 1845-July 22, 1861.   microfilm

Hanna, Agnes M., Old houses in Indiana, houses in Indianapolis and Marion county. (Clippings from the Indianapolis Star, 1929-1932). 134, [2]pp.   977.201 M341h

Hodges, Mrs. Laura F., ...Early Indianapolis. [1919?]. 1, 27pp.   IPL977.202 I388h

Spears, Jean E., Admission record, Indianapolis asylum for friendless colored children, 1871-1900. Trans. by Spears & Dorothy Paul. 1978. 159, [5]pp.   977.202 I388s

McKenzie, Anna, The greater Indianapolis blue book 1898-9. A complete list of club members, public officials, and prominent people....[1899]. 518pp.   IPL977.202 I388mc

...Coroner's book, 15 November 1884 to 13 December 1887, report of inquest proceedings. Abstracted by Jane E. Darlington. 1981. [14pp.]   p.f. 977.201 Muncat. no. 27

Pierson, Albert O., Local deaths, Jan. to Apr. 1939 from [Indianapolis] News, Times and Star papers. [13pp.]   p.f. 977.202 Iuncat. no. 3

The Harrison Home Statesman. President Benjamin Harrison Memorial Home, Indianapolis....(Scattered issues, vol. 4-, 1978-).   p.f. 977.202 Iuncat. no. 7

MARSHALL COUNTY

Formed 1835; organized 1836 from St. Joseph, Elkhart — County Seat—Plymouth

Deeds:

Deed indexes, 1834-1896.	microfilm
Deeds, 1835-1837, see DAR listing under "Family".	

Marriages:

Marriages, 1836-1850 (THG, #4-5, July-Aug., Sept.-Oct. 1962).	977.2 H789
Marriages, 1836-1898.	microfilm
Marriages, 1836-1850, see DAR listing under "Family".	
Marshall Co. Hist. Soc., Weddings...prior to 1850. [1962?]. [23pp.]	p.f. 977.201 M367 no. 4
McKay, Henrietta W., Weddings in county prior to 1850. (Clippings from the Daily Pilot, Plymouth, Ind., 1936). 6pp.	p.f. 977.201 Muncat. no. 1
Slevin, Ruth M., ...Marriage records, 1836-1888. [1975?]. 161, 160pp.	977.201 M367s
DAR, Marriage records...book "A" (1854-1862). Comp. by Theodora P. Artz. 1970/1. 2 pts.	p.f. 977.201 M367 no. 6

Probates:

Probates, 1836-1853; indexes, 1853-1899?	microfilm

Wills:

Wills, 1834-1899.	microfilm

Cemetery:

Durnan, Mary H., Survey of cemeteries....1979. 16pp.	977.201 m367d
[Ind. Hist. Soc., Cemetery records...]. 1941. 14 pts.	p.f. 977.201 M367 no. 1
DAR, [Cemetery records...]. 9 pts.	p.f. 977.201 M367 no. 2
Emerson, Frances E., Cemetery records....13pts.	p.f. 977.201 M367 no. 3
Morris, Erma H., Jacoby cemetery, Center township....1963. 13pp.	p.f. 977.201 M367 no. 5
Immanuel Lutheran cemetery, Polk township....15pp.	p.f. 977.201 Muncat. no. 3

Family:

DAR, Historical and genealogical records....(Includes marriage licenses, 1836-1850; deeds, 1835-1837). 1929. 104pp.	977.201 M367h
Marshall County Historical Society genealogy research file.	microfilm
Addenda to genealogy resources, Marshall County Historical Society Museum, Plymouth, Indiana. 1980. [5pp.]	p.f. 977.201 Muncat. no. 4 pt. 2

Miscellaneous:

Darlington, Jane E., ...Tax duplicate list for 1843 with some names from Starke county. 1981. n.p.	977.201 M367dam
"Old Settlers Society organized"....(Article from the Plymouth Democrat, vol. 23 #45...1878). [2pp.]	p.f. 977.201 Muncat. no. 2
Tract book, 1832-1875.	microfilm
Tax duplicate 1843 (THG, vol. 22 #3-4, Sept., Dec. 1982).	977.2 H789
WPA, Commissioners' record...1836-1844....3 vols.	Ind. Hist. Soc. Library

MARTIN COUNTY

Formed 1820 from Daviess, Dubois   County Seat—Shoals

Births:

Delayed births prior to 1941   miCrofilm

WPA, Index to birth records, 1882-1920.   977.201 M383u

Deaths:

WPA, Index to death records, 1882-1920.   977.201 M383u

Baker, Natalie M., ...Death records; 1882 thru Mar. 1900. 1977. 113pp.   977.201 M383b

Deeds:

Deeds, 1820-1863.   miCrofilm

Brown, Mrs. Immogene B., Land records of Indiana. 1965-1972. 5 vols. (Vol. 3, Martin County).   977.2 B878L

Marriages:

Marriages, 1846-1921.   miCrofilm

Marriage affadavits, 1883-1898.   miCrofilm

Marriages, 1820-1840 (THG, vol. 7 #4, July-Aug. 1967).   977.2 H789

WPA, Index to marriage records, 1850-1920.   977.201 M383u

WPA, Index to supplemental record, marriage transcripts, 1880-1920.   977.201 M383u

Baker, Natalie M., ...Marriage records, 1820-1925. 1977. 4 vols.   977.201 M383ba

Marriages, 1820-1850, see "Miscellaneous" entry by Stiles and Baker

Probates:

Complete probate, 1821-1847, 1853-1864.   miCrofilm

Probate indexes, 1824-1838.   miCrofilm

Probate order book, 1874-1920.   miCrofilm

Wills:

...Will records, books A-B [1840-1866, 1866-1894]. n.d. 36pp.   p.f. 977.201 M383 no. 6

Wills and probates, 1845-1930.   miCrofilm

Cemetery:

Clapp, Pauline, Emmons Ridge cemetery....1977. 9pp.   p.f. 977.201 M383c

Martin Co. Hist. Soc., Cemeteries....1963-1971. 3 vols.   977.201 M383ma

Jeffers, Phebe, ...Cemetery records. (Pleasant Valley, Spring Hill).   p.f. 977.201 M383 no. 1

Ingalls, Mrs. Robert, Cemetery records....2 pts. (McBride's Bluff, Dover Hill)   p.f. 977.201 M383 no. 2

Martin Co. Hist. Soc., Cemetery records....(Cemeteries in the Crane Naval Depot). 1966. 87pp.   p.f. 977.201 M383 no. 3

Chappell, Rachael, Jones cemetery...twp. of Lost River....1968. 4pp.   p.f. 977.201 M383 no. 4

Cislak, Gregory, Pleasant Grove cemetery, Crane Naval Depot....[1971?]. [4pp.]   p.f. 977.201 M383 no. 5

Tombstone inscriptions, Truelove cemetery (located in Rutherford township...). 1956. 16pp.   p.f. 977.201 Muncat. no. 3

Hamilton, Mrs. Minnie G., Jackson cemetery inscriptions....1pp.   p.f. 977.201 Muncat. no. 4

Arvin, Charles S., ...Cemetery inscriptions. 3 pts. (Holtsglaw, Mount Zion, Woods).   p.f. 977.201 Muncat. no. 5

Rector cemetery, Crane....1pp. (missing 1982)   p.f. 977.201 Muncat. no. 6

Miscellaneous:

...Handbook. Comp. by Stiles and Baker. [1967]. 100pp. (Gives marriages, 1820-1850).   977.201 M383m

Martin County, Indiana, Historical Society Collection.   microfilm
The Loogootee Tribune..., Dec. 28, 1950 and Aug. 24, 1950 [Obituaries]. 2pp.   p.f. 977.201 Muncat. no. 1
...Notes (a scrapbook of newspaper clippings, collected by Thelma Murphy). 1951.
    [42pp.]   977.201 Muncat. no. 2

MIAMI COUNTY

Formed 1832; organized 1834 from Cass   County Seat—Peru

Births:

WPA, Index to birth records, 1882-1920.	977.201 M618u

Deaths:

WPA, Index to death records, 1882-1920.	977.201 M618u
Wagner, Charles A., Index to official death records...1921-1974. 1978. 461pp.	977.201 M618ino

Deeds:

Deed indexes, 1836-1899.	microfilm

Marriages:

Marriages, 1843-1895.	microfilm
WPA, Index to marriage records, 1850-1920.	977.201 M618u
Index to marriage record...1840 to 1850... -newspapers; 1840 to 1849... -county clerk records. [19—]. [33pp.]	977.201 M618ind
Slevin, Ruth M., ...Marriage records, 1843-1855. 1970. 41, 42pp.	977.201 M618s

Probates:

Probates, 1843-1850; indexes, 1850-51, 1857-1889.	microfilm

Wills:

Wills, 1843-1900.	microfilm
Slevin, Ruth M., ...Will records, 1843-1900. [197-]. 278pp.	977.201 M618sL

Cemetery:

Ind. Hist. Soc., Pioneer Comm., ...Cemetery records. 11 pts. in 2 vols.	977.201 M618i
Tombaugh, Jean C., ...Cemetery inscriptions: (Allen & Perry twps.). 1977. 273pp.	977.201 M618t
Cemetery records...(South or Old Niconza, Geartie, Shoemaker, Enterprise, Niconza Church, Eikenberry Farm, name unknown in Perry twp.)	p.f. 977.201 M618 no. 1
Peru Public Lib., [Frances Slocum stone...]. [1967?]. [3pp.]	p.f. 977.201 M618 no. 2
———, Godfroy's cemetery....[1968]. [8pp.] (Also sup. of the plat of the Francis Godfroy cemetery). 5pp.	p.f. 977.201 M618 no. 3
Two unnamed cemeteries...(From THG, no. 1, 1963). 1pp.	p.f. 977.201 Muncat. no. 1
Old Clymer North cemetery, Jefferson township....(From Miami Co. Hist. Soc. Newsletter, vol. 6, 1980). 1pp.	p.f. 977.201 Muncat. no. 3

Census:

Ind. State Library, Index to 1840 census....1972. 10pp.	977.201 M618in
Bakehorn, Ray, 1840 federal population census....1977. xipp.	977.201 M618un
Smith, Robert D., 1850 federal population census....1977. 249, [4]pp.	977.201 M618una
———, 1860 federal population census....1977. 374pp.	977.201 M618uni
———, 1870 federal population census....1978. 458pp.	977.201 M618uns

Family:

Bakehorn, Ray, Early birth, marriage and death records....[19—]. vol. 1. 19pp.	977.201 M618b
Wagner, Charles A., ...Genealogies. 1978. 3 vols.	977.201 M618m
———, ...Encyclopedia. 1980- 3 vols.	977.201 M618mi
Smith, Robert D., Genealogical record...1763-1887; 1893-1914. 1977. 2 vols.	977.201 M618sm
Smith, Charles, Obituaries from the Bunker Hill (Indiana) Press, 1904-1926. 1981. [16], 165, 5pp.	977.202 B942o

Miscellaneous:

Land entry book, 1830-1852.	microfilm
Commissioners records, 1834-1853.	microfilm
Tract book (no date or names given)	microfilm
WPA, Index to enumeration of male voters, 1850-1920.	977.201 M618u
WPA, Index to supplemental record, male and female voters, 1922.	977.201 M618u
Wilmouth, Gillis L., North Grove United Brethren in Christ Church history (with supplemental denomination history). [19—]. 74pp.	977.202 N865w
The Converse Journal, the Indiana News-zine, Courier of Converse...centennial edition, Nov. 4, 5-6. 1948. 28pp.	p.f. 977.202 Cuncat. no. 1
Peru Public Lib., An annotated bibliography of Miami county, Indiana. n.d. [5pp.] pt. 2 [1980.] [revised.] [5pp.]	p.f. 977.201 Muncat. no. 2

MONROE COUNTY

Formed 1818 from Orange   County Seat—Bloomington

Births:

Delayed births prior to 1941.	miCrofilm
WPA, Index to birth records, 1882-1920.	977.201 M753u

Deaths:

WPA, Index to death records, 1886-1920.	977.201 M753u
Gromer, Doris, ...Death record index (1921-1950, 1951-1975). [1980?]. 2 vols.	977.201 M753gr

Deeds:

Deeds, 1817-1887.	miCrofilm
Deed indexes, 1817-1905.	microfilm

Marriages:

Ridlen, Colleen A., ...Early marriage records, 1818-1837. 1980. 43pp.	977.201 M753ri
DAR, An index to...marriage records, 1852-1859. Comp. by Mrs. Ruth C. Carter. 1976. 45pp.	977.201 M753daa
DAR, An index to...marriage records, 1818-1852. Comp. by Edith B. Cogswell. 1954. 145pp.	977.201 M753d
DAR, Marriage records...1882-1888. Comp. by Ruth Carter. [1972?]. 71pp.	977.201 M753c
DAR, Marriage records, book IV, October 2, 1859-September 9, 1867....Comp. by Ruth Carter. 1978. 93pp.	977.201 M753cm
DAR, Marriage records, book V...September 1867-November 1874. Comp. by Ruth Carter. 1979. 96pp.	977.201 M753cn
Marriages, 1818-1822 (IMH, vol. 34, 1938).	977.2 I39
Marriages, 1818-1835 (THG, vol. 18 #1, Mar. 1978).	977.2 H789
Marriages, 1818-1852.	microfilm
Marriages, 1818-1921.	miCrofilm
Marriage returns, 1882-1890.	miCrofilm
WPA, Index to marriage records, 1853-1920. (letters Jo-Z on microfilm)	977.201 M753u
WPA, Index to supplemental record, marriage applications, 1845-1920.	977.201 M753u

Probates:

Probate order books, 1818-1852; indexes, 1853-1873 [civil cases?].	microfilm
Probate records, final, 1838-1863; probate order books, 1818-1920 and index, 1870-1940.	miCrofilm

Wills:

Wills, 1818-1904.	microfilm
Wills, 1818-1851, 1873-1924.	miCrofilm
Carter, Ruth, Will abstracts...February 1873-February 1890....1974. 1 vol.	977.201 M753ca
Carter, Ruth, Will abstracts...February 1890-February 1904....1975. 55pp.	977.201 M753car
DAR, Will abstracts, will book 1...(1818-1841). Comp. by Mrs. Ruth Carter. [1971?]. 3 vols. (1818-1873 and index)	p.f. 977.201 M753 no. 5
Slevin, Ruth M., ...Will records, 1818-1904. [19—]. 242pp. (with index by Patricia Patton, 58pp.)	977.201 M753s

Cemetery:

Meredith, Mildred, Cemeteries....[1979?]. 63, 4, [4]pp.	977.2 M559c

DAR, Cemetery records...[Bean Blossom twp., Indian Creek twp., Presbyterian cem., Ellettsville]. [1957, 1959, 1969]. 3 vols.	977.201 M753da
Weaver, Elaine, [...Cemeteries...]. [1975?]. 1, 2, 1, 5, 5, 5pp. (Griffith, Hacker, Lipp, Pleasant View Baptist Church, Shilo, Stepp).	977.201 M753w
[Ind. Hist. Soc., Cemetery records...]. 1937. 13 pts.	p.f. 977.201 M753 no. 1
Richardson, Neva, ...Cemetery records. 10pts.	p.f. 977.201 M753 no. 3
Cowen, Mrs. Carl, [Cemetery records...]. (I U campus—God's Acre). 1961. 3pp.	p.f. 977.201 M753 no. 4
McCormick, Mrs. John F., Old Eller family cemetery near the Eller homestead...Van Buren township....1972. 1pp. (also 1975 correction, 1pp.)	p.f. 977.201 M753 no. 6
Matson, Donald K., Rose Hill cemetery. 1976. 343pp.	977.202 B655m
Old Liberty church cemetery....[5pp.]	p.f. 977.201 Muncat. no. 2
Wilson, Betty, Smithville, Indiana cemetery....1957. 1pp.	p.f. 977.201 Muncat. no. 3
Todd cemetery, Tower Ridge Road, Polk township....[2pp.]	p.f. 977.201 Muncat. no. 4
Wagner, Mrs. Emma F., Lowe cemetery....1pp.	p.f. 977.201 Muncat. no. 5
Adams, Mrs. Marie, Rawlins cemetery. 1pp.	p.f. 977.201 Muncat. no. 6
Emery, Mrs. Charles R., Records of the Chambers and Mt. Salem cemeteries. (From IMH, vol. 33, 1937). 1937. 4pp.	p.f. 977.201 Muncat. no. 7
Matson, Donald, Griffith cemetery, section 4, Bloomington twp. 1965. 1pp.	p.f. 977.201 Muncat. no. 8
Simpson Chapel cemetery (new), section 28, Washington twp. [9pp.]	p.f. 977.201 Muncat. no. 9
Matson, Donald, United Presbyterian cemetery, section 32, Bloomington twp. 1969. [17pp.]	p.f. 977.201 Muncat. no. 10
Hamm, Dorothy M., ...Cemeteries, Clear Creek and Polk townships. 1980. 3pp.	p.f. 977.201 Muncat. no. 11
Rice, Jane A.M., Hays cemetery, Polk township....1980. 1pp.	p.f. 977.201 Muncat. no. 13
Dunn cemetery, adjacent to Beck Chapel, Indiana University campus, Bloomington....1pp.	p.f. 977.201 Muncat. no. 14

Church:

Arpan, Mrs. Floyd G., Between then and now, 1819-1969: 150 years of Presbyterians in perspective: First United Presbyterian church...Bloomington....1969. 99pp.	977.202 B655ar
DAR, Membership roll of the First Baptist church, Bloomington...(1825-1890). [1971]. 20pp.	977.202 B655b
Ind. Hist. Soc., [Church records...]. 3 pts. (Ellettsville Baptist Church, Vernal Baptist Church, Richland Church).	p.f. 977.201 M753 no. 2
Tourner, Anne, [The First Baptist church of Bloomington...]. 7pp.	p.f. 977.202 B655 no. 1
Sanders, L.W., History of Vernal Baptist church...[with membership list, 1819-1900]. 22pp.	p.f. 977.201 Muncat. no. 1
Waldron, Mary A., History of Saint Charles Catholic Church, Bloomington....1934. 45pp.	977.202 B655w

Court:

Guardian docket and fee book, 1913-1930.	miCrofilm
Inquest records, 1895-1927.	miCrofilm
Naturalizations, 1854-1918.	miCrofilm
DAR, Records of declaration of intention...division of naturalization...October 1854-June 1890. Comp. by Ruth Carter. 1977. 20pp.	977.201 M753cat
Record of ear marks, brands [1818-1839]....1980. [26pp.]	p.f. 977.201 Muncat. no. 12

Miscellaneous:

WPA, Commissioners' record...1818-1832....2 vols.	Ind. Hist. Soc. Library

Farber, Renee, Index to commissioner's record...1818-1824...volume B, 1824-1932....1980. 86pp.   977.201 M753far

DAR, Bible records....[1973]. 18pp.   977.201 M753db

Monroe Co. Hist. Soc., Atlas of Monroe county...1856: indexed by townships. 1975. 51pp.   977.201 M753m

The Tree Climbers, Monroe county Genealogical Society, vol. 1-, November 1974-76 (continued as Monroe County Genealogical Society Newsletter). (scattered issues).   977.201 M753n

The Ellettsville Journal, vol. 12, no. 11, September 14, 1950, Ellettsville...(12th annual Monroe county Fall festival, Ellettsville, Sept. 14-16).   p.f. 977.202 Euncat. no. 1

[History and first annual reunion of Stanford school held August 28, 1938, at Stanford, Indiana]. 1939. [8pp.]   p.f. 977.202 Suncat. no. 1

MONTGOMERY COUNTY

Formed 1823 from Parke, Putnam   County Seat—Crawfordsville

Births:

WPA, Index to birth records, 1882-1920.   977.201 M788u

Deaths:

WPA, Index to death records, 1882-1920.   977.201 M788u

Walters, Crystal P., Deaths in southeastern part of...co...with a few from all over the county. 1971. 2 vols.   977.201 M788wa

Deeds:

Deed indexes, 1822-1907.   microfilm

...Original entry record book: dates 1821 & later. 1979. 86, 16pp.   977.201 M788mo 1979

Marriages:

DAR, ...Marriages, 1823-1860. 1953. n.p.   977.201 M788m

WPA, Index to marriage records, 1860-1920.   977.201 M788u

Shanklin, Mabel, ...Will and marriage records. (Wills, 1823-1883; marriages, 1823-1852). 1969-72. 3 vols. in 1.   977.201 M788s

DAR, Affidavits and consents for persons making applications for marriage license...(1823-1850). 1970. 4 vols.   q977.201 M788da

Probates:

Probate order books, 1824-1877.   microfilm

Wills:

Shanklin, Mabel, ...Will and marriage records. (Wills, 1823-1883...). 1969-72. 3 vols. in 1.   977.201 M788s

Shelby, Mrs. K.P., [Abstracts of] first wills....[1822-1831]. [4pp.]   p.f. 977.201 M787 no. 4

Hofmann, Roberta, ...Will indexes, 1822-1893. [197-]. [15pp.]   977.201 M788h

Wills, 1823-1831, 1852-1901.   microfilm

...Wills, book A [1825-1832]. (From THG, #4, July-Aug., 1962). 1pp.   p.f. 977.201 Muncat. no. 10

Cemetery:

DAR, Cemeteries....1963-73. 9 vols.   977.201 M788dc

[Cemetery records. 1961-62]. 2 pts. [1] Alamo cemetery...Ripley twp., Bunker Hill or Stonebraker cem., McCormick cem., O'Neal cem., Texas cem. and Willis cem., Yountsville cem. [2] Weir cem., Union twp.   p.f. 977.201 M788ce

Am. Legion, Montgomery county soldier dead....1941. 23pp. (also revisions of 1952, 1954, 1957, 1966, 1973).   p.f. 977.201 M787 no. 1

DAR, Cemetery records....5 pts.   p.f. 977.201 M787 no. 2

Herr, Ben, Cemetery records....2 pts.   p.f. 977.201 M787 no. 3

Meek, Steve, Cemetery records....2 pts. (Clouser, Deck).   p.f. 977.201 M787 no. 6

Evans, Mrs. Margaret, [Old Turkey Run cemetery, Coal Creek twp.: Grady cemetery, Wayne twp.: Moudy cemetery...]. [1953]. [3pp.]   p.f. 977.201 Muncat. no. 4

DAR, Location of cemeteries....2 pts. (1. Index of cemeteries by section, township, range. 2. Chart).   p.f. 977.201 Muncat. no. 6

Kerr, Mrs. Samuel W., A Family cemetery located in part of the northwest quarter of the northwest quarter, section 31, township 21 N, Range 3 West, Sugar Creek township....1pp.   p.f. 977.201 Muncat. no. 7

Ripley township, unnamed (4 miles from Crawfordsville on State Road 47), unnamed (northeast of Mace) cemeteries.... (From Illiana Gen., vols. 9, 5, 8, 1973, 1969, 1972). [5pp.]   p.f. 977.201 Muncat. no. 8

Peterson cemetery.... (From the Detroit Soc. for Gen. Res. Mag., vol. 32, 1969). 4pp.   p.f. 977.201 Muncat. no. 12

Linden cemetery.... (From the Detroit Soc. for Gen. Res. Mag., vol. 33, 1970). 1pp.   p.f. 977.201 Muncat. no .13

Church:

Linn, Mrs. W.H., St. John's church, Crawfordsville.... History of the Episcopal church from 1837 to 1927. 32pp.   p.f. 977.202 Cuncat. no. 1

Union Presbyterian church, Walnut township.... (From Bull. of the Seattle Gen. Soc., vol. 19, 1969). 4pp.   p.f. 977.201 Muncat. no. 11

History:

Walters, Crystal P., Fredericksburg (Mace) and Mace Station (Linnsburg) and vicinity... 1823 to 1969. 1970. 115pp.   977.201 M788w

———, History of Clark township, Ladoga and part of Scott township... 1828-1971. 1971. 196pp.   977.201 M788waa

———, History of New Ross and vicinity, 1829-1962. 1962. 65pp.   p.f. 977.202 N558 no. 1

———, History of Whitesville and community. [1963]. 16, 39pp. (and 1970 ed. of 71pp.)   977.202 W594w

Who's Your Ancestor Association..., Information sheet. [1974?]. 1pp.   p.f. 977.201 Muncat. no. 1

Young, Mrs. Katherine, Index of biographies and photographs for History of Montgomery County..., by Beckwith. 1950. [12pp.]   p.f. 977.201 Muncat. no. 2

Early settlers... as shown by signatures on petitions for pardon, Centerville, May 14, 1825. [1pp.]   p.f. 977.201 Muncat. no. 3

Montgomery... Your County Magazine. Sept. 1979.   p.f. 977.201 Muncat. no. 9

Mortuary & Obituaries:

Deaths and appointments of estate administrators in Crawfordsville newspapers, (June 1853-December 1858). (THG, vol. 18 #2, June 1978).   977.2 H789

DAR, Mortuary records.... [1] 1912-15. 1958. 114pp.   977.201 M788d

Naturalizations:

DAR, Immigration and naturalization records.... [1976?]. 8, 190pp.   977.201 M788di

Who's Your Ancestor, Genealogical and Hist. Soc., Naturalization applications... 1850-1930. [1979]. 67pp.   977.201 M788wh

Miscellaneous:

DAR, Family Bible records. 19pp. in v.p.   977.2 F198

Stockdale, Mrs. James, Index of 1850 census.... 1974. 48pp.   977.201 M788st

A List and sketch of all who have been granted pensions in this county—pensioners of 1812.... (From Saturday Evening Journal, Crawfordsville, 1879). [5pp.]   p.f. 977.201 Muncat. no. 5

WPA, Commissioners' record... 1823-1853.... 13 vols.   Ind. Hist. Soc. Library

MORGAN COUNTY

Formed 1822 from Delaware (N.P., unorganized), Wabash (N.P., unorganized)   County Seat—Martinsville

Births:

WPA, Index to birth records, 1882-1920.	977.201 M849u

Deaths:

WPA, Index to death records, 1899-1920.	977.201 M849u
Mertens, Mrs. F.C., ...deaths [1889-1927]. [4pp.]	p.f. 977.201 Muncat. no. 3

Deeds:

Deed indexes, 1822-1903.	microfilm

Marriages:

Weaver, Elaine, ...Marriage records, 1842-1851. [1975?]. 47pp.	977.201 M847we
Marriages, 1822-1835 (THG, vol. 10 #3, May-June 1970).	977.2 H789
Marriages, 1822-1901.	microfilm
WPA, Index to marriage records, 1850-1920.	977.201 M849u
WPA, Index to marriage records, 1921-1941.	977.201 M849u
WPA, Index to marriage affidavit record, 1881-1920.	977.201 M849u
Littell, Noble K., ...Marriage records, 1822-1851. 1971. n.p.	977.201 M847Lm
Ridlen, Colleen A., ...Early marriage records, 1822-1840. 1978. 41pp.	977.201 M847ri
Weaver, Elaine, ...Marriages, 1822-1842. [1972?]. 46pp.	977.201 M847w

Probates:

Probate order books, 1822-1836, 1843-1852; indexes, 1852-1901.	microfilm

Wills:

Wills, 1846-1904.	microfilm
Littell, Noble K., ...Will abstracts...1847-1887. 1980. 94pp.	977.201 M847Lim

Cemetery:

[Cemetery records...]. 1978. 2 vols. (Vol. 1, White Lick cemetery, Mooresville..., Vol. 2, West Union, Friendship Park, Slaughter, Wright, Patrick, Morgan, Butterfield).	977.201 M847ce
Sheetz, William E., ...Cemetery: Butterfield family cemetery records, Clay and Madison twp. line. 1974. 4pp.	p.f. 977.201 M847s
———, ...Cemetery: Morgan family cemetery records, Madison township. [1974?]. 3pp.	p.f. 977.201 M847sh
Ind. Hist. Soc., [Cemetery records...]. 2 pts. (Samaria, Centerton).	p.f. 977.201 M847 no. 1
Cowen, Carl and Janet, ...Cemetery records. 1968-69. 3 vols.	977.201 M847c
DAR, ...Cemetery records. 1960-66. 3 vols. (also index)	977.201 M847da
Morgan county, Indiana Historical Soc., ...Cemetery records. (includes North Branch, White Lick).	microfilm
Hoyt, Mrs. Leo, Cemetery records....11 pts. (pts. 4, 5, 6, 9, 10 missing 1982)	p.f. 977.201 M847 no. 4
Morlan, Mrs. W.M., Cemetery records....8 pts.	p.f. 977.201 M847 no. 5
Cowen, Carl C., Cemetery records....2 pts. (pt. 1 includes K.C. Pearce's Daily Journal, Aug. 15, 1862).	p.f. 977.201 M847 no. 6
Ind. Junior Hist. Soc., ...Cemetery records. (Hilldale, South Park, Baptist, Easthill). 4 pts.	p.f. 977.201 M847 no. 7
Hoyt, Mrs. Leo, Cemetery 9/10 of a mile south of Hall....[8pp.]	p.f. 977.201 Muncat. no. 4
Murphy, Thelma, Williams cemetery....2pp. (incomplete)	p.f. 977.201 Muncat. no. 5

DAR, Roll of honor of our Union dead buried in Mooresville cemeteries....10pp.	p.f. 977.201 Muncat. no. 6
Mertens, Mrs. Fred, ...Cemetery (West edge of Morgantown) and supplement. 2pp.	p.f. 977.201 Muncat. no. 7
Johnson, Jerry, Wilbur Road cemetery....1pp.	p.f. 977.201 Muncat. no. 8
Noble Hovious farm cemetery, SW of Martinsville...and Walter Myers farm cem., Owen county....1pp.	p.f. 977.201 Muncat. no. 9
Private cemetery in Baker twp....1pp.	p.f. 977.201 Muncat. no. 10
[Flake-Pierce cemetery]....[4pp.]	p.f. 977.201 Muncat. no. 11
McKinney, Mrs. Maurice E., [Inscriptions of the] Pruitt family cemetery. 1978. [2pp.]	p.f. 977.201 Muncat. no. 12
Ind. Junior Hist. Soc., Bethlehem cemetery, Jefferson twp....[3pp.]	p.f. 977.201 Muncat. no. 13
Ind. Junior Hist. Soc., ...Cemetery records (Butterfield, Centennial Church, Williams, Williams Graveyard, Sandcreek, Townsend, and Union). [51pp.]	p.f. 977.201 Muncat. no. 14

Church:

Friends, Soc. of., Minutes of White Lick Monthly meeting of women Friends for 1868-9. [24pp.]	977.201 M847fr
Taylor, Mary E.M., The Morgantown Methodist church. 1958. 7pp.	p.f. 977.202 M849 no. 1
Ind. Hist. Soc., Church records....1942. (missing 1982)	p.f. 977.201 M847 no. 2

School:

Adams, Oliver, School enumeration record for the twp. of Jackson...[1871-1889]. 1865. n.p.	977.201 M847a
Littell, Noble K., School enumeration...(1905, 1906...of Clay and Monroe townships and...Martinsville, 1908 of Martinsville). 2 vols.	977.201 M847L
Littell, Noble K., School enumeration...1977. 28-214, [51pp.]	977.201 M847Li

Taxes:

Darlington, Jane E., ...1840 tax duplicate book. 1982. n.p.	q977.201 M847mo
Littell, Noble K., Personal property assessment list...1900: Adams, Ashland, Baker, Brown, and Clay twps. 1976. [45pp.]	977.201 M847Lit
...Personal property assessment list, 1900. 27pp.	977.201 M847

Miscellaneous:

Ind. State Lib., Index to 1840 census....1972. 15pp.	977.201 M847i
Littell, Noble K., From the archives, with other clippings. (Xeroxed articles from the Morgan County Gazette primarily). 1972. vol. 2	977.201 M847Lf
McGuire, Donna L. and Donald, Abstracts of the Morgan County, Indiana Gazette. (1853-1858). 1982. 1 vol.	977.201 M847m
Mertens, Mrs. Frederick C., Account book of Dr. Griffitt and Dr. W.H. Murphy who practiced in Morgan and Brown counties...1878-1890, 1894-1899. 1950. [19pp.]	p.f. 977.201 Muncat. no. 1
———, Names of people living in and around Morgantown...1897, 1898, 1899. Taken from account book of Dr. Griffitt. [8pp.]	p.f. 977.201 Muncat. no. 2

NEWTON COUNTY

Formed 1859; org. 1860 from Jasper   County Seat—Kentland

Births:

WPA, Index to birth records, 1882-1937.   977.201 N567u

Deaths:

WPA, Index to death records, 1882-1937.   977.201 N567u

Deeds:

Deed indexes, 1839-1903.   microfilm

Deeds transcribed, 1838-1860.   microfilm

Lands transferred from Jasper County, 1855-58.   microfilm

Marriages:

Marriage licenses, 1860-1896.   microfilm

Miller, Mrs. Richard L., ...Marriage records, 1860-1897. 1974. 1 vol.   q977.201 N567m

WPA, Index to marriage records, 1860-1920.   977.201 N567u

Probates:

Probate order book indexes, 1861-1900.   microfilm

Wills:

Wills, 1860-1902.   microfilm

Miscellaneous:

Ind. Hist. Soc., Pleasant Grove & Doran cemeteries. 1955. 10, 1, 2pp.   p.f. 977.201 N567 no. 1

[Ind. Junior Hist. Soc., ...Cemetery records...]. [1] St. Joseph's cemetery. 1973. 2pp.   p.f. 977.201 N567 no. 2

Miller, Mrs. Richard L., ...Miscellaneous papers. n.d. 3pp.   p.f. 977.201 N567 no. 3

Ghrist, John R., "Roselawn...churches withstanding test of time". (Article from Register newspaper). 1979. 1pp.   p.f. 977.201 Nuncat. no. 1

Note: An earlier Newton County organized in 1835 from St. Joseph Co., dissolved in 1839.

NOBLE COUNTY

Formed 1835; organized 1836 from Elkhart, LaGrange, Allen   County Seat—Albion

Births:

Births, 1882-1901.	microfilm
Birth records, 1866-1913 from the Register of Dr.'s Salathiel and Warren S. Williams. Cop. by Adele C. Misselhorn. 1939. 49pp.	p.f. 977.201 Nuncat. no. 1 pt. 2

Deaths:

Deaths, 1882-1899.	microfilm

Deeds:

Deed indexes, 1834-1899.	microfilm

Marriages:

Marriage records, 1859-1875, see DAR listing under "Others".	
Marriages, 1859-1899.	microfilm
Slevin, Ruth M., ...Marriage records...1859-1899. 1971. 186, 191pp.	977.201 N747sL

Probates:

Probate indexes, 1859-1900.	microfilm

Wills:

Wills, 1854-1902.	microfilm
Slevin, Ruth M., ...Will abstracts, 1859-1894. [1974?]. 238pp.	977.201 N747s

Others:

DAR, ...Records. 7 vols. (Includes Cemetery records....324pp.	977.201 N747d
Bible records, obituaries and stories of early days....385pp.	977.201 N747db
Church histories, obituaries....375pp.	977.201 N747dc
Family records....363pp.	977.201 N747df
Marriage records...1859-1875...231pp.	977.201 N747dm
Mortuary and school records....330pp.	977.201 N747dmo
Obituaries and news items of early settlers....245pp.	977.201 N747do
Plat book, 1828-1875.	microfilm
Darlington, Jane E., ...Delinquent tax list 1847 including 1846. 1982. 25pp.	977.201 N747n
Harter, Stuart, Original land entries....1981. 15pp. 12 maps.	f977.201 N747h
Newhard, Malinda E.E., ...Veterans burial records, 1893-1923. 1981. 62pp.	977.201 N747ne
Owen, M.F., [Scrapbook of M.F. Owen indexing a few births, marriages, accidents, fires, etc....from late 1800's to early 1900's]. 144, [5]pp. 1976 photocopy	977.201 N747o
Sweet, Dale, Potter's Field, Lakeview cemetery. (Lakeview cemetery history included in church histories, obituaries...). 7pp.	p.f. 977.201 N747 no. 1
DAR Newspaper obituaries, miscellaneous clippings and chapter materials. 11 scrapbooks.	uncat.
Ind. State Lib., Index to 1840 census....1972. 10pp.	977.201 N747i
...1840 Census of Allen and Wayne townships....2pp.	p.f. 977.201 Nuncat. no. 1 pt. 1
The Noble County Genealogy Society Newsletter. (vol. 1 #1 1980).	p.f. 977.201 Nuncat. no. 2
Ligonier Centennial, 1835-1935. n.p.	p.f. 977.202 Luncat. no. 1

OHIO COUNTY

Formed 1844 from Dearborn   County Seat—Rising Sun

Births:

Births, 1882-1904.	microfilm
Delayed births prior to 1941.	miCrofilm

Deaths:

Billingsley, E.W., Death records...1882-1891. 1967.	977.201 O37bi
Deaths, 1882-1900.	microfilm
Deaths, 1911-Jan. 1970.	miCrofilm
Brown, Immogene, ...Death records...those born prior to 1850, abstracted... 1899-1920. 1964. 126pp.	977.201 O37b
Deaths, [1882-1910]; town of Rising Sun [1882-1910].	miCrofilm
Transcript of...deaths...[1901-1902] and record of returns of diseases dangerous to public health, in the city of Rising Sun...[1882-1909].	miCrofilm

Deeds:

Deed indexes, 1844-1899.	microfilm
Deeds, 1844-1981; indexes, 1844-1980.	miCrofilm

Marriages:

Marriages, 1844-1900.	microfilm
Marriages, 1844-1981.	miCrofilm
Marriage applications, 1903-1905.	miCrofilm

Probates:

Probate order books, 1844-1880, 1883-1981.	miCrofilm
Probate order book indexes, 1844-1900.	microfilm
Complete order books, 1844-1911.	miCrofilm

Wills:

Wills, 1843-1901.	microfilm
Wills, 1845-1981.	miCrofilm

Others:

Dorrell, Dillion R., ...Cemeteries. [1980?]. 131pp.	977.201 O37d
———, New Hope cemetery....4pp.	p.f. 977.201 Ouncat. no. 2
...Cemetery records. [1976?]. v.p.	977.201 O37e
Burial of soldiers, sailors, and marines under an Act...1889 (dates of death, 1886-1903).	miCrofilm
Sexton's reports, 1858-1939....	miCrofilm
...Records and family histories (from Ohio County Public Library).	miCrofilm
Family records (From Ohio County Historical Society).	miCrofilm
Milton Methodist church Bible....1pp.	p.f. 977.201 Ouncat. no. 1
Works, Andrew J., "Recollections of the Hill Country". (Series of articles originally published in the Ohio County News and Rising Sun Recorder, 1908-1909, and reprinted...1979...). 24pp.	p.f. 977.201 Ouncat. no. 3
Index to estates, 1860-1907.	miCrofilm
Naturalizations, 1848-1890, 1892-1912, 1914-1927; indexes, 1848-1926.	miCrofilm

ORANGE COUNTY

Formed 1816 from Knox, Gibson, Washington   County Seat—Paoli

Births:

Delayed births prior to 1941.	miCrofilm
WPA, Index to birth records, 1882-1920.	977.201 O63u
WPA, Index to birth records, 1882-1940.	977.201 O63u

Deaths:

WPA, Index to death records, 1882-1920.	977.201 O63u

Deeds:

Deeds, 1816-1886.	miCrofilm
Deed indexes, 1816-1887.	miCrofilm
Deed indexes, 1816-1902.	microfilm

Marriages:

Marriages, 1816-1835 (THG, vol. 17 #3, Sept. 1977).	977.2 H789
Marriages, 1816-1854.	microfilm
Marriages, 1816-1902.	miCrofilm
Marriages, 1816-1826 (IMH, vol. 37, 1941).	977.2 I39
Marriage records, 1816-1870, see DAR listing under "Miscellaneous".	
WPA, Index to marriage records, 1826-1920.	977.201 O63u
WPA, Index to supplemental record, marriage transcripts, 1880-1920.	977.201 O63u
Mavity, N.B., First marriage records...1816-1826. 1941. [17pp.] (missing 1982)	p.f. 977.201 O63 no. 2

Probates:

Probate indexes, 1874-1921.	miCrofilm
Probates, final record, 1852-1863.	miCrofilm
Probate order book, 1829-1850.	miCrofilm
Probates, 1817-1842, 1847-1874; indexes, 1874-1901.	microfilm
Probates, 1816-1825, see DAR listing under "Miscellaneous".	

Wills:

Wills, 1816-1852 (IMH, vol. 34, 35, 1938-39).	977.2 I39
Wills, 1816-1892, see DAR listing under "Miscellaneous".	
Early wills...(From IMH, vol. 34, 1938). [8pp.]	p.f. 977.201 Ouncat no. 2
Wills, 1816-1943.	miCrofilm

Cemetery:

Orange...cemeteries. 1981. [270pp.] Cop. by Stalker School Little Hoosiers and...Bedford North Lawrence History Hunters.	977.201 O63o
[Ind. Hist. Soc., Cemetery records...]. 1941. 2pts. (Murphy Family, Old Methodist).	p.f. 977.201 O63 no. 1
Richardson, Neva,...Cemeteries. 2 pts. (Gammon, private cem. in Northeast twp. on Wright farm).	p.f. 977.201 O63 no. 3
Harrison family cemetery...(From THG, vol. 5, 1965). 1pp.	p.f. 977.201 Ouncat. no. 4
See also under Miscellaneous, DAR, Vol. 3.	

Church:

DAR, Rock Spring Church membership record. Cop. by Mrs. Edith H. Key. 1974. [6pp.]	p.f. 977.201 O63 no. 5
Jeffers, Phebe, Lick Creek...migrations. 3pp.	p.f. 977.201 Ouncat. no. 1

Wilson, Pearl S., [Financial record of] Mt. Gilead United Brethren Church, Paoli twp...1874-1876. 1879. 2pp.   p.f. 977.201 Ouncat. no. 3

Fleming, Neva, "Quakers. Radical changes in the customs of these peaceful residents...have taken place in the lifetime of a beloved 97 year old pastor". (From Courier-Journal Magazine, 1953). 3pp.   p.f. 977.201 Ouncat. no. 5

Miscellaneous:

DAR, Genealogical records....1943-1981. 9 vols.   977.201 O63d

   (Vol. 1, Marriage records, 1816-1826; wills, 1816-1892. 93pp.

   vol. 2, Family Bible records. 115pp.

   vol. 3, Cemetery records. 464pp.

   vol. 4, Family Bible records. 216pp.

   vol. 5, First probate records, 1816-1825; marriages, 1826-1849; J.P. records, 1821-1822. 279pp.

   vol. 6, Marriage records, 1849-1870. 220pp.

   vol. 7, Church of Christ membership rolls in Orange & Crawford cos....Conference minutes.

   vol. 8, Church of Christ membership rolls of Liberty and Freedom.

   vol. 9, Descendants of William C. Senior & Mary F. (Swan) Cornwell.

   vol. 9a, Land records...from tract books 2 and 3. 216pp.

DAR, Funeral notices of residents of Orange-Crawford counties....Comp. by Mrs. D.L. Key. 1976 ed. [21pp.]   977.201 O63k
(also 1979 ed. [13pp.]).   977.201 O632k

Pluris, Gerene O., Booklet about Friends....1958. 69pp.   977.201 O63p

Vance, Mrs. Ronald, Earliest records of Paoli Public Library....1975. 25pp.   p.f. 977.201 O63v

Naturalizations, 1840-1905 (THG, vol. 22 #4, Dec. 1982).   977.2 H789

DAR, ...Tract book records (1808-1868). 1971. 12pp.   p.f. 977.201 O63 no. 4

WPA, Commissioners' record...1817-1828....2 vols.   Ind. Hist. Soc. Library

Partition, minute book, 1859-1873.   miCrofilm

Partition record, 1863-1898.   miCrofilm

Partition records, 1853-1918.   miCrofilm

Saline land records, 1836-1845.   miCrofilm

Apprentice records, 1848-1884.   miCrofilm

Negroe register, 1853-1861.   miCrofilm

Coroners record, 1897-1916.   miCrofilm

OWEN COUNTY

Formed 1819 from Daviess, Sullivan   County Seat—Spencer

Births:

WPA, Index to birth records, 1882-1920.	977.201 O97u

Deaths:

WPA, Index to death records, 1882-1920.	977.201 O97u

Deeds:

Deed indexes, 1819-1902.	microfilm
Deeds, 1819-1886; indexes, 1819-1890.	miCrofilm

Marriages:

Marriages, 1819-1834 (THG, vol. 7 #1-2, Jan.-Feb., Mar.-Apr. 1967).	977.2 H789
Marriages, 1819-1901.	microfilm
Marriages, 1819-1923.	miCrofilm
Marriage returns, 1882-1907.	miCrofilm
Marriage affadavits, 1875-1905.	miCrofilm
WPA, Index to marriage records, 1850-1920.	977.201 O97u
WPA, Index to supplemental record, marriage transcripts, 1880-1920.	977.201 O97u
...Marriage records, 1819-1834. Indexed by Ind. State Library....1967. 13pp.	p.f. 977.201 O97 no. 8
Franklin, Charles M., ...Early marriage records, 1819-1853. 1979/1981. 2 vols.	977.201 O97f

Probates:

Probates, 1819-1833 (Civil order book); 1833-1850 (probate order books).	microfilm
Probate order book, 1819-1919.	miCrofilm
Complete probate records, 1829-1847, 1849-1885.	miCrofilm
Probate indexes, 1819-1923.	miCrofilm
Partition records, 1854-1863.	miCrofilm

Wills:

Wills, 1819-1903.	microfilm
Wills, 1833-1920; indexes, 1833-1982.	miCrofilm
Franklin, Charles M., ...Will abstracts, 1819-1861. 1983. 57pp.	977.201 O97fw

Cemetery:

Cemetery records (from Spencer—Owen County Public Library).	miCrofilm
Church records (from Spencer—Owen County Public Library).	miCrofilm
Meredith, Mildred, Cemeteries....[1979?]. 63, 4, [4]pp.	977.2 M559c
McDonald, Nina Jo., Mannan cemetery, Harrison township....1962. [7pp.]	p.f. 977.201 O97m
...Cemeteries. 1942-1979. (Inscriptions from 199 cemeteries located in the thirteen townships...). 3 vols.	977.201 O97o
Steed, Ivan, Cemetery inscriptions of west half of Marion township....[1966]. 78pp.	977.201 O97s
[Ind. Hist. Soc., Cemetery records...]. 1941. 11 pts.	p.f. 977.201 O97 no. 1
Ind. Hist. Soc., [Church records]. 2 pts. (Bethel, Little Mount).	p.f. 977.201 O97 no. 2
Gibson, Mrs. Wayne, Old Owen cemetery...Spencer, Indiana....[1962]. [12pp.]	p.f. 977.201 O97 no. 5
Kline, Dixie G., Cemetery records....2 pts. (Barnes, Scott, White).	p.f. 977.201 O97 no. 6
Lundblade, Mrs. Philip A., (Cemetery inscriptions, Winters' cemetery....(Cop. from Bull. of the Seattle Gen. Soc., vol. 13, #1, Sept. 1963).	p.f. 977.201 O97 no. 7

Gibson, Mrs. E. Wayne, River "Hillgrove" cemetery, 1 mile south of Spencer, Indiana...Washington township....10pp.   p.f. 977.201 Ouncat. no. 1

Montgomery, Edna, Dunkin cemetery, Taylor township....2pp.   p.f. 977.201 Ouncat. no. 2

Houk, A.K., Jr. Stierwalt cemetery, Wayne township....2pp.   p.f. 977.201 Ouncat. no. 3

Lundblade, Mrs. Philip A., Cemetery inscriptions, Winters' cemetery, Jefferson township....(From the Bull. of the Seattle Gen. Soc., vol. 13). 5pp.   p.f. 977.201 Ouncat. no. 4

Old...cemetery. (From Ancestral Notes from Chedwato, vol. 15, 1968). 4pp.   p.f. 977.201 Ouncat. no. 5

Family:

DAR, Mills, Goss, Dyar Bible records, 1796-1953....1955. 13pp.   p.f. 977.201 O97 no. 3

Family records (from Spencer—Owen County Public Library).   miCrofilm

Long, Wayne, Tracing 24...families, 1820-1880. [1981?]. 107pp.   977.201 O97L

Lovell, Rosemary F., Owen county cousins [1578-1978]: A genealogical study concerning the families of Fulk, Hauser, Fiscur, Spainhower, Wright, Phipps, Elsberry, Abrell, Arney....1977-   . vol. 2. 814pp.   977.201 O97Lo

Miscellaneous:

Naturalizations, 1854-1937.   miCrofilm

Enrollment record of the army (listed in 1886).   miCrofilm

PARKE COUNTY

Formed 1821 from Vigo, Wabash (N.P., unorganized).   County Seat—Rockville

Births:

WPA, Index to birth records, 1903-1920.	977.201 P237u

Deaths:

WPA, Index to death records, 1882-1920.	977.201 P237u

Deeds:

Brown, Mrs. Immogene B., ...Land entries, [1816-1836]. 5 vols.	977.201 P237b
DAR, Old land entree book....Cop. by Lilian L. Weller. 1981. 254, [40]pp.	977.201 P237o

Marriages:

DAR, Marriages...[1829-1979]. 1949-1980. 12 vols.	977.201 P237d
WPA, Index to marriage records, 1850-1920.	977.201 P237u
WPA, Index to supplemental record, marriage applications, 1850-1920.	977.201 P237u
Sanders, Evea, ...Marriage records...(1833-1844). [1969?]. 37pp. (missing 1982).	977.201 P237s

Probates:

Probates, 1833-1853; indexes, 1853-1900.	microfilm

Wills:

Wills, 1833-1849 (THG, vol. 9 #1-2, Jan.-Feb., Mar.-Apr. 1969).	977.2 H789
Wills, 1834-1909.	microfilm
Weller, Lillian, ...Will abstract...1833-1853. 1979. 70pp.	977.201 P237w
Slevin, Ruth M., ...Will record, 1834-1906. [197-]. 282pp.	977.201 P237sL
...Wills, 1833-1849 (From THG, vol. 9, 1969). [10pp.]	p.f. 977.201 Puncat. no. 5

Cemetery:

DAR, Cemetery records....12 pts.	977.201 P237dc
———, Cemetery records...early nineteenth century to the present time; roster of the...seventy-eighth regiment, Indiana volunteers, sixty day men of 1862. Cop. by Kathryn Y. Rice. [1968?]. 202pp.	977.201 P237dca
———, Containing, cemetery records; a history of Scotch Irish families; miscellaneous genealogical materials. Cop. by Kathryn Y. Rice. 1969. 147pp.	977.201 P237dce
———, Memory Garden cemetery....1982/83. 119pp.	977.201 P237m
———, Florida township....1982. 33pp. (Boatman and Loree cem., prepared by Mrs. John Seville; Numa cem., prep. by Mary Jo Harney and Karen Lewis), [also Jackson twp.—Bemis and Hamilton cem.; Liberty twp.—Brockway, Ephlin, Harvey, Thompson, Whitford cem.; Penn twp.—Robbins cem.; Reserve twp.—Warner cem, prepared by...].	977.201 P237f
———, Cemetery registers...veterans of American Revolution, War of 1812, Spanish American War, Mexican War, Indian Wars, Whiskey Insurrection, Civil War. [19—]. [12pp.]	p.f. 973 I385d
———, Montezuma, Indiana, cemetery records, 1879-1960. Cop. by Eva C. Saunders. 1961. 52pp.	977.202 M781s
———, Rockville, Indiana, cemetery records, 1825-1960. Cop. by Eva C. Saunders. 1961. 193pp.	977.202 R683s
[Ind. Hist. Soc., Cemetery records...]. 12 pts.	p.f. 977.201 P235 no. 1
Philadelphia Lutheran cemetery, Green township....2pp.	p.f. 977.201 Puncat. no. 1
Smelser, Dolly D., Dooley cemetery....1950. 1pp.	p.f. 977.201 Puncat. no. 2
Two unnamed...cemeteries. (From Sycamore Leaves, vol. 5, 1974). 1pp.	p.f. 977.201 Puncat. no. 3

[Maps showing location of Russell cemetery...]. 1pp.　　　　　　　　　p.f. 977.201 Puncat. no. 4

Miscellaneous:

DAR, Bibles.... 1960. n.p.　　　　　　　　　977.201 P237db

———, Genealogical records. 1962/3, 1970/1. 2 pts. (Includes some family histories, cemetery records, local DAR roster, 1851 tax list).　　　　　　　　　977.201 P237g

———, Mortuary records, Rockville...; Barnes 1939-1970, Butler 1961-1977. Cop. by Kathryn Y. Rice. 1977. 124pp.　　　　　　　　　977.201 P237r

Thomson, Mary V., Three sections of indexes of the Parke county...atlas of 1874 which was compiled from the 1870 census. [1969]. 115pp.　　　　　　　　　977.201 P237t

WPA, Index to supplemental record, federal census, 1880. (Lists names, sex, color, ages).　　　　　　　　　977.201 P237u

Weller, Lilian H., Abstracts of...guardian bonds, 1832-1858. 1979. 113pp.　　　　　　977.201 P237wa
　　(Also Guardian bond record book...1832-1858. 1979. [2], 124pp. Cop. by Lilian H. Weller for DAR).　　　　　　　　　977.201 P237wa 1979a

PERRY COUNTY

Formed 1814 from Gibson, Warrick   County Seat—Cannelton

Births:

Births, 1889-1894, 1899-1905.	microfilm
WPA, Index to birth records, 1882-1920.	977.201 P465u

Deaths:

WPA, Index to death records, 1882-1920	977.201 P465u
(Also 1980 reprint. 131pp.)	977.201 P465u 1980

Deeds:

Deeds, 1815-1835.	microfilm

Marriages:

Marriages, 1814-1830 (THG, vol. 13 #1, Jan.-Mar. 1973).	977.2 H789
Marriages, 1815-1861.	microfilm
Perry Co. Hist. Soc., Marriage records...1814 to...1850. [1945]. 184pp.	977.201 P465m
WPA, Index to marriage records, 1850-1920.	977.201 P465u
WPA, Index to supplemental record, marriage transcripts, 1887-1905.	977.201 P465u
Leistner, Doris, Marriages...1814-1852. 1977. 176pp.	977.201 P465L
Baertich, Frank, ...Marriage records, 1814-1823. 1972. [17pp.]	p.f. 977.201 P465 no. 1

Wills:

Wills, 1813-1843.	microfilm

Cemetery:

Baertich, Frank, ...Cemetery records, 1972. 2 vols.	977.201 P465b
Chappell, Mrs. Ray, List of markers found in McFall graveyard about five miles from Cannelton toward German Ridge recreation area. 1pp.	p.f. 977.201 Puncat. no. 1
Baertich, Frank, St. Michael's cemetery....1972. 16pp.	p.f. 977.201 Puncat. no. 3
Enlow cemetery.... 1pp.	p.f. 977.201 Puncat. no. 4
Landrum, Bernard, Powell cemetery, Troy township....1976. 2pp.	p.f. 977.201 Puncat. no. 5
Landrum, Bernard, Scull cemetery, Troy township....1976. 1pp.	p.f. 977.201 Puncat. no. 6

Miscellaneous:

Circuit court order book, 1815-1832; complete record, 1817-1834.	microfilm
Commissioners record, 1847-1851.	microfilm
Darlington, Jane E., ...Assessors book 1835. 1981. [13pp.]	977.201 P465dar
Wanhainen, Jeanne and Doris Leistner, ...1850 federal census. 1982. 177, [35]pp.	977.201 P465p
Baertich, Frank, Troy school town enumeration for school year 1899 and 1900, Troy....[5pp.]	p.f. 977.202 Tuncat. no. 1
Waggoner, Charles, [Marriages and deaths from the Cannelton Enquirer, 6-4-1870, 5-25-1872...]. [12pp.]	p.f. 977.201 Puncat. no. 2

PIKE COUNTY

Formed 1817 from Gibson, Perry   County Seat—Petersburg

Births:

WPA, Index to birth records, 1882-1920.   977.201 P636u

Deaths:

WPA, Index to death records, 1896-1920.   977.201 P636u

Woodhull, Joan, Index to...death records, 1896-1899 (i.e. 1907) (incomplete). 1978. 2, 17pp.   977.201 P636wo

Index to...death records, 1887 to 1895 (incomplete)....3pp.   p.f. 977.201 Puncat. no. 4

Deeds:

Deed indexes, 1817-1901.   microfilm

Marriages:

Marriages, 1817-1844 (THG, vol. 15 #2, Apr.-June 1975). (Also a few 1844-1848 marriages).   977.2 H789

Marriages, 1817-1903.   microfilm

WPA, Index to marriage records, 1900-1920.   977.201 P636u

———, Index to supplemental record, marriage transcripts, 1882-1920. (Reprinted 1980. 131pp.)   977.201 P636u
977.201 P636u 1980

Malett, Marjorie,...Marriage records, 1817-1886. 1980. 143pp.   977.201 P636mL

Slevin, Ruth M.,...Marriage record, 1859-1905. [197-]. 2 vols.   977.201 P636se

Probates:

Probates, 1831-1851; indexes, 1851?-1890.   microfilm

Wills:

Wills, 1817-1902.   microfilm

Slevin, Ruth M.,...Record of wills, 1817-1902. [1974?]. 144pp.   977.201 P636s

Cemetery:

Woodhull, Joan,...Cemetery records, 1976-1980. 9 vols. (Also 1980 edition. 2 vols.)   977.201 P636w
977.201 P636w 1980

Ind. Hist. Soc., [Cemetery records...]. pt. 1. 1949. 3pp. (Old Town Graveyard of Petersburg).   p.f. 977.201 P636 no. 1

Persinger, Patricia, [Cemetery records...]. 2 pts. (1, Lick Creek cemetery, Washington twp.; 2, Smith cemetery, Washington twp.). [1965].   p.f. 977.201 P636 no. 3

DAR, New Lebanon and Velpen cemeteries....1974. 3pp.   p.f. 977.201 P636 no. 4

Family:

McClellan, Ruth M., Our people of Pike county...1978. 1978. 268,16pp.   977.201 P636mc

Kendall, Agnes L, Some...families, including Smith, Chappell, Foster, Capehart families. 1962. v.p.   p.f. 977.201 P636 no. 2

Taylor, Philip, Pioneer families of Pike and Warrick counties...with ancestors and related families of Philip Taylor. 1981. 116, [59pp.]   977.201 P636t

Miscellaneous:

Pike County [Indiana] Historical Material (from Petersburg Public Library).   microfilm

Naturalizations, Sept. 1857-Nov. 1906 (THG, vol. 19 #4, Dec. 1979).   977.2 H789

WPA, Index to supplemental record, registered voters, 1919-1920.   977.201 P636u

Estates and guardianship. n.d.   microfilm

Pike and Gibson county...school enumerations, 1837-1852. 15pp.   p.f. 977.201 Puncat. no. 1

The Pike County Historian (and our Newsletter). 1974-1977, 1979-1981. p.f. 977.201 Puncat. no. 2-3
WPA, Commissioners' record...1817-1839....2 vols. Ind. Hist. Soc. Library
Farber, Renee, Index to county commissioners' records...1817-1839....[1981?].
   43pp. 977.201 P636f

PORTER COUNTY

Formed 1835; organized 1836 from St. Joseph   County Seat—Valparaiso

Births:

Semanick, Mrs. Carl, Index to...birth records, 1884-1919. 1970. 195pp. (also 101pp. index)	977.201 P849sb

Deaths:

Semanick, Mrs. Carl, Index to...death records, 1884-1930. 1970. 214pp. (also 104pp. index)	977.201 P849s

Deeds:

Deed indexes, 1833-1910.	microfilm

Marriages:

DAR, Marriage records...[1836-1905]. 14 vols. (also 166pp. index)	977.201 P849dm
Marriages, 1836-1850 (THG, #3-4, May-June, July-August 1961 vol. 17 #2, June 1977).	977.2 H789

Wills:

DAR, Wills...Dec. 26, 1839-Nov. 1, 1880. 1961. 127pp.	977.201 P849d

Cemetery:

D.A.C., Cemetery inscriptions, Lake, Porter and Starke cos....1968. 117pp.	977.201 L192c
Hassmer, Franklin, ...Cemetery records. 1965-70. 10 pts. (St. Patrick, Spencer, St. Paul, Sacred Heart, Essex, Blake, Cornell, Hebron-North, Hebron-South, Kouts).	977.201 P849ha
Barnard, Campell, Glen Kingery Farm, Lakeshore property and Chesterton cemetery records...in the files of the Valparaiso Public Library. [197-]. [92pp.]	977.201 P849b
Hoyt, Arabelle C., Surname index to cemetery records in Valparaiso-Porter County Public Library genealogy collection. 1978. [3], 226pp.	977.201 P849ho
Swanson, Alice W., Cemeteries in Porter township....n.d. 128pp.	977.201 P849sw
Ind. Hist. Soc., [Cemetery records...]. 14 pts.	p.f. 977.201 P849 no. 1
Map of Porter county...[with location of county cemeteries north of Valparaiso pencilled in]. n.d.	p.f. 977.201 P849 no. 2
DAR, Cemetery records....11 pts.	p.f. 977.201 P849 no. 4
———, [Cemetery records...]. Cornell cemetery. 1962. 19pp.	p.f. 977.201 P849 no. 5
Mefford, Phyllis, [Cemetery records...]. 8 pts.	p.f. 977.201 P849 no. 6
Blachly, Mrs. Josephus C., [Cemetery records...]. (East side of Blachly cemetery). 1959. [7pp.]	p.f. 977.201 P849 no. 7
DAR, Record of Hebron and Cornell cemeteries. 1939. [21pp.]	p.f. 977.201 P849 no. 8
Phares, Marvin, Old City cemetery, Valparaiso....[1968?]. [14pp.]	p.f. 977.202 V211 no. 1
DAR, Mosier cemetery inscriptions, Union township....5pp.	p.f. 977.201 Puncat. no. 1
[List of] cemeteries....[3pp.]	p.f. 977.201 Puncat. no. 2

Census:

Ind. State Lib., Index to 1840 census....1972. 4pp.	977.201 P849i
Hiday, Mrs. Nellie, Index to 1850 census....1966. n.p.	977.201 P849h
Valparaiso-Porter Co. Pub. Lib., 1880 Census....[1978]. 108pp.	977.201 P849v

Obituary:

Imel, Madge, Western Ranger newspaper, Valparaiso...deaths, 1847-1950. 1974. [5pp.]	p.f. 977.201 P849 no. 9
McCarron, Helen, Surname index to obituaries, 1980, Chesterton Tribune....[1982]. [196pp.]	977.2 M115s

Miscellaneous:

Mefford, Phyllis, GAR applications....[1978]. 16pp.	973.7 I39me
DAR, Genealogies of William Henry Harrison Chapter. Comp. by Lucy Putnam. n.d.. 140pp. (also 1961 addenda of 4pp.)	977.201 P844g
Griffiths, Kaye, Abstracts, Porter county Vidette, June 4, 1874-Dec. 13, 1877. 1982. 22, 23pp.	977.201 P844ga
Lundstrom, Mary E., Index, naturalization records...1854-1955....[1979?]. 94pp.	977.201 P849L
Mefford, Mrs. Robert R., Genealogical notes from the Western Ranger, April 10, 1847-July 25, 1849, and the Practical Observer...August 1, 1849-December 27, 1852. [1982?]. 38, 15pp.	977.201 P844mg
Skinner, Hubert M., History of Valparaiso from the earliest times to the present, by a citizen. 1876. 30pp.	977.202 V211s
Adams Church, Morgan Prairie, Morgan township...[1904-1950]. 6pp.	p.f. 977.201 Puncat. no. 3
WPA, Commissioners' record...1836-1845....4 vols.	Ind. Hist. Soc. Library

POSEY COUNTY

Formed 1814 from Warrick   County Seat—Mount Vernon

Births:

Births, 1882-1907.	microfilm
WPA, Index to birth records, 1882-1920.	977.201 P855u

Deaths:

WPA, Index to death records, 1882-1920.	977.201 P855u

Deeds:

Deeds, 1812-1832.	microfilm

Marriages:

Marriages, 1814-1831 (THG, vol. 11 #2, Apr.-June 1971).	977.2 H789
DAR, Marriage records...1815-1825. 1949-53. 2 vols.	p.f. 977.201 P855 no. 2
Marriages, 1815-1846.	microfilm
WPA, Index to marriage records, 1847-1920.	977.201 P855u
WPA, Index to supplemental record, marriage applications, 1850-1920.	977.201 P855u
...Marriage returns, 1899-1900.	977.201 Puncat. no. 1
Phillips, J. Oscar, ...Marriage records, 1814-1831. 1980. 70pp.	977.201 P855phi
Slevin, Ruth M., ...Marriages...1832-1846. [1974?]. 36, 36pp.	977.201 P855s

Probates:

Probate order book, 1815-1834.	microfilm
DAR, Index of...probate records, Abbott to Allison. 8pp.	p.f. 977.201 Puncat. no. 2

Wills:

Wills, 1816-1852.	microfilm

Cemetery:

Cox, Gloria M., Additional...cemetery records (with inscriptions from scattered cemeteries in Illinois, Kentucky, Warrick and Spencer counties, Indiana). 1976. [139pp.]	q977.201 P855coa
Cox, Carroll O., ...Cemetery records, 1814-1979. 1979. 477,106pp.	977.201 P855cop
Cox, Carroll B., [Cemetery records...]. 2 pts.-115,121pp.	p.f. 977.201 P855 no. 1
Cemetery records. 1953.	p.f. 977.201 P855 no. 3
Cox, Carroll O., Posey and Gibson county...cemetery records (and a few scattered records from Daviess, Vanderburgh and Warrick counties....). n.d. 2 pts.	p.f. 977.201 P855 no. 5
———, ...Cemetery records (Beech, Dixon, Greathouse, Johnson, Laurel Hill, Mt. Pleasant, Unnamed-Mt. Vernon). 1967. v.p.	p.f. 977.201 P855 no. 7
Persons buried in Harmonie on the Wabash [New Harmony...]. 1pp.	p.f. 977.202 Nuncat. no. 1
List of cemeteries....[8pp.]	p.f. 977.201 Puncat. no. 4
Miller, Mrs. Don E. Smith cemetery, Smith township....1976. [3pp.]	p.f. 977.201 Puncat. no. 5
Maple Hill cemetery....(From Geneal. Ref. Builders Newsletter, vol 2). 1pp.	p.f. 977.201 Puncat. no. 11

Court:

Cox, Gloria M., ...Court record. 1974. 1 vol.	977.201 P855co
———, Miscellaneous...court record. 1976. 290, [116]pp.	q977.201 P855cox
Names of persons granting "power of attorney" to Frederick Rapp, May 1, 1824. Trans. by Harry O. Garman....1940. 13pp.	977.201 P855n
Circuit court order book, 1815-1829.	microfilm

Commissioners record, 1817-1855. microfilm
WPA, Commissioners' record...1820-1829....2 vols. Ind. Hist. Soc. Library

History:

Cox, Carroll O. & Gloria M., ...A documented history, 1815-1900. 1982. 2 vols.
(Contains probate records, divorce records, tax lists, poor farm inmates for 1900, etc.). 977.201 P855capc

Cox, Gloria M., History of Robb, Smith, Harmony, Center townships....1955. 12pp. p.f. 977.201 P855 no. 4

Cox, Carroll O., Some early settlers....36pp. p.f. 977.201 P855 no. 6

Cox, Gloria M., Genealogical data on men in 1820 census....1972. n.p. p.f. 977.201 P855 no. 8

Young, Otis E., Personnel of the Rappite community of Harmony...in...1824
(From IMH, vol. 47, 1951). p.f. 977.201 Puncat. no. 1

Miscellaneous:

[Cox, Gloria M.], Misc....information. [1980?]. [98pp.] 977.201 P855m

Darlington, Jane E., ...Tax duplicate list, 1842. [1982]. 99pp. 977.201 P855d

Cox, Gloria M., New Harmony, Indiana, newspaper gleanings. [1980?]. 3 vols.
(1825-1943). (also 1980 ed. of 268pp.) 977.202 N5325c

Murphy, Thelma M., Obituaries and local news from the Poseyville (Indiana) News, October 27, 1944 to December 27, 1946. 1981?. [51pp.] 977.202 P855m

Bethel Baptist Church list of members taken from the book of minutes, 1820....[5pp.] p.f. 977.201 Puncat. no. 3

...School petitions, 1833. [35p.] p.f. 977.201 Puncat. no. 6

Notation from volume 3 of the Posey county Recorder's book relating to the "Farmer's Elevator Co. of Mt. Vernon, Indiana". [3pp.] p.f. 977.201 Puncat. no. 7

Free inhabitants in Harmony township in the county...enumerated...[August... 1850...]. (From IMH, vol. 42, 1946). 30pp. p.f. 977.201 Puncat. no. 8

Military history....[18pp.] p.f. 977.201 Puncat. no. 9

Cox, Gloria M., Some...first land purchases. 1981. v.p. p.f. 977.201 Puncat. no. 10

PULASKI COUNTY

Formed 1835; organized 1839 from Cass, St. Joseph — County Seat—Winamac

Deaths:

WPA, Index to death records, 1882-1920.	977.201 P981u

Deeds:

Deeds, 1840-1849; indexes, 1840-1897.	microfilm

Marriages:

Marriages, June 1839-June 1853 (THG, vol. 19 #4, Dec. 1979).	977.2 H789
Marriages, 1839-1900.	microfilm
WPA, Index to marriage records, 1842-1920.	977.201 P981u
DAR, Marriage record...1839-1847. 1970. 8pp.	977.201 P981d

Probates:

Probates, 1839-1852; indexes, 1853-1900.	microfilm

Wills:

Wills, 1843-1899.	microfilm
Burgess, Betty, Genealogical gleanings extracted from will records A and B, Pulaski Circuit Court....1976. 39pp.	977.201 P981bug

Cemetery:

Binkley, Julia Ann, Indian Creek cemetery...Indian Creek township....1971. 31pp.	977.201 P981b
Drybread, Bernice, St. Peter's Catholic cemetery, Winamac, Ind. 1972. 85pp.	977.201 P981dr
Pulaski Co. Hist. Soc., ...Cemetery inscriptions: with historical and genealogical notes. 1975-1980. 6 vols.	977.201 P981p
Mothers Club of Winamac, Winamac cemetery records....[1948?]. 27,95pp. (also supplement)	q977.202 W758m
Ind. Hist. Soc., [Cemetery records...]. (1, Victor Chapel United Brethren cemetery, Van Buren twp. 1942; 2, Buck cemetery, Van Buren twp. 1947).	p.f. 977.201 P981 no. 1
Binkley, Julia Ann, Buck cemetery, Van Buren twp....[1974?]. 55pp.	p.f. 977.201 P981 no. 2
———, Victor Chapel cemetery, United Brethren, Van Buren township....1971. 24pp.	p.f. 977.201 P981 no. 3
Henry, Mrs. Herschel E., Listed graves of the Pulaski cemetery, Pulaski, Indiana. 1952. [22pp.] (also 1963 supplement)	p.f. 977.202 P981 no. 1
Krasner, Jack, [Inscriptions from Dead Man's Hollow cemetery located two miles south of Winamac...]. 2pp.	p.f. 977.201 Puncat. no.1

Miscellaneous:

Howe, Zera E.H., Medaryville town records, 1900-1916. 1976. 71pp.	977.202 M488h
———, The Medaryville Methodist Church and its circuits, 1860-1890. 1977. 117pp.	977.202 M488m
Burgess, Betty, 1850 census...added genealogical gleanings....1972. 112pp.	977.201 P981bu
DAR, Genealogical records of Star City area....1971. 269pp.	977.201 P981dg
Ind. State Lib., Index to 1840 census....1973. 2pp.	977.201 P981i
Nale, Iona H., Some Pulaski county...people, 1860-1886, [1887-1895]: from news clippings in the Winamac Public Library. 1981 3 vol.	977.201 P981ns
WPA, Index to supplemental records, registered voters, 1922.	977.201 P981u
Tract book, 1838-1876.	microfilm
Swamp land patent record, 1852-1857.	microfilm
Swamp land tract book, 1853-1883.	microfilm

PUTNAM COUNTY

Formed 1822 from Vigo, Owen, Wabash (N.P., unorganized)　　　　County Seat—Greencastle

Births:

Delayed birth records prior to 1941.	miCrofilm
WPA, Index to birth records, 1882-1920.	977.201 P989u

Deaths:

WPA, Index to death records, 1880-1920.	977.201 P989u

Deeds:

Deed indexes, 1824-1903.	microfilm

Marriages:

Marriages, 1822-1923.	miCrofilm
DAR, Marriage records...1822-1843. 1940. 151pp.	977.201 P989d
Wright, Minnetta L., Marriage records...Apr. 1843-Dec. 1849. 1949. 97pp.	977.201 P989m
WPA, Index to marriage records, 1850-1920.	977.201 P989u

Probates:

Probate complete record, 1825-1868, 1880-1911.	miCrofilm
Probate order books, 1825-1918.	miCrofilm
Probate order books, 1825-1852; indexes, 1852-1899.	microfilm

Wills:

Wills, 1844-1902.	microfilm
Wills, 1844-1921.	miCrofilm
Slevin, Ruth M.,...Will records, 1823-1902. [19—]. 321pp.	977.201 P989s

Cemetery:

Wright, Minnetta L., Revolutionary soldiers buried in Putnam...records. Rev. 1975. [58pp.]	973.34 I385wr
Meredith, Mildred, Cemeteries....[1979?]. 63,4,[4]pp.	977.2 M559c
Buis, Worth M., Mill Creek cemetery, Jefferson township....65pp.	p.f. 977.201 P989b
Mt. Carmel cemetery. [197-]. 8, [2]pp.	p.f. 977.201 P989mt
Wilson, Robert L., Palestine cemetery....1976. 12pp.	977.201 P989w
Putnam Co. Hist. Soc., Cemetery records....[1955-56]. 2 vols.	977.201 P989p
[Ind. Hist. Soc., Cemetery records...]. 1940. 7 pts.	p.f. 977.201 P989 no. 1
Martindale, Harry H., Tombstone records of Howard family and related families, cemetery opposite Baptist Church, Barnard....n.d. [2pp.]	p.f. 977.201 P989 no. 3
DAR, Sutherlin cemetery, Russell twp....Plotted by Jeanette M. Sutherlin. 1961. 9pp.	p.f. 977.201 P989 no. 5
Ramsay, Margaret, Cemetery records....(1, Hebron cemetery. 1962; 2, Russellville cemetery. 1962).	p.f. 977.201 P989 no. 6
O'Gara, Mrs. Helen Toney, Burial list of Little Walnut cemetery....[1965]. 14pp.	p.f. 977.201 P989 no. 7
DAR, Wesley Chapel cemetery, Floyd township....[9pp.]	p.f. 977.201 P989 no. 8
Williams, Mrs. Leon E., Doe Creek cemetery of Cloverdale, Indiana. 1971. [3pp.]	p.f. 977.201 P989 no. 9
Allee, Enos, Mill Creek cemetery records, located in Jefferson twp....1939. 4pp.	p.f. 977.201 P989 no. 10
Wilson, Mrs. John H., On Old Case farm, near New Maysville, Indiana. 1pp.	p.f. 977.201 Puncat. no. 1
Charles Sheckles Farm cemetery...(1 mile northwest of New Maysville). 1pp.	p.f. 977.201 Puncat. no. 2
Revolutionary soldiers buried in Putnam county...(newspaper clipping). 1pp.	p.f. 977.201 Puncat. no. 3

Pitts, Mrs. William, Pickle cemetery.... 1pp.   p.f. 977.201 Puncat. no. 5

Cooper, Mary F., Burials in Bethel Methodist cemetery in Warren township....3pp.   p.f. 977.201 Puncat.no. 6

Burials in cemetery located in Monroe township...about 1 mile east of Bainbridge. 1pp.   p.f. 977.201 Puncat. no. 7

Pisgah cemetery, Russell township....[10pp.]   p.f. 977.201 Puncat. no. 11

Miscellaneous:

DAR, Brief history...and genealogies of Washburn Chapter. Comp. by Lenore Alspaugh. [1928], 1934. 2 vols.   977.201 P989a

Naturalizations, 1905-1906; declaration of intention, 1854-1904.   miCrofilm

Accounts current record, 1895-1917.   miCrofilm

...1845 Tax list. 1982. 92pp.   977.201 P989pu

...Revolutionary War patriots. [1976?].   p.f. 973.34 I385p

Ind. Hist. Soc., [Church records...]. (1, Presbyterian Church, Bainbridge. Poplar Spring Church).   p.f. 977.201 P989 no. 2

...1841 Tax list for Jefferson, Warren and Washington townships. Cop. by Macy. 1957. 7pp.   p.f. 977.201 P989 no. 4

[Miscellaneous births, marriages, and deaths of Putnam county...]. [8pp.]   p.f. 977.201 Puncat. no. 4

Millcreek township...[list of those who agreed to "pay...for the purpose of hiring men to fill the places of those drafted in the above named township"], October 27, 1864. 2pp.   p.f. 977.201 Puncat. no. 8

Series remembers those who fought; newspaper articles....(Three clippings from the Greencastle Banner Graphic, May, 1972).   p.f. 977.201 Puncat. no. 9

Darlington, Jane E., [Index to] James Townsend account book, general store, Putnamville...1830-1832. 1979. [9pp.]   p.f. 977.201 Puncat. no. 10

RANDOLPH COUNTY

Formed 1818 from Wayne   County Seat—Winchester

Births:

Births, 1882-1907   microfilm
    (Includes a few Parker, Windsor, Losantville, Winchester, and Modoc births and
        some of later dates)

Deaths:

Deaths, 1882-1900.   microfilm

Deeds:

Deed indexes, 1820-1901.   microfilm

Marriages:

Marriage records...[1819-1827]. [10pp.]   p.f. 977.201 Runcat. no. 3

Marriages, 1819-1895.   microfilm

Marriage returns, 1882-1900.   microfilm

...Marriages, 1819-1852. n.d. 111pp.   977.201 R192

Heiss, Willard, Index of women's marriages..., 1819-1852. [1957]. [38pp.] (Also with
    men's index of 40pp.)   977.201 R192i

Wills:

Wills, 1819-1842, 1847-1900.   microfilm

Slevin, Ruth M., ...Will records...1821-Jan. 1906. 1973. 327pp.   977.201 R192s

Cemetery:

Fields, Ann, Weimer cemetery, near Saratoga in Ward township....[1979]. 5,[4]pp.   977.201 R192fi

Hamm, Thomas D., Records of Fairview, Rees cemeteries of Delaware county...and
    Cherry Grove Friends, New Liberty, Snow Hill, Cabin Creek A.M.E., Union
    Chapel, White River Christian, and Bethel A.M.E. of Randolph county....
    [1977]. [214pp.]   977.201 D343h

The Original Pleasant Hill cemetery. 1976. 26pp.   977.201 R192o

Wisener, Minisa, Reitenour, New Reitenour, Lawndale, Prospect, Pleasant View
    (Riverside), Old Ridgeville (Race Street), and Saratoga cemetery records....
    1980/81. [282pp.]   977.201 R192r

Union City, city cemetery, burial records, 1874-1913. 291pp.   977.202 U58b

Lumpkin, LaVora, Cemetery records....3 pts. (Salem, Little Creek (Maulsby), cem.
    s. of Losantville).   p.f. 977.201 R192 no. 1

Church of Jesus Christ of Latter Day Saints, [Cemetery records...]. pt. 1, Union
    cemetery. 75pp.   p.f. 977.201 R192 no. 3

Dennis, Mary W., Huntsville cemetery. 1963. 24pp.   p.f. 977.201 R192 no. 4

Niccum, Norman, [Hoover cemetery, Jackson township...]. 1pp.   p.f. 977.201 Runcat. no. 2

Dennis, Mary, Soldiers buried in Huntsville cemetery, Carlos....1963. 4pp.   p.f. 977.201 Runcat. no. 4

Census:

Ind. State Lib. Index to 1840 census....1972. 35pp.   977.201 R192ind

U.S. Census office, Index 1850 census....n.d. 30pp.   977.201 R192in

Church:

Heiss, Willard, Records of White River Monthly meeting....1956-. 2 pts.   977.201 R192f

———, Extracts of the records of Arba Monthly meeting of Friends, Greensfork
    township....1828-1835. 1957. n.p.   977.201 R192fa

———, [Records of] Cherry Grove Monthly meeting, Washington township.... 1958. n.p.   977.201 R192fc

Jericho Friends meeting and its community...1818 to 1958. [1958]. 162pp.   977.201 R192fj

Heiss, Willard, ...Pioneer Quakers. 1956. v.p.   977.201 R192h

Lumpkin, LaVora, Abstract of Nettle Creek-Little Creek Baptist Church. [1963]. 13pp.   p.f. 977.201 R192 no. 2

Miscellaneous:

Common pleas and circuit court records, 1819-1881.   microfilm

Ft. Wayne Pub. Lib., Record of Reynard Funeral home, Modoc, Indiana. 1974. 129, [32]pp.   977.202 M692f

[Heiss, Willard], Land entries (tract book)....[1964]. 134pp.   q977.201 R192L

Wilke, Katherine, Newspaper gleanings...1873-1883. 1969. [89pp.]   977.201 R192w

Wolfe, Barbara E., ...Record: district 1, Jackson township, 1863-1878, school attendance. 1974. 66pp. (Also 8pp. index)   977.201 R192wo

DAR, Some of the first records....1929. 4pp.   p.f. 977.201 Runcat. no. 1

RIPLEY COUNTY

Formed 1816; organized 1818 from Dearborn, JeffersonCounty Seat—Versailles

Births:
Births, 1882-1906.	microfilm
Delayed births (prior to 1941).	miCrofilm

Deaths:
Deaths, 1882-1900. [some Batesville to 1903].	microfilm
Gibbs, A., [Index to] book 1...death records, Feb. 1882-Jan. 1900. 1979. [19pp.]	p.f. 977.201 Runcat. no. 3

Deeds:
Deed indexes, 1818-1898.	microfilm
Deeds, 1818-1886; indexes, 1818-1889.	miCrofilm

(also see listing under "Miscellaneous")

Marriages:
Fletcher, Charles W., ...Marriage records, 1818-1840. [1968]. 30pp.	977.201 R589f
Marriage applications, 1882-1901.	microfilm
Toph, Violet E., ...Marriage records...[1818-1949]. 1949-1951. 2 vols. (also index of 189pp).	q977.201 R589tma
Fletcher, Charles W., ...Marriage records, 1841-1850. 1971. 35pp.	977.201 R589fa
Marriages, 1818-1922.	miCrofilm
Marriage affidavits, 1881-1906.	miCrofilm
Ridlen, Colleen A., ...Early marriage records, 1818-1839. 1980. 42pp.	977.201 R589rii

Probates:
Probate indexes, 1834-1900.	microfilm
Probate order books, 1818-1918.	miCrofilm
Complete probate books, 1834-1907.	miCrofilm
Partition record, 1854-1917.	miCrofilm
Fee book index, 1832-1845.	microfilm

Wills:
Wills, 1818-1900.	microfilm
DAR, ...Abstracts of wills, 1909-1922 and Dec. 1931-Nov. 1944. [1975?]. 40, 85pp.	977.201 R589da
Gibbs, Ann, Will book B...May 1839-May 1862. 1974. 33,22pp.	977.201 R589gw
Slevin, Ruth M., ...Will records, 1821-1896. [197-?]. 1 vol.	977.201 R589s
DAR, Will book I...1821-1837. 1974. [9pp.]	p.f. 977.201 Runcat. no. 2
Wills, 1819-1839 (THG, vol. 12 #2, Apr.-June 1972).	977.2 H789
Wills, probate entries...to 1850 (THG, vol. 19 #3, Sept. 1979).	977.2 H789
Wills, 1839-1922.	miCrofilm

Cemetery:
DAR, ...Cemetery records. [1963]. [vol. 1], Akers Friendship cemetery.	977.201 R589d
———, 1850 Brown township census and Brown township cemeteries....1976. 45, 81pp.	977.201 R589dau
Ind. Hist. Soc., [Cemetery records...]. [1935, 1941]. 19 pts.	977.201 R589i
Ripley Co. Hist. Soc., Adams twp. cemetery directory....[197—]. [68pp.]	977.201 R589ri
Charlton, Adena, Graves in Old Milan cemetery on State Road 101....1974. 3pp.	p.f. 977.201 R589 no. 2
DAR, Marked graves of Revolutionary soldiers buried in Ripley co....[1975]. 2pp.	p.f. 977.201 R589 no. 3

Census:

Ind. State Lib., Index to 1840 census....1973. 16pp.	977.201 R589in
Gibbs, Ann, ...1860 census index. 1978. [42pp.]	p.f. 977.201 R589gr
———, ...1870 census index. 1981. [52pp.]	q977.201 R589gs
———, 1853 White male inhabitants....1982. 26pp.	977.2 G437e
Jackson township...enumeration of males, colored, and white over 21 in 1919. 3pp.	p.f. 977.201 R589 no. 1

Church:

Toph, Violet E., ...Church record. 1937. 53pp.	977.201 R589tc
Hill, Mary, St. Magdalen's Catholic Church baptisms...for the year of 1869. 1941. 2pp.	p.f. 977.201 Runcat. no. 1

Court:

Miscellaneous...court records, 1839-1851. [2 pts. and index]. 650pp.	q977.201 R589
Gibbs, Ann, ...Early unnumbered court record....1974. [9pp.]	977.201 R589g
———, Apprentice book A...May 1833-May 1853 indentures. 1976. [18pp.]	p.f. 977.201 R589ga
———, Naturalization records...up to 1900, missing 1822-1836. 1974. [3], 50, [14]pp.	977.201 R589n
Naturalizations, 1851-1905, 1907-1928.	miCrofilm
Naturalizations, 1818-1843 (THG, vol. 22 #3, Sept. 1982).	977.2 H789
Record of indentures, 1853-1905.	miCrofilm
Coroner's inquest, 1897-1928.	miCrofilm

Family:

Toph, Violet E., Genealogy....1946. [6 vols.]	977.201 R589t
———, ...Family genealogies. n.d. 3 vols.	977.201 R589tf
———, ...Miscellaneous family notes. n.d. 63pp.	977.201 R589tm
[Ripley County...family records]. (Records from Historical Museum, Ripley County, and includes family histories, Toph records, apprentice book, church records, etc.). 1982.	miCrofilm

Miscellaneous:

Gibbs, Ann, Miscellaneous...notes. n.d. v.p.	977.201 R589gm
———, ...Revolutionary soldiers. 1974. n.d.	977.201 R589r
Holmes, Maurice, Early landowners....1977. 90pp.	977.201 R589h
Toph, Violet E., ...Obituaries. n.d. 2 vols.	977.201 R589to

RUSH COUNTY

Formed 1822 from Delaware (N.P., unorganized)   County Seat—Rushville

Deaths:

See listing under Probates and Miscellaneous.

Deeds:

Deed indexes, 1822-1907.	microfilm

Marriages:

Marriages, 1822-1829 (THG, vol. 3 #6, Nov.-Dec., 1963, vol. 4 #1, Jan.-Feb. 1964).	977.2 H789
Marriages, 1822-1901.	microfilm
Ridlen, Colleen A., ...Early marriage records, 1822-1835. 1979. 43pp.	977.201 R952ri
Slevin, Ruth M., ...Marriage record, 1862-1901....2 vols.	977.201 R952s

Probates:

Probates, 1823-1853; indexes, 1853-1901.	microfilm
Deaths from probates, 1823-1856 (THG, vol. 15 #4, Oct.-Dec. 1975).	977.2 H789

Wills:

Wills, 1822-1838, 1843-1907.	microfilm

Cemetery:

DAR, ...Cemetery records prior to 1885....[1940]. [461pp.]	977.201 R952d
Ind. Junior Hist. Soc., ...Cemetery records. 1973-75. 3 vols. in 1.	977.201 R952i
Articles of association and by-laws, East Hill cemetery company, Rushville...and the names of owners of lots up to December, 1910. 1910. 47pp.	977.202 R954r
Ind. Hist. Soc., Names of persons buried in Friends cemetery, Carthage, 1840-1939. [1939]. [7pp.]	p.f. 977.201 R952 no. 2
Miner, Mrs. Fairy, Shiloh cemetery, Center township....14pp.	p.f. 977.201 Runcat. no. 1
Hutton, Russell, Overleese cemetery inscriptions....[2pp.]	p.f. 977.201 Runcat. no. 2
Irvin, Mildred L., "Barrett cemetery stones show data of pioneer residents" (article from Knightstown Daily Banner, 1953).	p.f. 977.201 Runcat. no. 3

Court:

Holmes, Maurice, Court records...1822 to 1857. 1975. 310pp.	977.201 R952hc
Naturalizations, 1875-1890, 1899-1906.	microfilm
Naturalizations, 1857-1868 (THG, vol. 20 #1, Mar. 1980).	977.2 H789
WPA, Commissioners' record...1822-1844. 5 vols.	Ind. Hist. Soc. Library

Miscellaneous:

Rush County Historical Society Bicentennial Microfilm Project (Rushville Public Library)	microfilm
Holmes, Maurice, Early landowners....1975. 35, 44pp.	977.201 R952h
Poisal, M.A., Mortuary record; a complete list of deaths in southern Rush and northern Decatur cos....1925. 58pp. (missing 1982)	p.f. 977.201 R952 no. 1
Sutton, Donna C., "Rural Roots" (from Rushville Republican, April 2, and 9, 1979). 1pp.	p.f. 977.201 Runcat. no. 4

ST. JOSEPH COUNTY

Formed 1830 from Cass   County Seat—South Bend

Births:

WPA, Index to birth records, 1882-1920.	977.201 S143u
———, Index to birth records; Mishawaka, 1882-1902; South Bend, 1882-1920.	977.201 S143u

Deaths:

WPA, Index to death record, 1882-1920.	977.201 S143u
———, Index to death records; Mishawaka, 1882-1920; South Bend, 1882-1920.	977.201 S143u

Deeds:

Deed indexes, 1831-1899.	microfilm
DAR, Abstract of deeds....[1830-1860] [197-]. 8 vols.	977.201 S143da

Marriages:

Marriages, 1830-1844 (THG, vol. 17 #1, Mar. 1977).	977.2 H789
Marriages, 1830-1868.	microfilm
DAR, Marriage records...1887-1889....1966. 61pp.	977.201 S143dm
WPA, Index to marriage records, 1860-1920.	977.201 S143u
———, Index to supplemental record, marriage applications, 1882-1920.	977.201 S143u

Probates:

Probates, 1832-1851; indexes, n.d.	microfilm

Wills:

DAR, Abstract of wills...1830-1912. 1968-72. vols. 2-8.	977.201 S143dw
Wills, 1830-1895.	microfilm

Cemetery:

DAR, Death records...cemeteries. [1938-40]. 3 vols. and index.	977.201 S143d
Bowman cemetery, South Bend...1910-1973. n.d. 1 vol.	977.202 S726b
City cemetery, South Bend...1828-1938. n.d. 2 vols.	977.202 S726c
Burrell, Mrs. Joseph, Cemetery records....1979. 106pp.	977.201 S143bu
Interments, Cedar Grove cemetery, Notre Dame, South Bend....n.d. 2 vols. (1938-1973) and index, 1974.	977.202 S726i
Northern Ind. Hist. Soc., Southlawn cemetery (on U.S. 31, south edge of South Bend)....[Interments, 1959-1974 and old lot book]. 1975. 2 vols.	q977.202 S726n
Ind. Hist. Soc., [Cemetery records...]. pt. 1, List of St. Joseph county cemeteries. pt. 2, Map.	p.f. 977.201 S143 no. 1
Hoyt, Mrs. Leo, Olive Chapel cemetery records, Olive township, near Carlisle.... 1957. 9pp.	p.f. 977.201 S143 no. 2
Garman, Harry O., Salem Church cemetery located four miles northwest of Elkhart...names on gravestones....1934. 12pp.	p.f. 977.201 S143 no. 3
Morse, Irving, Earl C. Webb & Dr. P.C. Traver, Road map...1955. [Cemeteries located and listed...]. [1957?]. map.	f977.201 S143s
Markers in...the South Bend City cemetery. 6pp.	p.f. 977.201 Suncat. no. 1
Traver, Perry C., [Cemetery records of soldiers in the American Revolution, War of 1812, Mexican and Indian Wars buried in St. Joseph county...]. [13pp.]	p.f. 977.201 Suncat. no. 3
Hamilton cemetery....[24pp.]	p.f. 977.201 Suncat. no. 4
Mount Pleasant cemetery (old part), German township...(from South Bend Area Geneal. Soc. Quart., vol. 5 #2, 1980). [6pp.]	p.f. 977.201 Suncat. no. 5

Church:

DAR, Vital statistics from records of births, marriages, and deaths of First Methodist Church, First Presbyterian Church, Grace Methodist Church, St. James Episcopal Church, St. Paul's Methodist Church...1940-41. n.p. 977.202 S726d

History of the Hamilton Church....[15pp.] p.f. 977.201 Suncat. no. 2

Kiracoffe, J.H., A History of the Osceola Methodist Church from 1851-1951. [1951]. 40, [1]pp. p.f. 977.202 O81 no. 1

Family:

Michiana Roots. (scattered issues). 977.2 M624

South Bend Area Genealogical Society, Quarterly. vol. 1-(6). 977.201 S143so

DAR, Bible records...Mishawaka....1961. 59pp. 977.201 S143db

———, ...South Bend; genealogies and early history. 1929. 219pp. 977.201 S143g

Miscellaneous:

Farber, Renee, Index to county commissioners' records...1830-1844. 1980. 135pp. 977.201 S143f

WPA, Commissioners' record...1830-1844....7 vols. Ind. Hist. Soc. Library

———, Index to supplemental record, registered voters 1921, 1923. 977.201 S143u

SCOTT COUNTY

Formed 1820 from Clark, Jefferson, Jennings, Washington, Jackson   County Seat—Scottsburg

Births:

Births, 1882-1907.	microfilm

Deeds:

Deeds, 1820-1874.	miCrofilm
Deeds, 1819-1828; indexes, 1820-1910.	microfilm

Marriages:

Marriages, 1820-1840 (THG, vol. 5 #6, vol. 6 #1, Nov.-Dec., 1965, Jan.-Feb., 1966).	977.2 H789
DAR, ... Marriage books, 1840-1850. 1970. [18pp.]	977.201 S431dm
The Researchers, ... Marriages, 1820-1850. [198?]. [13,9]pp.	977.201 S431si
Marriages, 1820-1908.	microfilm
[Gioe, Joan], ... Marriages, 1820-1850. 23pp.	p.f. 977.201 Suncat. no. 3

Probates:

Greear, William R., Probate court records...1820-1847. 1969. 52pp.	977.201 S431g
Probate order books, 1820-1852; indexes, 1852-1892, 1899-1900.	microfilm
Probates, complete record, 1838-1854, 1856-1905.	miCrofilm
Civil and probate order book, 1866-1870.	miCrofilm

Wills:

Bogardus, Carl R., ... Will book records...1821-1889. 1970. 38, [43]pp.	977.201 S431ba
———, Wills...1821-1889. 1968. 7, 23pp.	977.201 S431b
Wills, 1838-1923.	microfilm

Cemetery:

Scott Co. Hist. Soc., Cemetery records. 1978. 165pp.	977.201 S431s
Ind. Hist. Soc., Cemetery records....17 pts.	p.f. 977.201 S431 no. 1
Bennett, Wilma, Mount Pleasant cemetery....[1965]. 2pp.	p.f. 977.201 S431 no. 3
Bogardus, Carl R., Cemetery records....15 pts.	p.f. 977.201 S431 no. 5
Paulus, Mrs. Raymond, [Incomplete cemetery records...]. 1958. 4pp. (Scottsburg, Kimberlin, Estell, Zoa—all partial).	p.f. 977.201 Suncat. no. 1
Henry, Mrs. Donald W., Parks family cemetery....1pp.	p.f. 977.201 Suncat. no. 2

Census:

1860 Census index....[197-?]. 16pp.	977.201 S431e
1870 Census index....[197-?]. 19pp.	977.201 S431ei
Gioe, Joan C., The Key to the 1900 census of Scott county....1978. 6pp.	977.201 S431gi
———, An Index to the 1880 census....[18pp.]	p.f. 977.201 Suncat. no. 4

Family:

Bogardus, Carl R., Persons of foreign birth in ninetenth century Scott county...1817-1894. 1969. 29pp.	977.201 S431bo
DAR, Bible records....1971. v.p.	977.201 S431d
Family history (Scott Co. Public Library).	miCrofilm

Miscellaneous:

Assessor's book, 1839 (THG, vol. 21 #3, Sept. 1981).	977.2 H789
Assessors book for 1839 by J.E. Roe, assessor. [123]pp. on [63].	q977.201 S431sa 1839a

Accounts current record, 1885-1895, 1917-1919.	miCrofilm
Bogardus, Carl R., Pioneer life in Scott county....1957. 30pp.	p.f. 977.201 S431 no. 2
Darlington, Jane E., ...Assessor's book for 1839. [1981]. 35pp.	977.201 S431dr
DAR, Mortuary records. 1970. 3 vols. (Lexington register, Mar. 1904-Apr. 1933; Stewarts Mortuary records, 1918-1940; Vest Mortuary records, 1947-1958).	977.201 S431dmo
Greear, William, Old Ox Primitive Baptist Church....1965. 7pp.	p.f. 977.201 S431 no. 4
Commissioners records, 1841-1865.	microfilm
Land entry book. n.d.	microfilm

SHELBY COUNTY

Formed 1822 from Delaware (N.P., unorganized)　　　　　　　　　　County Seat—Shelbyville

Births:

WPA, Index to birth records, 1882-1920.	977.201 S544u

Deaths:

WPA, Index to death records, 1882-1920.	977.201 S544u

Deeds:

Deed indexes, 1822-1902.	microfilm

Marriages:

Marriages, 1822-1836 (THG #6, Nov.-Dec. 1962, vol. 10 #5, Sept.-Oct. 1970).	977.2 H789
Marriages, 1822-1852.	microfilm
Peck, Mrs. A.D., ...Marriage records...1828 to 1839. [34pp.]	p.f. 977.201 S544 no. 3
WPA, Index to marriage record, 1856-1920.	977.201 S544u
Weinantz, Mrs. Russell, ...Marriage records [1849-1856]. [1963]. 18,9pp.	p.f. 977.201 S544 no. 14
Zerfas, Mrs. Leon G., ...Marriage records, [1822-1830]. [17pp.]	p.f. 977.201 S544 no. 1
Fox, Mrs. John L., ...Marriages (1827-1850) and index....1981. 136pp.	977.201 S544fo
Heiss, Willard C., ...Marriage records, 1822-1856. n.d. 160pp.	977.201 S544h
Holmes, Maurice, Marriage returns...1883-1889. 1978. 489pp.	977.201 S544hos
(Marriages...1889-1893. 1978. 211pp.)	977.201 S544hot
(Marriages...1895-1898. 1979. 187pp.)	977.201 S544hou
Ridlen, Colleen A., Early...marriage returns, 1822-1839. 1976. 42pp.	977.201 S544r
DAR, ...Marriages, 1827-1829. 1971. n.p.	p.f. 977.201 S544 no. 20

Probates:

Probates, 1822-1852; indexes, 1853-1900.	microfilm

Wills:

Wills, 1858-1906.	microfilm
Holmes, Maurice, Will records...1822-1906. 1976. 365pp.	977.201 S544how

Cemetery:

...Cemetery records. 1975. 2 vols.	977.201 S544s
City cemetery, Shelbyville, Ind. [1954]. n.p.	977.202 S544s
Records of the Forest Hill cemetery, Shelbyville...1884-1978.	microfilm
DAR, Norristown, Indiana...Washington township. Cop. by Mildred Harrod. 1979. [55pp.]	977.202 N861no
Holmes, Maurice, [...Cemeteries]. 1974. 6pp. (Campell, Wilkins, Ruggels, Patterson cems.)	p.f. 977.201 S544hoc
Ind. Hist. Soc., [Cemetery records...]. 1. Little Blue River. 1948.	p.f. 977.201 S544 no. 2
Harper, John E., Cemetery records....8 pts.	p.f. 977.201 S544 no. 4
Wintin, Gendron, Genealogy of Van Pelt or Ogden cemetery, in Noble township.... [1955]. 20pp.	p.f. 977.201 S544 no. 5
———, Winterrowed cemetery. [1956?]. n.p.	p.f. 977.201 S544 no. 6
Montgomery, Mrs. Harry, Cemetery records....11 pts.	p.f. 977.201 S544 no. 7
Wintin, Gendron, Cemetery at Middletown....[1960]. 3pp.	p.f. 977.201 S544 no. 8
Hoyt, Mrs. Leo, Cemetery records....14 pts.	p.f. 977.201 S544 no. 9
Wintin, Gendron, Ensminger cemetery. [1961?]. [2pp.]	p.f. 977.201 S544 no. 10

Jordan, Mrs. James, Cemetery records....4 pts. (Branson, Cotton, DeWitt, Nave).	p.f. 977.201 S544 no. 11
Weinantz, Mrs. Russell, Cemetery records....(1, Knowlton cemetery. 1962; 2, Roberts Chapel cemetery (new). 1962; 3, Shepherd cemetery. 1962).	p.f. 977.201 S544 no. 12
Wintin, Gendron, Hough cemetery....n.d. n.p.	p.f. 977.201 S544 no. 15
Holmes, Maurice, Grave markers in Parrish cemetery....3pp.	p.f. 977.201 S544 no. 16
Crabtree, H.C., Brockman cemetery...Jackson township. 1967. 8pp.	p.f. 977.201 S544 no. 17
Holmes, Maurice, Gatewood cemetery....1968. 2pp.	p.f. 977.201 S544 no. 18
Ind. Junior Hist. Soc., ...Cemetery records. 1970-74. 29 pts.	p.f. 977.201 S544 no. 19
DAR, Cemetery records....1, Boggstown cemetery, Sugar Creek twp. [1972]. [9pp].	p.f. 977.201 S544 no. 21
Holmes, Maurice, Law cemetery inscriptions, Hendricks twp....[1972]. 3pp.	p.f. 977.201 S544 no. 22
Murphy, Thelma, Boggstown...Indiana, old cemetery. 2pp.	p.f. 977.201 Suncat. no. 1
[Records of] Jackson cemetery, and Maple Shyrock cemetery....3pp.	p.f. 977.201 Suncat. no. 3
Wintin, Mrs. Walter, ...Cemetery records. 2 pts. (Bilby family; cemetery NE of Lewis Creek, Washington twp.). 1956.	p.f. 977.201 Suncat. no. 4
Murphy, Thelma, ...Cemetery records. 2 pts. (Brandywine cem., Cem. on State Road 9).	p.f. 977.201 Suncat. no. 5
Hoyt, Mrs. Leo C., Reed cemetery, Noble township....2pp.	p.f. 977.201 Suncat. no. 6
Montgomery, Mrs. Harry, Family cemetery...Shelby township...section 34, Range 7 East on Forrest Monroe farm. 1pp.	p.f. 977.201 Suncat. no. 7
Holmes, Maurice, Grave inscriptions, Sand Hill cemetery [or Keith], Sugar Creek township....7pp.	p.f. 977.201 Suncat. no. 8
Wintin, Mrs. Walter, [...Bible records]. (Ensley, Pope, Wray, and Tindell families). 2pp.	p.f. 977.201 Suncat. no. 9
Holmes, Maurice, Gravestone inscriptions....12 pts.	p.f. 977.201 Suncat. no. 10
———, St. Vincent de Paul Catholic Church....[cemetery records]. 25pp.	977.201 S544sv
Sand Hill or Keith cemetery...(from THG, #6, 1962). 1pp.	p.f. 977.201 Suncat. no. 11
[Incomplete listing of Davis cemetery inscriptions...]. [5pp.]	p.f. 977.201 Suncat. no. 12
Winterroad cemetery, Norristown, Indiana...Washington township, and index. [16pp.]	p.f. 977.201 Suncat. no. 13

History:

Gordon, Robert, and Holmes, Maurice, Excerpts from Shelbyville...newspapers, 1853-1859. 1973. 217, 27pp.	977.202 S544go
Holmes, Maurice, Shelbyville...newspaper items, 1860-1862. 274pp. 1981.	977.202 S544ho
———, Newspaper items from Shelbyville...newspapers, 1866 to 1870. 1978. 263pp.	977.202 S544hon
History of Shelby county...from 1822 to 1876, by a Comm. of citizens [reprint of the 1876 ed.]. 1976. 40pp.	p.f. 977.201 S544sh
Kimberling, Zerillin L., Purchasers' pass book, leading business firms of Shelbyville, Indiana. 1878. [9pp.]	p.f. 977.202 Suncat. no. 1

Miscellaneous:

Holmes, Maurice, Early landowners....1973. 43pp. (and rev. ed. 1975. 41,43pp.)	977.201 S544ho
———, Court records...1822 to 1862. 1974. 348pp.	977.201 S544hol
———, Court records...1862-1876. 1977. 462pp.	977.201 S544hom
WPA, Index to supplemental record, federal census, 1880. (Lists names, sex, color, ages).	977.201 S544u
1847 Tax List....[1962] n.p.	p.f. 977.201 S544 no. 13
Lemmon, J.G., ...Assessment roll, 1828....1954. n.p.	p.f. 977.201 Suncat. no. 2

SPENCER COUNTY

Formed 1818 from Perry, Warrick   County Seat—Rockport

Births:

WPA, Index to birth records, 1882-1920.	977.201 S746u

Deaths:

WPA, Index to death records, 1882-1920.	977.201 S746u

Deeds:

Deeds, 1818-1835.	microfilm

Marriages:

...Marriages, 1863-1868. [1981?]. 70pp.	977.201 S746yob
Marriages, 1818-1835 (THG, vol. 11 #3, July-Sept. 1971).	977.2 H789
Young, Christine, Marriage records...1818-1855. 1974. 109pp.	977.201 S746yo
Young, Christine, ...Marriages, 1855-1863....1976. 62pp.	977.201 S746yoa
DAR, ...First 200 marriages, [1818-1826], with index. 1943. [5], 20pp.	p.f. 977.201 S746 no. 1
Marriages, 1818-1863.	microfilm
Marriage returns, 1882-1890.	microfilm
WPA, Index to marriage records, 1850-1920.	977.201 S746u
WPA, Index to supplemental record, marriage transcript, 1880-1920.	977.201 S746u
Phillips, J. Oscar, ...Marriages...1818-1850. 1980. 42,16,12pp.	977.201 S746ps

Probates:

Probate and will records, 1818-1830. *adm Bonds 1847, 52*	microfilm
Young, Christine, ...Probate records. [1965]. 2 vols. (vol. 1, 1818-1833; vol. 2, 1833-1849).	p.f. 977.201 S746 no. 4
Young, Christine, ...Complete probate record, 1842-1850; complete circuit court, 1842-1856. [1965?]. n.p.	p.f. 977.201 S746 no. 5

Wills:

Young, Christine, ...Wills, 1833-1875. [1965?]. 33pp.	p.f. 977.201 S746 no. 6
Young, Christine, Early wills and estate settlements, ...1818-1831...1833-1839. 1971. 37pp.	977.201 S746yw
DAR, ...Will records, December 1853-1874. 1974. 54, 4pp.	p.f. 977.201 S746da
Phillips, J. Oscar, Early will book (1818-1831) and will book (1853-1880)....1980. 50, 58pp.	977.201 S746phi

Cemeteries:

Phillips, J. Oscar, ...Cemeteries. 1980. vol. 1 (Carter, Clay, Grass and Jackson townships). 154pp.	977.201 S746p
Young, Christine, Cemetery inscriptions....[1971-] 13 vols. (and index. 1975. 28pp.)	977.201 S746y
Ind. Hist. Soc., [Cemetery records...]. 5 pts.	p.f. 977.201 S746 no. 2
DAR, Cemetery records....1, Roth family cemetery. 1964. 2pp.	p.f. 977.201 S746 no. 3
Baertich, Frank, ...Cemetery records. 1972. 15pp.	p.f. 977.201 S746 no. 8

Miscellaneous:

A Partial list of voters, Harrison township...1842. 1pp.	p.f. 977.201 Suncat. no. 1
Members and friends of Little Pigeon Baptist Church...1816-1840. (From THG, vol. 8, 1968). [6pp.]	p.f. 977.201 Suncat. no. 2
..."Home coming and family reunion", Jones-McCoy families, 1925 (From The Rockport Journal, July 10, 1925). 1pp.	p.f. 977.201 Suncat. no. 3

DAR, 1820 census....[1982?]. 16pp.   977.201 S745etw
———, 1830 census....[1982?]. 24pp.   977.201 S745eth
Young, Christine, Records of...courthouse. [1965?]. n.p.   p.f. 977.201 S746 no. 7

STARKE COUNTY

Formed 1835; organized 1850 from St. Joseph County Seat—Knox

Births:

WPA, Index to birth records, 1894-1938.   977.201 S795u

Deaths:

WPA, Index to death records, 1894-1938.   977.201 S795u

Deeds:

Deed indexes, 1858-1900 (grantor only, 1850-1858).   microfilm

Marriages:

WPA, Index to marriage records, 1896-1938.   977.201 S795u

WPA, Index to marriage applications, 1840-1920.   977.201 S795u

WPA, Index to marriage transcript, 1899-1938.   977.201 S795u

Marriages, 1850-1890.   microfilm

Slevin, Ruth M., ...Marriage records, 1850-1890....1974. 35,35pp.   977.201 S795sl

Probates:

Probate indexes, books 1-3. n.d.   microfilm

Wills:

Wills, 1850-1898.   microfilm

Slevin, Ruth M., ...Will records, 1855-1898. 1973. 45pp.   977.201 S795s

Others:

McCormick, Joseph N., ...Early land entries. n.d. 10pp.   p.f. 977.201 S795 no. 1

D.A.C., Cemetery inscriptions, Lake, Porter and Starke cos....1968. 117pp.   977.201 L192c

DAR, Cemetery records....[1963?]. v.p.   977.201 S795d

Enumeration of children in Center twp...between 1866 and 1895. Comp. by George F. Harden. 1962. 47pp.   p.f. 977.201 Suncat. no. 2

1913 Enumeration of white and colored males in Center twp....Comp. by G.F. Harden. 1961. 8pp.   p.f. 977.201 Suncat. no. 1

U.S. Bur. of the Census, Census...1850. [1964?]. 20pp.   p.f. 977.201 S795 no. 2

Swampland record, 1853?-1876?.   microfilm

WPA, Commissioners' record...1850-1860....3 vols.   Ind. Hist. Soc. Library

STEUBEN COUNTY

Formed 1835; organized 1837 from LaGrange | County Seat—Angola

Deeds:

Deed indexes, 1836-1899. | microfilm

Marriages:

Kirk, Hazel, Marriage records...[1837-1867]. [1959]. 2 vols. (Index by K. Doll, ISL). | 977.201 S842s

Lewis, Audree S., Marriage record...1832-1890. 1967. 611pp. | 977.201 S842Lm

Marriages, 1837-1897. | microfilm

Marriage returns, 1882-1890. | microfilm

Probates:

Probate indexes, 1853-1899. | microfilm

Wills:

Wills, 1845-1892. | microfilm

Others:

Lewis, Audree S., Tombstone inscriptions...Carleton, Jackson Prairie, Memorial Grove cems. 1967. 5,23,21pp. | 977.201 S842L

Ind. Junior Hist. Soc., ...Cemetery records. 1970. 21 pts. | p.f. 977.201 S842 no. 1

DAR, Cemetery records....1, Bower cemetery (Slaybaugh farm). 1971. 2pp. | p.f. 977.201 S842 no. 2

Court docket, 1845-1855 (see Noble County entry "Others" of Mortuary and school records by DAR)

Steuben County pioneers (articles from Steuben Republican, Aug. 13, 1890 and Aug. 19, 1891). 2 pts. | p.f. 977.201 Suncat. no.1

SULLIVAN COUNTY

Formed 1817 from Knox   County Seat—Sullivan

Births:

WPA, Index to birth records, 1882-1920.   977.201 S952u

Deaths:

WPA, Index to death records, 1880-1920.   977.201 S952u

Deeds:

Deed indexes, 1850-1901 (books 2-3 missing).   microfilm

Marriages:

WPA, Index to marriage records, 1850-1920.   977.201 S952u

———, Index to supplemental record, marriage applications, 1880-1920 [?].   977.201 S952u

———, Index to supplemental record, marriage transcript, 1880-1920.   977.201 S952u

Zerfas, Mrs. L.G., ...Marriage records, 1850-1852. 6pp.   p.f. 977.201 Suncat. no. 1

Sullivan Co. Hist. Soc., Marriage records...1850-1902. [1982?]. 112,6pp.   977.201 S952mr

Probates:

Probate indexes, 1860-1901.   microfilm

Wills:

Wills, 1846-1901.   microfilm

Will abstracts, July 1844-Apr. 1855 (THG, vol. 21 #2, June 1981).   977.2 H789

Cemetery:

DAR, Old cemeteries....1954. [4pp.]   977.201 S952d

Maple, James B., Cemetery records of pioneer families buried in southern part of Sullivan county....1957. 29pp.   977.201 S952m

Maple, Dr. J.B., Old cemetery records in southern Sullivan county...from the research notes of Mr. & Mrs. Geo. R. Miles. 58pp.   977.201 S952o

Willis, Sharon, Cemeteries of Haddon township....[197-]. [12pp.]   977.201 S952w

Ind. Hist. Soc., Cemetery records....17 pts.   p.f. 977.201 S952 no. 1

Hoyt, Mrs. Leo, Cemetery records....1, Mt. Moriah cemetery. [1957]. 6pp.   p.f. 977.201 S952 no. 2

Jewell, Mrs. Denver, Pirtle graveyard [also Lund cem. of Greene co. and Clayton of Sullivan]. [4pp.]   p.f. 977.201 S952 no. 3

Sole, Mrs. H.M., Grave markers, old town cemetery, Carlisle....[1968]. 7pp.   p.f. 977.201 S952 no. 4

Jeffers, Phoebe, Friendship cemetery, Farmersburg....2pp.   p.f. 977.201 Suncat. no. 3

Halberstadt, L.C., et al., Cemetery record of the old Harris cemetery located southeast of Fairbanks....2pp.   p.f. 977.201 Suncat. no. 5

Patterson, Leafy D., Tombstone inscriptions [incomplete] of Deckard cemetery....1pp.   p.f. 977.201 Suncat. no. 6

Aydelotte, Mrs., Farnsworth cemetery....(From Sullivan Co. Hist. Soc. Newsletter, vol. 4 #4, 1977). [2pp.]   p.f. 977.201 Suncat. no. 9

Johnson (Haddon township), Johnson (Turman township), and Paxton (Neal) cemeteries...(from Sycamore Leaves, vol. 5-6, 1974, 1975, 1976). [9pp.]   p.f. 977.201 Suncat. no. 10

A Neglected graveyard. (From Sullivan Co. Hist. Soc. Newsletter, vol. 4 #5, 1977). 1pp.   p.f. 977.201 Suncat. no. 11

Johnson, Harold W., Letter to the editor concerning Walls cemetery....(From Sullivan Daily Times, July 21, 1978). 1pp.   p.f. 977.201 Suncat. no. 13

Mt. Zion cemetery, Gill twp....[30pp.]   p.f. 977.201 Suncat. no. 14

Burnett cemetery, Gill twp....[8pp.]	p.f. 977.201 Suncat no. 15
Cooper, Marjore B., Hail-Hale cemetery. 1981. [4pp.]	p.f. 977.201 Suncat. no. 16
List of soldiers in various graveyards near Carlisle. 3pp.	p.f. 977.201 Suncat. no. 17
Burials in McClellan-Snyder cemetery....3pp.	p.f. 977.201 Suncat. no. 18
Buckley family plot in the town cemetery of Carlisle....1pp.	p.f. 977.201 Suncat. no. 19

Church:

DAR, History of Carlisle Methodist Church, Carlisle....[1968]. 23, [31]pp.	977.202 C283d
Morgan, Chloe S., A Minute book for the Christian Church on Busseron Creek—record of the Christian Church at Palmers Prairie, Sullivan county....(From IMH, vol. 47, 1951). [18pp.]	p.f. 977.202 Puncat. no. 1
Maple, James B., The Sullivan Methodist Church: the events leading to its origin and the church itself through the years. [1981?]. 47pp.	977.201 S952ms
Turman, Robert E., Church in the Wildwood (article on the Hopewell Presbyterian Church in Sullivan, Indiana Union, April 22, 1954). 1pp.	p.f. 977.201 Suncat. no. 4

Miscellaneous:

DAR, Historical data reported on the admission of Indiana to the Union from the files of the Sullivan Union, Sullivan, Indiana, December 14, 1950, marking the 134 years of admittance also interesting items of descendants of pioneers of that time. 1958. 38pp.	977.201 S952s
Poll list for Fairbanks township...for the year, 1934. 1pp.	p.f. 977.201 Suncat. no. 2
Sullivan County Historical Society Newsletter. Volumes 1-9, 1974-1982.	p.f. 977.201 Suncat. no. 7
"...The Names of men living in Sullivan county who have passed the 70th mile-stone". (Article from the Sullivan Democrat, Sullivan, vol. 28 #22, Jan. 16, 1902). 2pp.	p.f. 977.201 Suncat. no. 8
Col. Dames of XVII Century, Abstracted from leading citizens and farmers' directory, Sullivan county...1896. 1977. 64pp.	p.f. 977.201 Suncat. no. 12
Curtis Gilbert's list for marks and brands on stock [taken from his account books at Fort Harrison...]. (From Leaves of Thyme, vol. 20, 1969). 1pp.	p.f. 977.202 Funcat. no. 1

SWITZERLAND COUNTY

Formed 1814 from Dearborn, Jefferson   County Seat—Vevay

Births:

Births, 1882-1907.	microfilm
Delayed birth records prior to 1941.	miCrofilm

Deaths:

Deaths, 1882-1900.	microfilm

Deeds:

Deeds, 1815-1886; indexes, 1817-1900.	miCrofilm
Deed indexes, 1814-1900.	microfilm

Marriages:

Marriages, 1814-1925.	miCrofilm
Marriage returns, 1882-1895.	miCrofilm
Marriage applications, 1905-1925.	miCrofilm
Knox, Louise A.L., A Record of marriage licenses issued...[1814-1855, 1885-1900]. 60pp. (Also 1948 index of 97pp.)	977.201 S979k
Marriages, 1854-1885.	microfilm
Marriage applications, 1882-1900.	microfilm
Marriages...[1814-1817]. [2],4pp.	p.f. 977.201 S979 no. 1
Knox, Mrs. James S. and Ruth M. Slevin, ...Marriage records, 1831-1885. 1970. 357pp.	977.201 S979sm
Marriages, 1814-1830 (THG, vol. 4 #4-5-6, vol. 5 #1, July-Aug., Sept.-Oct., Nov.-Dec. 1964, Jan.-Feb. 1965).	977.2 H789

Probates:

Complete probate records, 1835-1947.	miCrofilm
Probate records, 1827-1834.	miCrofilm
Probate order books, 1814-1824, 1831-1919.	miCrofilm
Probate indexes, 1827-1902.	microfilm

Wills:

[handwritten: estate Record 1919-38]

Wills, 1825-1900.	microfilm
Wills, 1823-1919.	miCrofilm
Slevin, Ruth M., ...Will records, 1825-1903. n.d. v.p.	977.201 S979s

Cemetery:

Switzerland county, Indiana cemetery records.	microfilm, MiCrofilm
Haskell and Morrison Funeral Home, Vevay cemetery records.	miCrofilm
Ind. Junior Hist. Soc., ...Cemeteries. 3 pts. (missing 1982)	p.f. 977.201 S979 no. 3
Danner, Mrs. Effa M., The Caledonia Church and cemetery (From IMH, vol. 41, 1945). [2pp.]	p.f. 977.201 Suncat. no. 1
Cook, Mrs. Ivan M., Shaw family cemetery. 2pp.	p.f. 977.201 Suncat. no. 2
Jennings, Francis, Vevay cemetery inscriptions....(From IMH, vol. 46, 1950). 2pp.	p.f. 977.201 Suncat. no. 3
Byrer, Irene, Inscriptions from a small private cemetery....1972. 1pp.	p.f. 977.201 Suncat. no. 4

Family:

Switzerland County Historical Collection, 1976 (From Switzerland County Public Library and Switzerland County Museum).	microfilm

Switzerland County, Indiana, Records and Family Histories (Switzerland County Public Library)   miCrofilm q977.201 S979

[Memoirs of some...families...]. Recorded in Vevay, 1928. 1967. n.p.

DAR, Twelve Conewago, Pa., families who came to Kentucky and Indiana. 1957. 71pp.   977.201 S979d

Miscellaneous:

Edgerton, Mildred H., The...census for 1820. 1963. 21pp.   p.f. 977.201 S979 no. 2

Names...for the expenses of soldiers reunion...at Vevay, Aug. 6th and 7th, 1915. 2pp.   p.f. 977.201 Suncat. no. 5

Naturalizations, 1825-Apr. 1829 (THG, vol. 22 #2, June 1982).   977.2 H789

TIPPECANOE COUNTY

Formed 1826 from Wabash (N.P., unorganized), Parke   County Seat—Lafayette

Births:
WPA, Index to birth records, 1882-1920.   977.201 T595u

Deaths:
WPA, Index to death records, 1882-1920.   977.201 T595u

Deaths from cholera, 1849 (THG, vol. 18 #2, June 1979).   977.2 H789

Deeds:
Deed indexes, 1826-1901.   microfilm

Marriages:
DAR, Marriage records, 1830-1850....1952. 3 vols. [a few 1829 marriages].   977.201 T595m

Marriages, 1826-1830 (IMH, vol. 32, 1936).   977.2 I39

WPA, Index to marriage records, 1850-1920.   977.201 T595u

WPA, Index to supplemental records, marriage transcripts, 1880-1906.   977.201 T595u

Esarey, Myra, Marriage records...1826-1830 (From IMH, vol. 32, 1936). 3pp.   p.f. 977.201 Tuncat. no. 1

Probates:
Tippecanoe Co. Area Geneal. Soc., Index to...probate final records...1830-1849. [12pp.]   p.f. 977.201 Tuncat. no. 4

Civil probate records, 1827-1853; indexes, 1853-1890.   microfilm

Wills:
Index to wills, June 1825-1844, Apr. 1845-1864 (THG, #6, Nov.-Dec. 1961, #2, Mar.-Apr. 1962).   977.2 H789

Index of wills...1825-1864 (From THG, #6-7, 1961, 1962). [3pp.]   p.f. 977.201 Tuncat. no. 6

Wills, 1842-1902.   microfilm

DAR, Typed copy of will book I, 1828-1834....[1981?]. 133pp.   977.201 T595ty

Cemetery:
Cemetery records (Grandview, 1908-1932; Springvale, 1869-1917).   microfilm

DAR, ...Cemetery records of Shelby township....1960. 94pp.   977.201 T595ds

———, Inscriptions from cemeteries of Sheffield township....[1957?]. [128pp.]   977.201 T595di

———, Record of the cemeteries of Tippecanoe township....[1956]. v.p. [Includes Battle Ground, Liberty Chapel, Methodist Camp Ground, Pretty Prairie cems.].   977.201 T595dr

———, Cemetery records of Burton, McCormick, Mt. Zion, Sandridge cemeteries, Wabash township....1954. v.p.   977.201 T595da

Warren, Elza, ...Cemetery records: West Point, Fink, Sickler, Spring Grove, Wild Cat, Lafayette. 1966. 105pp.   977.201 T595w

Tippecanoe Co. Hist. Assoc., [Cemetery records...]. 1, Greenbush cem. 1946. 31pp.   p.f. 977.201 T595 no. 1

Cox, Carroll O., [Cemetery records...]. [1955]. 23pp. (Cemeteries in Illinois; Isley cemetery...).   p.f. 977.201 T595 no. 2

Tippecanoe Co. Hist. Assoc., Cemetery records, Wea township....1, Spring Grove cemetery. [1962]. 6pp.   p.f. 977.201 T595 no. 3

Williamson, Wallace F., Pierce cemetery index. 1965. [13pp.]   p.f. 977.201 T595 no. 4

D.A.C., Gravestone records of Concord cemetery....1965. 23pp.   p.f. 977.201 T595 no. 5

Blachly, Mrs. Josephus C., [Cemetery records...]. (Battle Ground. 1967. 1pp.) p.f. 977.201 T595 no. 7

Ind. Junior Hist. Soc., ...Cemetery records. 1, Shambaugh cemetery, Shelby twp. 1pp.   p.f. 977.201 T595 no. 8

DAR, Cemetery on the old Harvey farm. 1pp.	p.f. 977.201 Tuncat. no. 2
Warren, Mrs. E.P., Sickler cemetery, Wea township....5pp.	p.f. 977.201 Tuncat. no. 3
Durkee cemetery...(From THG, #2, 1962). 1pp.	p.f. 977.201 Tuncat. no. 5

Church:

Raub, Nellie T., A History of Farmers Institute monthly meeting of Friends and its community. [1951?]. 48pp.	p.f. 977.201 T595r
DAR, A Copy of the register of St. John's Episcopal church, Lafayette, Ind., from June 1837 to June 1898. 1940. [47], 85pp.	977.201 T595s
D.A.C., Records of membership of the Dayton, Indiana, Presbyterian church, 1832 to 1940....1965. v.p.	p.f. 977.201 T595 no. 6

Family:

DAR, Historical and genealogical records....1929. 153pp.	977.201 T595d
———, Abstracts of alien declarations...for the decades 1830 and 1840. [1982]. 131pp.	977.201 T595a
"Ancestors" column in the Wabash magazine of the Lafayette Journal and Courier, Sunday edition. (scattered issues).	p.f. 977.2 Auncat no. 1
DAR, ...Bible records, Finkle, Howell, McBride, Oglebay, Moran, and Shortridge, McCollough, Smiley, Taylor. 1973. 14pp.	p.f. 977.201 T595 no. 9
Smith, Lora R., Records...copied from documents....[1971?]. [7pp.] [Lafayette]	p.f. 977.202 L161 no. 1

Miscellaneous:

DAR, [Early land owners (1840-1843)...]. [1978?]. 3 vols.	977.201 T595dau
Farber, Renee, Index to county commissioners' record....1980. 302pp.	977.201 T595f
Tipp. Co. Historical Assoc., Commissioners' record...1826-1846....6 vols.	Ind. Hist. Soc. Library
DAR, Land transactions: abstracted from the 1st entry tract book...beginning date, 1823....[1981?]. 100pp.	977.201 T595Lat
WPA, Index to supplemental record, registered voters, 1922.	977.201 T595u
Merritt, Grace H., Index to census of 1830 and 1840....[1967]. 24,43pp.	977.201 T595me

TIPTON COUNTY

Formed 1844 from Hamilton, Cass, Miami   County Seat—Tipton

Deeds:

Deed indexes, 1844-1902.   microfilm

Marriages:

Marriages, 1844-1856 (THG, vol. 16 #3, Sept. 1976).   977.2 H789

Marriages, 1844-1905.   microfilm

Marriage affidavits, 1867-1905.   microfilm

Marriage applications, 1896-1900.   microfilm

Slevin Ruth M., ...Marriages, 1870-1905. [19—]. 339pp.   977.201 T596s

Slevin, Ruth M., ...Marriages, 1844-1870. [1980?]. 108pp.   977.201 T596sa

Probates:

Probates, 1844-1864; indexes, 1865-1904.   microfilm

Wills:

Wills, 1847-1913; book 1, 1891-1925, incomplete?   microfilm

Slevin, Ruth M., ...Will records, 1847-1913....[197-]. 151pp.   977.201 T596sL

Cemetery:

Dickey, Lee W., Richardson cemetery, Liberty township....1968. 8pp.   977.201 T596d

DAR, ...Cemetery inscriptions and histories. 1979-80. 7 vols., and index of 338pp.   977.201 T596da

Wolford cemetery at Goldsmith. 1pp.   p.f. 977.201 Tuncat. no. 1

Brown, Jennifer, "DAR, EHA women index graves in Tipton county's 32 cemeteries".
  (From Tipton Tribune, July 6, 1978). 1pp.   p.f. 977.201 Tuncat. no.2

DAR, Pleasant Hill cemetery...Madison township. 1978. [27pp.]   p.f. 977.201 Tuncat. no. 3

Miscellaneous:

Freeman, Ruth, ...Picture of a pioneer people: census 1850, marriages 1844-1850,
  wills 1844-1850. [1976]. 8,99pp.   977.201 T596f

McKinney, Julia, Declaration of intentions to become citizens: (naturalization
  intentions)...1854-1904. 15,[2]pp.   977.201 T596m

Tri-Central High School, Sharpsville, Pioneers...[cemetery records]. 1972. n.p.   977.201 T596t

Hoyt, Alma E., The Nichols Funeral home records, 1881-1931, Tipton, Indiana. 1978.
  92pp.   977.202 T595n

Nelson, Elaine J., [Directory of Sharpsville High School 1961 class members]. 1981.
  6pp.   p.f. 977.201 Tuncat. no. 4

UNION COUNTY

Formed 1821 from Fayette, Franklin, WayneCounty Seat—Liberty

Deeds:

Deed indexes, 1821-1900.	microfilm

Marriages:

Marriages, 1821-1900.	microfilm
Marriages, 1821-1830 (IMH, vol. 50, 1954).	977.2 I39
Slevin, Ruth M., ...Marriages, 1860-1918. [197-?] 70, 69pp.	977.201 U58s
Riker, Dorothy, ...Marriages, 1821-1826 (From IMH, March 1954). [5pp.]	p.f. 977.201 Uuncat. no. 1
...Marriages, 1826-1830 (From IMH, vol. 50, 1954). [7pp.]	p.f. 977.201 Uuncat. no. 2
Heiss, Willard, Marriage record of Salem (originally called Silver Creek) Monthly meeting...1817-1885. 14pp.	p.f. 977.201 Uuncat. no. 3
Marriages in Union and Henry counties...1860-1861, taken from the diaries of Aggie A. Lafuse, of Liberty, Union county. [1pp.]	p.f. 977.201 Uuncat. no. 5

Probates:

Probates, 1821-1845; indexes, 1846-1852, 1863-1881.	microfilm

Wills:

Wills and inventories, 1821-1827, 1845-1901	microfilm

Cemetery:

DAR, Cemeteries....1934. 148pp.	977.201 U58d
Ind. Hist. Soc., Names of burials in cemeteries in Harmony township....1938. [21pp.]	977.201 U58m
Ind. Junior Hist. Soc., Union county...cemetery survey. 1981-82. 129pp. (Includes Christian Union, United Methodist Church, Calvary, College Corner, Crawford, Drook, Dunlapsville, Keffer, New Hope, Nutter, Old Bath Springs, Pentecost, Philomath, Railsback, Ranck, Richland, Salem Church, Sering, Silver Creek, Sims, Smoker, Thomas, Universalist, Witter, West Point, Woods Chapel).	977.201 U58u
Genealogical notes....2pp. (Includes some incomplete cemetery listings in Sims, Lineagar, Railsback, Brown, Dunlapsville cems.)	p.f. 977.201 Uuncat. no. 4

Miscellaneous:

Manuscripts relating to Union county..., history and families (from Treaty-Line Museum).	microfilm
Holmes, Maurice, Early landowners....1978. 85pp.	977.201 U58ho
Lafuze, Maurice S., Union county people, c1804-1870. n.d. v.p.	977.201 U58L
Ind. Junior Hist. Soc., Union county....1981. 7pp.	977.201 U58u

VANDERBURGH COUNTY

Formed 1818 from Gibson, Posey, Warrick   County Seat—Evansville

Births:

WPA, Index to birth records, 1882-1920.	977.201 V229u

Deaths:

WPA, Index to death records, 1882-1920.	977.201 V229u

Deeds:

DAR, Deed book #1 with index...1854. 1955-56. 14pp.	977.201 V229dd

Marriages:

See also under Church, and Family.

Marriages, 1818-1840 (THG, vol. 15 #3, July-Sept. 1975).	977.2 H789
DAR, ...Marriage records [1840-1850, 1854-1859, 1859-1864]. 1950-51. 4 vols.	977.201 V229dm
Riker, Dorothy, ...Marriages, 1819-1840. 1961. n.p.	977.201 V229da
WPA, Index to marriage records, 1846-1920.	977.201 V229u
WPA, Index to supplemental record, marriage transcripts, 1882-1898.	977.201 V229u
Marriages, 1818-1880.	microfilm
Slevin, Ruth M., ...Marriage records, 1818-1840. 1974. 22, 22pp.	977.201 V229s

Wills:

DAR, Abstracts of wills...[1823-1873]. 1952. 89pp.	977.201 V229v

Cemetery:

Kolb, Doris, James cemetery....1970. 5pp.	977.201 V229k
Lantaff, Carol A., Cemetery records....1980. 1 vol. 326pp.	977.201 V229La
Cox, Carroll O., [Cemetery records...]. (1, Park Lawn, Powell, Unnamed). 1967. [8pp.]	p.f. 977.201 V229 no. 3
DAR, [Cemetery records...]. Hornsby Graveyard. 1967. [8pp.]	p.f. 977.201 V229 no. 4
McCutchan, Kenneth P., Cemetery records....5 pts. (Blue Grass, Hornby, Sansom, Ingle-Browning, McCutchanville, Episcopal).	p.f. 977.201 V229 no. 5
Knight township trustee restoring abandoned cemetery south of levee. (Clipping from Evansville Courier, 1959). 1pp.	p.f. 977.201 Vuncat. no. 1
Becker, David, Old Protestant German cemetery, German township....2pp.	p.f. 977.201 Vuncat. no. 2

Church:

Cook, Michael L., Church records....1979. 1 vol. 373pp.	977.201 V229c
DAR, St. Paul's Episcopal Church records, Evansville, Ind.: Marriages 1835-1863, 1865-1882, 1894-1900. 1961. 7pp.	977.202 E92e
———, Marriage records 1868-1917, Holy Innocents Episcopal Church, Evansville, Ind. 1962. 10pp.	977.202 E92ev
The Records of First Presbyterian Church of Evansville, Indiana.	microfilm

Family:

DAR, ...Records. 1949. [20], 1pp. [Includes marriages, 1835-1839, probates, 1821-1847, Bible records, wills].	977.201 V229d
———, Index of records from Vanderburgh chapter, DAR [1960?]. [21pp.]	p.f. 977.201 V229 no. 1
———, Bible records, biography and family history. 1964. 44pp.	p.f. 977.201 V229 no. 2

Miscellaneous:

DAR, ...Tract book #1, land purchases 1805-1853. 1968. 99pp.	977.201 V229dt

Johnson, Charles E., One hundred years of Evansville, Indiana, 1812-1912 with miscellanea. 188pp. (missing 1982)   p.f. 977.202 Euncat. no. 1

Bigham, Darrel E., ...A preliminary inventory, old Vanderburgh county courthouse...a bicentennial project. 1975. 17pp.   p.f. 16.977201 B592v

WPA, Commissioners' record...[1818]-1844....8 vols.   Ind. Hist. Soc. Library

VERMILLION COUNTY

Formed 1824 from Parke   County Seat—Newport

Births:

WPA, Index to birth records, 1882-1920.   977.201 V526u

Deaths:

WPA, Index to death records, 1882-1920.   977.201 V526u

Marriages:

Newton, Mrs. Claude, ...Marriage records, 1824-1850....1948. [109pp.]   977.201 V526v

Volkel, Lowell M., ...Land and marriage records, [1824-1861]. 1967?-70. 3 vols. in 2. 977.201 V526vo

WPA, Index to marriage records, 1850-1904.   977.201 V526u

WPA, Index to supplemental record, marriage applications, 1904-1920.   977.201 V526u

WPA, Index to supplemental record, marriage transcripts, 1882-1920.   977.201 V526u

Cemetery:

Volkel, Lowell, [...Cemetery inscriptions]. [1963]. 18pp.   p.f. 977.201 V526 no. 3

———, Hicks cemetery, Highland township....1966. 66pp.   977.201 V526vh

Illiana Geneal. & Hist. Soc., History of the Hopewell Primitive Baptist church and
    cemetery records, 1829-1968. 1970. 45pp.   977.201 V526i

Ind. Hist. Soc., [Cemetery records...]. 1, Riverside cemetery. 1949. [5pp.]   p.f. 977.201 V526 no. 1

Williams, Opal H., Indiana cemetery records, Pisgah cemetery, Helt twp....1947.
    2pp.   p.f. 977.201 V526 no. 2

Illiana Geneal. & Hist. Soc., Hopewell cemetery inscriptions. 1966. 30pp.   p.f. 977.201 V526 no. 4

Old Hopewell cemetery stones. [12pp.]   p.f. 977.201 V526 no. 5

Cemetery on Holder farm, near Perrsyville....2pp.   p.f. 977.201 Vuncat. no. 1

Lebanon Methodist, Lower Mound, Shelby and Spangler cemeteries....(From
    Illiana Genealogist, vols. 4-6, 1968-1970). [30pp.]   p.f. 977.201 Vuncat. no. 2

...Burials. (From Illiana Genealogist, vol. 17, 1981). 2pp.   p.f. 977.201 Vuncat. no. 3

Miscellaneous:

O'Donnell, Harold L., Excerpts from the Cayuga Herald...1892-1924. 1964. 338pp.   977.201 V526c

Lineage book, Brouillet chapter, DAR, Clinton, Indiana. n.d. 84pp.   973.346 D2i2nL

Commissioners records, 1824-1826 (THG, vol. 8 #2, Mar.-Apr. 1968).   977.2 H789

WPA, Commissioners' record...1824-1844....8 vols.   Ind. Hist. Soc. Library

VIGO COUNTY

Formed 1818 from Sullivan   County Seat—Terre Haute

Births:
WPA, Index to birth records, 1882-1920.   977.201 V689u

Deaths:
WPA, Index to death records, 1882-1920.   977.201 V689u

Deeds:
Brown, Mrs. Herbert E., Deed records from deed book 1, [1816-1821]. 1947. n.p.   p.f. 977.201 V689 no. 3

Brown, Mrs. Herbert E., Land entries from "tract book" [1816-1820]. 1947. [38pp.] p.f. 977.201 V689 no. 2

Marriages:
Marriages, 1818-1830 (THG, #2, Mar.-Apr. 1963).   977.2 H789

[handwritten: + Mrs. M. M. Greenwood, marriage records Brides & Grooms #9-1920-1930]

Johns, Mae and Markle, A.R., ... Marriage licenses from 1818 to 1850. 1936. 72pp.   977.201 V689j

WPA, Index to marriage records, 1840-1920.   977.201 V689u

———, Index to supplemental record, marriage transcripts, 1880-1920.   977.201 V689u

Wills:
D.A.C., Will book A, ...1818-1831. 1972. 12pp.   p.f. 977.201 V689 no. 5

Brown, Maxine, ...Will book A, 1818-Jan. 1831. [1978]. 11, [1]pp.   977.201 V689b

[Vigo...wills, 1818-1848]. [42pp.]   p.f. 977.201 V689 no. 1

Cemetery:
Clark, Dorothy J., Tombstone orders and inscriptions, 1865-1866 of Wabash Valley. 1967. 14,4pp.   977.201 V689c

Some Wabash Valley cemeteries in Park [i.e. Parke], Sullivan, and Vigo counties....1977-Book 1. 57pp.   977.201 V689s

Wilhoite, Virginia, Cemeteries....1980-82. Vol. 1, Northeast section; vol. 2, Northeast [i.e. South] section; vol. 3, Middle section; vol. 4, Northwest section.   977.201 V689w

DAR, Complete index of names found in 1877 plat maps of Woodlawn cemetery, Terre Haute....Comp. by Dorothy J. Clark. 1959. n.p.   977.202 T325d

Lansaw, Simona, Woodlawn cemetery, Terre Haute...index of burials, 1839 thru 1899. 1980 254pp.   977.202 T325L

Ind. Hist. Soc., A List of inscriptions...in a cemetery...Riley township....3pp.   p.f. 977.201 Vuncat. no. 1

Clark, Mrs. Robert I., [McClintock cemetery, Nevins township...]. 2pp.   p.f. 977.201 Vuncat. no. 2

The List of the dead patriots buried in Woodlawn cemetery, Terre Haute....(From The Terre Haute Express, May 27, 1886). [8pp.]   p.f. 977.202 Tuncat. no. 3

Some...cemeteries...with list of cemeteries....(From issues of Sycamore Leaves). 1977. [44pp.]   p.f. 977.201 Vuncat. no. 8

Smith, Lena, [Inscriptions from] Stewart Lawn cemetery. (From Sycamore Leaves, vol. 8 #4, 1978). 6pp.   p.f. 977.201 Vuncat. no. 9

Evans cemetery, Otter Creek township....(From Sycamore Leaves, vol. 10 #4, 1980). 1pp.   p.f. 977.201 Vuncat. no. 10

Names and locations of some cemeteries in Otter Creek township....(From Sycamore Leaves, vol. 10 #4, 1980). 2pp.   p.f. 977.201 Vuncat. no. 11

Watson cemetery....(From Sycamore Leaves, vol. 3 #1, 1981). 3pp.   p.f. 977.201 Vuncat. no. 12

Census:
First census of the town of Terre Haute, Indiana, October 9, 1829. 4pp.   p.f. 977.202 Tuncat. no. 1

Census of August 5, 1835 [of Terre Haute...]. 8pp.   p.f. 977.202 Tuncat. no. 2

Church:

Clark, Dorothy J., Index of minutes book of Union Baptist church, Pierson twp....1966. 4, [28pp.]	p.f. 977.201 V689 no. 4
Friends, Society of, Honey Creek Monthly meeting, minutes, 1820-1825. 1930. 62pp.	977.201 V689fr
Heiss, Willard, Honey Creek Monthly meeting of Friends...1820. [1961]. 26pp.	977.201 V689frh

Family:

Farwell, Bonnie and Markle, Augustus, Genealogical and historical sketches...with a list of monuments in old burying grounds and county records up to 1820. 1929. 268pp.	977.201 V689f
Vigo Co. Hist. Soc, Family Bible records. Comp. by Mrs. Robert I. Clark. 1952-75. 5 vols.	977.201 V689v
Brown, Mrs. Herbert E., ...Family records. 1966. 51, [5]pp.	977.201 V689vb
DAR, ...Family records. 1945. 221pp.	977.201 V689d
Clark, Dorothy J., Terre Haute Sunday Tribune-Star, genealogy columns, Sept. 17, 1978 thru April 15, 1980. 1982. 176, [8]pp.	977.202 T329c
Genealogy surnames and subjects: Vigo county Library special collections, Terre Haute...[197-].	p.f.16.929 G3264

History:

Complete list of the graduates from the Terre Haute High school since 1867. (From Terre Haute Gazette, July 6, 1895). 1pp.	p.f. 977.202 Tuncat. no. 4
Legal notices appearing in the Terre Haute Star, Wednesday, April 30, 1969, listing residents (and some heirs) of Terre Haute. 1pp.	p.f. 977.202 Tuncat. no. 5
...Death obituary. (Clippings from the Terre Haute Tribune Star, 1939).	p.f. 977.201 Vuncat. no. 3
Routes to Terre Haute early 19th century. 1pp.	p.f. 977.201 Vuncat. no. 4
[A History of...] pioneers, 1814-1830. [37pp.]	p.f. 977.201 Vuncat. no. 5
Markle, Augustus R., Sons of American Revolution seek traces of some early settlers. (Clippings from Terre Haute Star, May 11, 1947). 1pp.	p.f. 977.201 Vuncat. no. 6
Men who voted 100 years ago [at an election for Harrison township...held in the court house, February 1, 1832]. (Clipping from Terre Haute Star, Sept. 3, 1933). 1pp.	p.f. 977.201 Vuncat. no. 7

Miscellaneous:

Darlington, Jane E., ...1828 tax list with delinquencies returned 15 December 1828: including power of attorney....[1982]. [22pp.]	977.201 V689dv
WPA, Commissioners' record...1818-1844. 7 vols.	Ind. Hist. Soc. Library
Vigo county records.	microfilm

WABASH COUNTY

Formed 1832; organized 1835 from Cass, Grant* County Seat—Wabash

Births:

LaSalle, Robert, ...Births: from the records of Dr. Robert LaSalle, Sr., Wabash county health officer. [19—]. 8pp.   977.201 W112L

Deeds:

Deed indexes, 1835-1897.   microfilm

Marriages:

Marriages, 1835-July 1840 (THG, vol. 21 #1, Mar. 1981).   977.2 H789

Wabash Co. Hist. Museum. ...Marriage records...[1835-1882]. 1958-67. 2 vols.   977.201 W112m

Marriages, 1856-1899.   microfilm

Probates:

Probate indexes, 1850-1900.   microfilm

Wills:

Wills, 1847-1894.   microfilm

Cemetery:

Binnie, Lester H., Cemetery records for Pleasant, Chester and Paw Paw townships....1971. 432pp.   977.201 W112b

DAR, Cemeteries....1964-67. 2 pts.   977.201 W112d

Cemeteries of Noble township....1979. 256pp.   977.201 W112c

Four Waltz township cemeteries not included in Mississinewa Memorial cemetery. 1979. 32pp.   977.201 W112f

Fourteen cemeteries of Lagro township....1979. 252pp.   977.201 W112fo

Ind. Junior Hist. Soc., ...Cemetery records of Lagro, Noble, and Waltz townships. 3 pts. [197-]. 90, [108, 21]pp.   977.201 W112in

McPherson, Robert D., Mississinewa Memorial cemetery...includes Bank cemetery, Captain Dixon cemetery, Chester E. Troyer cemetery, Mt. Vernon cemetery, Ogan cemetery, Pleasant Grove cemetery, William Ted Hosier cemetery. 1977. 206pp.   977.201 W112mc

Gray, Alice M., Records of St. Patrick cemetery, Lagro, Ind. (Aug. 1, 1846-Apr. 15, 1883). 1973. 43pp.   977.202 L179gr

Wabash Cem. Soc., Record of interments, Falls cemetery, Wabash, Ind., 1838-1971. 1972. 3 vols.   977.202 W112r

Woodward, Ronald L., Records relating to the Rodef Sholem cemetery, Wabash, Indiana. 1977. 28,8, [8]pp.   977.202 W112w

Ind. Hist. Soc., Cemetery records....[pt. 1], Waucoon Indian Church. [13pp.]   p.f. 977.201 W112 no. 1

O'Hair, Mary C., Cemetery records....16 pts.   p.f. 977.201 W112 no. 2

Ind. Junior Hist. Soc., ...Cemetery records. 1, Cemetery located on the F. Draper farm, Liberty twp.; Center Grove; Friends of Lagro twp.; I.O.O.F., LaFontaine; Leedy; Matlock; Mississinewa Memorial; Murphy. Lutheran; Rennaker; Stone; Waggoner; Wallace; 2, Treaty cemetery; Richvalley cemetery; America cemetery; 3, Falls cemetery.   p.f. 977.201 W112 no. 7

Seven cemeteries (South Old Niconza, Niconza Church, Shiloh, Reed, Jack, Soap Hill, Stockdale) Paw Paw township....[1971]. [16pp.]   p.f. 977.201 W112 no. 8

Kelly, Stephen R., The Hoff cemetery of Noble township....1973. 19pp.   p.f. 977.201 W112 no. 9

*Note: Not the Wabash County created from the New Purchase, see Footnote 2.

Rhodes, Mrs. Hazel, Stockdale cemetery...near Roann....1954. 2pp.   p.f. 977.201 Wuncat. no. 2 pt. 1

Shiloh cemetery....1955. 3pp.   p.f. 977.201 Wuncat. no. 2 pt. 2

Beachler, Lowell H., Renicker cemetery, Lagro township....1979. 6pp.   p.f. 977.201 Wuncat. no. 3

Census:

Ind. State Lib., Index to 1840 census....1972. 10pp.   977.201 W112i

Census and list of taxables, 1840.   microfilm

O'Hair, Mary C., Heads of families and list of taxables....1840. [19—]. 22pp.   977.201 W112o

Woodward, Ronald L., 1870 Census....1978. 2 vols.   977.201 W112u

Church:

Early records of the Bachelor Creek Christian church, June 1845-April 1871. [19—]. 14pp.   977.201 W112ba

Gray, Alice McN., Baptismal records, May 24, 1846-Aug. 1973, St. Patrick church, Lagro, Indiana and surrounding communities. 1974. 109pp.   977.202 L179g

Mortuary & Obituaries:

Ft. Wayne P.L., Abstracts from Jones Funeral Home records, Wabash, Ind. 1972. 2 vols.   977.202 W112a

McPherson, Robert D., Abstracts from Eddingfield Mortuary, Wabash, Indiana, September 1953-September 1977. [1978?]. 355pp.   977.202 W112m

———, Wire Funeral Home records, 1930-1959, Wabash, Indiana....1977. 149pp.   977.201 W112w

Woodward, Ronald L., Obituaries from Wabash Weekly Gazette, 1848-1856. [197-]. [14pp.]   977.201 W112w

Miscellaneous:

Duplicate tax list, 1835 (THG, vol. 22 #2, June 1982).   977.2 H789

McPherson, Robert D., Declaration of intention and applications for citzenship...1854-1929. 1977. 94pp.   977.201 W112w

Assessment record, 1847.   microfilm

Commissioners records, 1835-1868.   microfilm

Marks and brands, 1846-1878.   microfilm

Tract book, 1826-1850.   microfilm

Tibbs, Helen, List of uncalled for letters published...in the various newspapers... 1846...1861. [1963?]. v.p.   p.f. 977.201 W112 no. 5

Roll of old settlers attending the first old settler's meeting held in Wabash county, Sept. 11, 1879. 10pp.   p.f. 977.201 W112 no. 6

Hackleman, Elijah, A Historical sketch...December 1, 1860. 1pp.   p.f. 977.201 Wuncat. no. 1

Mortgages [miscellaneous late 1800's...]. [38pp.]   p.f. 977.201 Wuncat. no. 6

Wabash Trails. vol. 1 #1, 3, 1980-   p.f. 977.201 Wuncat. no. 7

[O'Hair, Mrs. Mary], Wabash newspapers, 1849-Apr. 10, 1863. [Abstracts of articles]. notebook.   p.f. 977.201 Wuncat. no. 4

———, Abstracts of newspaper articles from Wabash Plain Dealer, January 6, 1876-December, 1896. [74pp.]   p.f. 977.201 Wuncat. no. 5

WARREN COUNTY

Formed 1827 from Fountain   County Seat—Williamsport

Births:
WPA, Index to birth records, 1882-1920.	977.201 W286u

Deaths:
WPA, Index to death records, 1882-1920.	977.201 W286u

Deeds:
Deed indexes, 1830-1900.	microfilm

Marriages:
Marriages, 1827-1904.	microfilm
DAR, Marriages...1828-1846. Cop. by Lydia M. Earl...and Mrs. A.S. Dolch. 1931. 80pp.	977.201 W286d
Marriages, 1828-1836 (THG, #3-4, May-June 1962, July-Aug. 1963).	977.2 H789
WPA, Index to marriage records, 1853-1920.	977.201 W286u
WPA, Index to supplemental marriage applications, 1882-1911.	977.201 W286u
WPA, Index to supplemental record, marriage transcript, 1882-1900.	977.201 W286u

Probates:
Probates, 1829-1850.	microfilm

[handwritten: Guardianship. 1863-1907]

Wills:
Wills, 1830-1897.	microfilm
Leath, Mrs. Wilbur T., ...Will abstracts 1830-1858. [1969?]. 20,6pp.	977.201 W286L

Cemetery:
Ind. Junior Hist. Soc., ...Cemetery records. 1976. [48pp.]	977.201 W286i
Denges, Jeanette, Mound cemetery, Pine Village...1837-1969. 1969. 31pp.	977.201 W286de
Jenkins, Rosella R., Sacred to the memory. Inscriptions from eastern Warren county...cemeteries, 1826-1974. 1975. 183pp.	977.201 W286j
Swisher, Emelyn, A Partial listing of graves in the West Lebanon cemetery, West Lebanon...data from gravestones. 1978. 14pp.	977.202 W516s
Ind. Hist. Soc., [Cemetery records...] 3pts. (Sisson, Tomlinson, Gopher Hill, Bumgarner).	p.f. 977.201 W294 no. 1
Williams, Grover, Lyons cemetery...Steuben twp....[1965?]. [7pp.]	p.f. 977.201 W294 no. 2
Cunningham, Irish Catholic, Old Baltimore Burying Ground, Rodgers, and Upper Mount cemeteries....(From Illiana Genealogist, 1974, 1975, 1965, 1967). [30pp.]	p.f. 977.201 Wuncat. no. 3
Tombstone records....3pp.	p.f. 977.201 Wuncat. no. 1
Williams, Grover, Dixon or Foster cemetery, Mound township....1pp.	p.f. 977.201 Wuncat. no. 2
Ind. Junior Hist. Soc., ...Cemetery records (Davis, Foster, McConnell, McKenzie, Pond Grove, Independence). [24pp.]	p.f. 977.201 Wuncat. no. 4

Miscellaneous:
Darlington, Jane E., ...Stock marks recorded Oct. 1827 to May 1931. 1983. 25,6pp.	
Salts, Walter and Warren Co. Hist. Soc., Warren county...and its people. 1980. 112pp.	977.201 W286w
Tract book, 1825-1852.	microfilm

WARRICK COUNTY

Formed 1813 from Knox   County Seat—Boonville

Births:

Births, 1899-1907.	microfilm
WPA, Index to birth records, 1882-1920.	977.201 W295u
(published 1980 in 4 vols.)	977.201 W295i

Deaths:

WPA, Index to death records, 1882-1920.	977.201 W295u
(published in 1980, 199pp.)	977.201 W295wa

Deeds:

Deeds, 1813-1834.	microfilm

Marriages:

DAR, Early marriage records, 1813-1818....1955. 5pp.	977.201 W295w
Dillingham, Thomas J., ...Marriages...[1813-1860]. 1943-44. 2 vols.	p.f. 977.201 W295 no. 2
Marriages, 1813-1884.	microfilm
Marriage returns, 1882-1891.	microfilm
WPA, Index to marriage records, 1900-1920.	977.201 W295u
WPA, Index to supplemental record, marriage transcript, 1880-1920.	977.201 W295u
DAR, ...Marriages, 1813-1854. [1972?]. 165pp.	977.201 W295dm

Probates:

Probate order book, 1817-1834.	microfilm

Wills:

Dillingham, Thomas J., ...Wills made and probated, 1814-1859. 29pp.	p.f. 977.201 W295 no. 3 pt. 2
Wills, 1814-1839 (abstracts in IMH, vol. 44, 1948).	977.2 I39
Wills, 1831-1859.	microfilm
DAR, Will book 1, 1831-1859....[1972]. 207pp.	977.201 W295dw

Cemetery:

DAR, ...Cemeteries. [1] Boon township. 1970. 147pp.	977.201 W295dc
———, Maple Grove cemetery, Boonville....1969. 304pp.	977.202 B724d
Ind. Hist. Soc., [Cemetery Records in Warrick County]. (From Indiana State Library).	miCrofilm
Phillips, Opal B., They came to Warrick Co., In.: The Revolutionary War soldiers and patriots buried in Warrick county...and some of their descendants. [1976?]. 3 vols.	977.201 W295p
Phillips, J. Oscar, ...Cemeteries. 1980. Vol. 1, Greer and Campbell townships. 90, 65pp.	977.201 W295ph
Ind. Hist. Soc., [Cemetery records...]. (Anderson township, 12 pts.; Boon township, 46 pts.; Campbell township, 16 pts.; Greer township, 10 pts.; Hart township, 11 pts.; Lane township, 3 pts.; Ohio township, 19 pts.; Owen township, 10 pts.; Pigeon township, 9 pts.; Skelton township, 17 pts.)	p.f. 977.201 W295 no. 1
Foster, Hallie, Brackenridge cemetery, west of Boonville. 1pp. (missing 1982)	p.f. 977.201 Wuncat. no. 2
Miller, Norma S., Those believed to be buried on the Small farm....[3pp.]	p.f. 977.201 Wuncat. no. 3

Census:

Lynn, Mrs. Gene, The 1830 census....[1969]. 12pp.	p.f. 977.201 W295 no. 4

Phillips, J. Oscar, ...1850 census. 1980. 219pp.	977.201 W295phc
U.S. Census Office, 1870 census....1 vol.	977.201 W295us
U.S. Census Office, 1880 federal census....1971. 3 vols.	977.201 W295un

Court:

Commissioners record, 1813-1852.	microfilm
Common Pleas and circuit court records, 1813-1838.	microfilm
DAR, Circuit court records...1813-1823....1955. [43pp.] [Includes circuit court records, 1813-1823; order book, August 1818; index of wills, 1831-1859].	977.201 W295c
Miller, Mrs. Mabel H., [Index to]...estates, record book no. 2, 1844-1848. 2pp.	p.f. 977.201 Wuncat. no. 1
Dillingham, Thomas J., [...Records]. 4 pts. (pt.1, Stock marks, 1819-1887; pt.2, wills...1814-1859; pt.3, estate inventories or sale bills of personal properties made or held, 1813-1832; pt.4, Dr. Alva Pasco).	p.f. 977.201 W295 no. 3

Family:

DAR, ...Bible and family records. 1964-75. 5 vols. (published 1980 in 4 vols.)	q977.201 W295d
Lant, Kay F., ...Genealogical records. 1963. 104pp.	977.201 W295L
Revolutionary War pensions. n.d.	microfilm

Mortuary & Obituaries:

Miller, Mabel H., Keyhole to the past, Boonville Standard. 1968. 47pp. [obituaries].	977.201 W295m
Phillips, J. Oscar, Records of Shafer Bros. Funeral home, Boonville, Indiana, 1885-1919....1980. 127pp.	977.202 B724phi

Miscellaneous:

DAR, Gleanings from the Boonville Standard, 1878-1897. 1977. 275pp.	977.201 W295da
Parish records of German Evangelical United Immanuel Church (Susott Church). 1980. 160pp.	977.201 W295ge
Raleigh, Eldora M., History of Newburgh and Warrick county...[1965?]. 39pp.	977.201 W295r
Taylor, Phillip, Pioneer families of Pike and Warrick counties...with ancestors and related families of Philip Taylor. 1981. 116, [59 pp.]	977.201 P636t

WASHINGTON COUNTY

Formed 1814 from Clark, Harrison, Jefferson   County Seat—Salem

Births:

WPA, Index to birth records, 1882-1920.	977.201 W317u
Delayed birth records prior to 1941.	miCrofilm
Births, 1882-1907.	microfilm

Deaths:

WPA, Index to death records, 1882-1920.	977.201 W317u
Burns, Clara M., Death records...1882-1950. 1970. 2 vols.	977.201 W317bu

Deeds:

Deeds, 1814-1830; indexes, 1814-1911.	microfilm
Deeds [indentures], 1814-1887.	miCrofilm
Deed indexes, 1814-1897.	miCrofilm
Deeds [indentures], lands transferred from Clark county, 1838-1874.	miCrofilm

Marriages:

Marriages, 1815-1867, 1881-1888.	microfilm
WPA, Index to marriage records, 1850-1920.	977.201 W317u
WPA, Index to supplemental record, marriage applications, 1882-1890.	977.201 W317u
WPA, Index to supplemental record, marriage transcripts, 1894-1907. Appendix 1904-6.	977.201 W317u
Slevin, Ruth M., ...Marriage records, 1815-1847....1970. 95,79pp.	977.201 W317s
Marriages, 1815-1922.	miCrofilm
Marriage affidavits and consent, 1884-1918.	miCrofilm
Short, Lorraine, K., Affidavits, consents, certificates and marriage returns...1883 through 1890. 1979. 309pp.	977.201 W317sh
Morris, Harvey and Trueblood, Lillie, Marriage record of Blue River Monthly meeting. 2 vols. [Vol 1, 1816-1920, Hicksites after 1829; vol. 2, 1829-1882, Orthodox].	977.201 W317f
DAR, ...Marriages to 1821. 1970. 3pp.	p.f. 977.201 W319 no. 18
Marriages, 1815-1833 (THG, vol. 12 #1, Jan.-Mar. 1972).	977.2 H789

Probates:

Probate order books, 1814-1824, 1837-1841.	microfilm
Probates, 1814-1824, 1830-1852; indexes, 1865-1884, 1887-1899.	microfilm
Probate court minute book, probate record, common pleas minutes and order book, probate order books, 1814-1919.	miCrofilm
Common pleas, circuit court, and probate final records, 1831-1869.	miCrofilm
Circuit court and civil probate vacation record, 1887-1927.	miCrofilm

Wills:

DAR, Abstracts of wills...1814-1900. 1952-53. 240pp.	977.201 W317w
Wills, 1821-1830, 1860-1902.	microfilm
Davis, Lulie, Abstracts of wills...1808-1902. 1971. 214pp.	977.201 W317da
Wills, 1821-1830 (THG, #3-4, May-June, July-Aug. 1963).	977.2 H789
Intestate records, 1814-1830 (THG, #5, Sept.-Oct. 1963).	977.2 H789
Wills, 1873-1925.	miCrofilm

Index to estates, 1874-1895.	miCrofilm
Early...wills, 1821-1830; intestate records, 1814-1830 (From THG, 1963). 6pp.	p.f. 977.201 Wuncat. no. 10

Cemetery:

Burns, Clara M., Claysville cemetery, Vernon township....1969. 26pp.	977.201 W317b
———, Partial listing of burial plots of Crown Hill cemetery, Salem, Indiana. 1974-75. 151pp.	977.201 W317bp
Wash. Co. Hist. Soc., Cemeteries of Washington township....[1981?]. 171pp.	977.201 W317cem
DAR, Cemeteries, Washington, Clark, Scott, and Floyd counties....1956. 97pp.	977.201 W317d
———, ...Condensed obituaries [1930's]. Bible records and cemetery records. 1968-69. 2 vols.	977.201 W317dr
Wash. Co. Hist. Soc., Salem cemeteries....1980. 378pp.	977.202 S163sc
Trueblood, Lillie D., [Cemetery records of Friends cemeteries...]. 3 pts. (Includes Blue River Monthly meeting, Highlands Friends, and Old Blue River).	977.201 W317t
Taylor, Ben F., Beech Grove cemetery, Franklin township....[1967] 19pp.	977.201 W317ta
...Cemetery records. 1 vol. (Includes readings copied from gravestones in Smith/Miller cemetery, Big Spring cemetery, Kansas cemetery, and Hop cemetery....).	977.201 W317was
Ind. Hist. Soc., Cemetery records....28, [3]pp.	p.f. 977.201 W319 no. 2
Richardson, Neva, ...Cemeteries. 1, Fleener-Winslow cem.	p.f. 977.201 W319 no. 6
Ingalls, Mrs. Robert, Cemetery records....1, Smedley cemetery. [1962]. 4pp.	p.f. 977.201 W319 no. 7
Buley, Earl R., Bethlehem cemetery, Jackson township....1963. [9pp.]	p.f. 977.201 W319 no. 9
Taylor, Ben F., Martinsburg cemetery, Martinsburg, Jackson township....[1965-66]. 2 pts.	p.f. 977.201 W319 no. 10
———, Rodman cemetery, Franklin township....[1966]. 3pp.	p.f. 977.201 W319 no. 11
Driskell, Arthur N., Old Prowsville cemetery, about five miles northeast of Campbellsburg....[1966?]. [3pp.]	p.f. 977.201 W319 no. 12
Cook, Mrs. Claude E., Cemetery records....11 pts.	p.f. 977.201 W319 no. 13
Cox, Carroll O., Cemetery records....1, Martin, Livonia cemeteries. 1967. 2pp.	p.f. 977.201 W319 no. 17
Mottis, Mary A., Plaque of Mount Carmel cemetery located on Rural Route 1, Campbellsburg, Indiana....1966. v.p. (Additional dates added by Violet Cook, 1974).	p.f. 977.201 W319 no. 21
Old Sparksville cemetery....n.d. 2pp.	p.f. 977.201 W319 no. 22
Taylor, Ben, Wilcoxson cemetery, Jackson township....1pp.	p.f. 977.201 Wuncat. no. 2
Boston, Mrs. Earl R., Inscriptions from the Newby cemetery, Howard township....3pp.	p.f. 977.201 Wuncat. no. 3
Gaitor cemetery, Gibson twp....5pp.	p.f. 977.201 Wuncat. no. 9

Church:

St. Patrick's observe 100th anniversary [Washington, Indiana]. (From The Washington Democrat, Aug. 23, 1940).	p.f. 977.202 Wuncat. no. 1
DAR, First book of births, Blue River Friends church. 1973. 18,18pp.	977.201 W317bl
———, Records of the Salem Presbyterian Church...copied from first book, 1817-1853....1955. 82pp.	977.202 S163s
Baptisms, Weir Methodist Church, Salem, Ind., [1863-1879]. n.p.	p.f. 977.201 W319 no. 15

Court:

Circuit court minute book, 1814-1818.	microfilm
Commissioners records, 1817-1855.	microfilm

Cook, Claude E., ...Commissioners book "B"...1824-1839. 1965. 120pp.   977.201 W317wc
(Also a 1969 index by Mary Crismore).

———, Records...Pt.1, Recs. of Board of Co. commissioners...1817-1923; Pt.2,
Civil case 1814...misc. probate records, 1818-1821. 1969. v.p.   977.201 W317cr

———, Indentures...1828-1891. 1965. [9pp.]   p.f. 977.201 W319 no. 19

Indentures, 1828-1891.   miCrofilm

Coroners record, 1926-1938.   miCrofilm

Negro register, 1853-1861.   miCrofilm

Naturalizations, 1892-1929.   miCrofilm

Record of administration, guardians, wills and bonds, 1852-1877.   miCrofilm

Enumerations:

Cook, Claude E., Records of Brown township....[1967]. v.p.   977.201 W317c
(Also Enumeration of males over 37 in 1913. 8pp.)   977.201 W317ce

———, School enumerations [Brown twp., 1882-95; Jackson twp., 1866-95; Jefferson
twp., 1882-95; Vernon twp., 1882-95; Posey twp., 1882-95; Madison twp.,
1882-95; Howard-Pierce-Polk twp., 1882-95; Washington twp., 1882-95.]
1868-70. 9 pts.   977.201 W317cs

———, ...Poll lists, 1844-73. 1966. n.p.   977.201 W317wp

———, ...Tax lists, years 1843-46, 1849. 1965. n.p.   977.201 W317wt

...Jackson township, enumeration of male inhabitants over the age of 21 years—year
1889 & year 1901; enumeration of school children year 1900. [Cop. by Clara M.
Burns. 1968]. n.p.   977.201 W317

Ind. State Lib., Index to 1840 census....1973. 45pp.   977.201 W317i

Family:

Lagenaur, Frank, Birth, marriage and death dates of residents of Washington &
Orange counties, Indiana. Cop. by Mrs. Clara Burns. 1968. 75pp.   977.201 W317L

McCoskey, Mary E., Mary E. McCoskey's record of births, deaths, obituaries, &
miscellaneous data, 1865-1920...(mostly Canton community connections).
[1970?]. n.p.   977.201 W317m

Birth, death, and marriage records, Vernon and Posey twps....[Cop. by Will H.
Mitchell...taken from an old...account book...]. [1945]. [34pp.]   p.f. 977.201 W319 no. 1

DAR, Family Bible records....1954. 8pp.   p.f. 977.201 W319 no. 4

———, Family and Bible records from Washington county...and adjoining counties,
Clark and Floyd. 1956. 10, [2]pp.   p.f. 977.201 W319 no. 5

———, Our pioneer ancestors; family Bible records....13pp.   p.f. 977.201 Wuncat. no. 1

Some Washington county...families. (Family history of several of the students at the
Eastern High school, Pekin, Ind.). 1967. 13 pts.   p.f. 977.201 W319 no. 16

Washington County, Indiana, Family Records (Washington Co. Historical Society).   miCrofilm

Mortuary & Obituaries:

DAR, Coffin accounts, 1873-1880....Cop. from an old ledger by Lennie Martin
Berkey, Berkey's store, Salem, Ind. [1954]. 9pp.   p.f. 977.201 W319 no. 3

———, Condensed obituaries....1963-65. 5 vols. (1960-63; 1950-59; 1849 [sic]-1956;
1950-60; 1950-65).   p.f. 977.201 W319 no. 8

Casket list from account book of Stratton Brothers, Campbellsburg, Brown
twp...1906-1910. Abstracted by C.E. Cook. 1971. 4pp.   p.f. 977.201 W319 no. 20

Obituaries, 1895-1904, 1934-1968.   microfilm

Miscellaneous:

Morris, Mrs. Harvey. Archaeological and historical survey....[1925?]. 929pp.	977.201 W317a
Wash. Co. Hist. Soc., Index to...tract book, 1810-1859. 1 vol. n.p.	977.201 W317wa
Tract book [1811-1852].	microfilm
Cook, Mrs. Claude E., Copy of clippings from Campbellsburg Graphic. Deaths, 1908-1909. [2pp.]	p.f. 977.201 W319 no. 14
Skelley, Mrs. Thomas, Miscellaneous autographs and autobiographies taken from "A Book of Memoirs", by Dr. Thomas H.B. Baker...doctor of Pekin, Indiana....38pp.	p.f. 977.201 Wuncat. no. 4
The First settlement at South Boston. (From The Salem Leader, August 19, 1964). 1pp.	p.f. 977.201 Wuncat. no. 5
Washington County Historical Society. Newsletter. vol. 5 #3, 1977.	p.f. 977.201 Wuncat. no. 6
Records of the Hardin family, Providence Methodist church, and Wilcoxin cemeteries. (From IMH, 1936, 1939). 5pp.	p.f. 977.201 Wuncat. no. 7
Clippings from Blue River Gazette and Palmyra Gazette.	microfilm

WAYNE COUNTY

Formed 1811 from Clark, Dearborn   County Seat—Richmond

Births:
WPA, Index to birth records, 1882-1920.   977.201 W359u

Deaths:
WPA, Index to death records, 1882-1920.   977.201 W359u

Deeds:
Deed indexes, 1816-1879.   microfilm

Deed indexes—lots (includes Richmond), 1820-1910.   microfilm

Marriages:
Marriages, 1811-1830 (THG, vol. 16 #1, Jan.-Mar. 1976).   977.2 H789

Marriages, 1811-1860.   microfilm

WPA, Index to marriage records, 1860-1920.   977.201 W359u

Yount, Beverly W., Marriage records...March 11, 1811 to March 23, 1860. 1974.
    242pp.   977.201 W359yo

Marriages, 1811-1822 (IMH, vol. 40, 1944). (Reprinted by Ind. Hist. Society).   p.f. 977.201 W359 no. 3

Probates:
Probate indexes, 1818-1830. *Prob. Court Rec. 1845-64*   microfilm
Inv. + Sales Bills 1843-47

Wills:
Wills, 1812-1819 (abstracts in IMH, vol. 46, 1950).   977.2 I39

Wills, 1812-1900.   microfilm

Cemetery:
DAR, Cemetery records of eastern Wayne....Comp. by Hazel R. Gennett. 1948.
    32pp.   977.201 W359da

Yount, Beverly W., Tombstone inscriptions....1968-70. 4 vols.   977.201 W359y

History of Riverside cemetery. Rev. ed. 1908. 91pp. [Cambridge City].   977.202 C178c

Whitewater Valley Junior Hist.Soc., Capital Hill cemetery, Cambridge City,
    Ind....1977. [28pp.]   977.202 C178ca

Pike, Edna J., Crown Hill cemetery, Centerville....194- -1955. 3 vols. (and index).   p.f. 977.201 W359 no. 2

DAR, ...Cemetery records. 11 pts.   p.f. 977.201 W359 no. 4

———, Cemetery records....1955. (Beulah, Shiloh, Bulla). 3pp.   p.f. 977.201 W359 no. 6

Dennis, Mary W., ...Cemeteries. (Nettle Creek Friends burying ground). 28pp.   p.f. 977.201 W359 no. 7

D.A.C., Cemetery records. Comp. by Mrs. Robert Shoemaker, Sr. 1964. 10pp.
    (Family graveyard, 10 mi. east of Lisbon, Ohio; Quaker cemetery, Milton, Ind.;
    Milton City cemetery; Keesling cem., Henry county, Ind.).   p.f. 977.201 W359 no. 8

Cox, Carroll O., Cemetery records....[1], Graveyard at Jacksonburg. 4pp.   p.f. 977.201 W359 no. 9

Hibner, Janet L., Ridge cemetery....1967. 8, [5]pp.   p.f. 977.201 W359 no. 10

Ind. Junior Hist. Soc., ...Cemetery records. [1], Saint Marys cemetery, Ridge
    cemetery, Boston cemetery.   p.f. 977.201 W359 no. 11

Farm, Manlove, United Brethren cemeteries....(From Illiana Genealogist, 1967,
    1968, 1970). [4pp.]   p.f. 977.201 Wuncat. no. 1

Jeffers, Phoebe, East cemetery, Dublin....1pp.   p.f. 977.201 Wuncat. no. 2

Census:
Ind. State Lib., Index to 1840 census....1973. 69pp.   977.201 W359i

Ind. State Lib., Index to 1850 census....60pp.   977.201 Wuncat. no. 4

WPA, Index to supplemental record, federal census, 1880. (Lists names, sex, color, ages).   977.201 W359u

Church:

Friends, Soc. of, Milford Monthly meeting, [Records—birth and marriages]. 2 pts.   977.201 W359fm

Friends, Soc. of, New Garden Monthly meeting, Birth and death records [and minutes]....[220pp.]   977.201 W359fn

Friends, Soc. of, Springfield Monthly meeting, Records of Springfield Monthly meeting....220pp. (Includes births, deaths, marriages, and minutes).   977.201 W359fs

Friends, Soc. Of, Whitewater Monthly meeting, [Records] of White Water Monthly meeting....2 pts. (missing 1982).   977.201 W359fw

[Heiss, Willard, Quaker marriage records...]. 1958. 2 pts. (Chester MM, 1823-1890; Dover MM, 1837-1870).   p.f. 977.201 Wuncat.no. 3

Record of Indiana Quakers, covering the Springfield Monthly meeting; the Economy Monthly meeting; and the Whitewater Monthly meeting.   microfilm

Court:

Commissioners court, [first record, 1811-1817]. [1914]. [13pp.] (Missing 1982)

Farber, Renee, Index to county commissioners' records....151pp.   977.201 W359far

Naturalizations, 1833-1840 (THG, vol. 19 #2, June 1979).   977.2 H789

WPA, Commissioners' record...1811-1835. 4 vols.   Ind. Hist. Soc. Library

History:

[Inventory of] town records of Cambridge City, Dublin, Lewisville, Milton and Mount Auburn....1pp.   p.f. 977.201 Wuncat. no. 5

Crabtree, Caroline, ...Stock marks, record A, Mar. 1815-Apr. 1822. 2pp.   p.f. 977.201 Wuncat. no. 6

Whitewater Valley Jun. Hist. Soc., [Surname] index to the minutes of the Board of Trustees, 1841-1867, Cambridge City....[1975]. [6pp.]   p.f. 977.202 Cuncat. no. 1

———, [Surname index to the] minutes of the Board of Trustees, 1893-1900 (1913-1927), Dublin....[1975]. 2 pts.   p.f. 977.202 Duncat. no. 1

———, [Surname index to the] Dublin, Indiana (Jackson township...) roll book, 1901-1943. [1975]. [2pp.]   p.f. 977.202 Duncat. no. 2

———, [Surname index to the] Dublin, Indiana (Jackson township...), Board of Health minutes, 1882-1888. [1975]. [2pp.]   p.f. 977.202 Duncat. no. 3

———, [Surname index to the] Milton, Indiana (Washington township...) minutes of the Board of Trustees, 1897-1907....[1975]. [5pp.]   p.f. 977.202 Muncat. no. 1

———, [Surname] index [to] minutes of the Board of Trustees, Milton, Indiana (Washington township...) 1907-1930....[1975]. [5pp.]   p.f. 977.202 Muncat. no. 1 pt. 2

Membership of Presbyterian Church, Cambridge City....Funerals, weddings, Reports [1882-1885]. [7pp.]   p.f. 977.202 Cuncat. no. 2

Whitewater Valley Jun. Hist. Soc., [Surname index to the] Mount Auburn, Indiana (Jackson township...) minutes of the Board of Trustees, 1880-1887....[1975]. [2pp.]   p.f. 977.202 Muncat. no. 1 pt. 1

———, [Surname] index [to] Mount Auburn, Indiana (Jackson township...) Board of Trustees minutes, 1891-1893....[1975]. [2pp.]   p.f. 977.202 Muncat. no. 1 pt.2

———, [Surname] index [to] Mount Auburn, Indiana (Jackson township...) Board of Trustees minutes 1899-1909. [1975]. [3pp.]   p.f. 977.202 Muncat. no. 1 pt.3

———, [Surname] index [to] Mount Auburn, Indiana (Jackson township...) Board of Trustees claim docket 1899-1950....[1975]. [3pp.]   p.f. 977.202 Muncat. no. 1 pt.4

———, [Surname] index to the Mount Auburn, Indiana (Jackson township...) Board of Trustees ordinances 1880-1916....[1975]. [2pp.]   p.f. 977.202 Muncat. no. 1 pt.5

———, [Surname] index [to] Mount Auburn, Indiana (Jackson township...) Treasurer's book 1881-1905....[1975]. [3pp.]   p.f. 977.202 Muncat. no. 2 pt.1

———, [Surname] index [to] Mount Auburn, Indiana (Jackson township....) Treasurer's book 1905-1916....[1975]. [2pp.]   p.f. 977.202 Muncat. no. 2 pt.2

———, [Surname] index [to] Mount Auburn, Indiana...Board of Trustees tax duplicates, assessments, and order book 1880-1899....[1975]. 3pp.   p.f. 977.202 Muncat. no. 3

Miscellaneous:

DAR, Family Bible records....2 pts. (Brown, Doughty, Thornborough, Skinner, Cooper, Toney).   p.f. 977.201 W359 no. 5

Ranck, Cecilia, Doddridge Chapel community, yesterday and today. 1950. 172pp.   977.201 W359r

WELLS COUNTY

Formed 1835; organized 1837 from Allen, Delaware, Randolph   County Seat—Bluffton

Births:

WPA, Index to birth records, 1883-1920.	977.201 W456u

Deaths:

WPA, Index to death records, 1883-1920.	977.201 W456u

Deeds:

Deed indexes, 1838-1899.	microfilm

Marriages:

Higgins, Hilda T., Marriage records...1899 thru 1974. 1977. 6 vols. (with bride index).	977.201 W456hia
Higgins, Hilda T., Marriage records...1837-1900. 1976. 2 vols.	977.201 W456hi
DAR, Marriage records...1837-1900. [19—]. 2 vols.	977.201 W456da
Wells Co. Hist. Soc., ...Marriages, 1838-1868. [1966?]. 36pp.	p.f. 977.201 W453 no. 1
WPA, Index to marriage records, 1837-1920.	977.201 W456u
———, Index to supplemental record, marriage applications, 1905-1920.	977.201 W456u
Marriages, 1837-1861 (THG, vol. 6 #4, 5, 6, July-Aug., Sept.-Oct., Nov.-Dec. 1966).	977.2 H789

Probates:

Probates, 1838-1852; indexes, 1853-1900.	microfilm

Wills:

Wills, 1838-1901.	microfilm

Cemetery:

Minniear, Ingabee B., ...Cemetery records. 1972. 4 vols. (also 241pp. index by Dorothy Pemberton).	977.201 W456m
DAR, Cemetery records....[1] Elhanan cemetery, Jefferson twp. [1971].	p.f. 977.201 W453 no. 2
Old cemetery located on the west bank of the Wabash river...between the Lake Erie & Cloverleaf Railroad....1940 on the south side, Bluffton....7pp.	p.f. 977.202 Buncat. no. 1

Mortuary & Obituaries:

DAR, G.M. Gavin's Undertakers report, Poneto...1899-1907. [1976?]. 10pp.	p.f. 977.201 W456d
———, Death records, 1865-1877, book 1, McBride Funeral home, Bluffton, Ind. Cop. by Mrs. Ervin Lochner. 1970. 12pp.	p.f. 977.202 B658 no. 1
Meyer, Kimberly, Records of McBride Funeral home, Bluffton...Jan. 1, 1888-Mar. 12, 1975. 1976. 390pp.	977.201 W456mea
———, McBride Funeral home coffin records, Bluffton...1865-1887. 1976. 72pp.	977.201 W456me
Minniear, Ingabee B., ...Obituaries, 1969 to 1975. 1978. 301pp. (also 92pp. index by Dorothy Pemberton).	977.201 W456mi
———, ...Obituaries, 1975-1979. 1981. 436pp.	977.201 W456miw

Miscellaneous:

DAR, Land patents...Comp. by John W. Carnall and Sons, Inc. 1976. [72pp.]	977.201 W456j
Tract book, 1830-1853.	microfilm
Edwards, Melba M., Zanesville, Indiana, history, 1849-1976. 253pp. (also in Allen county).	977.202 Z28e

WHITE COUNTY

Formed 1834 from Carroll   County Seat—Monticello

Births:

WPA, Index to birth records, 1882-1920.   977.201 W589u

Deaths:

WPA, Index to death records, 1882-1920.   977.201 W589u

Deeds:

Deed indexes, 1834-1900.   microfilm

Marriages:

Brewer, Pequetti H., ...Marriage records, 1834-1852. n.d. [13pp.]   p.f. 977.201 W582 no. 3

Scott, Bixler and Glick, Early...marriages, 1834-1906. 1968. 4 vols. (and 135pp. index by Ind. State Lib.).   977.201 W589

Marriages, 1834-1852.   microfilm

WPA, Index to marriage records, 1850-1920.   977.201 W589u

Probates:

Probates, 1835-1850; indexes, 1850?-1900?.   microfilm

Wills:

Wills, 1835-1895.   microfilm

Original wills and estate papers (these survived the 1974 tornado). [197-?.] 27pp. (Housed at White County Historical Museum).   977.201 W589o

Others:

Brewer, Pequetti H., ...Cemeteries. 1970. vol. 1, Liberty and Cass townships. 35pp.   977.201 W589b

Ind. Hist. Soc., Cemetery records....13 pts. in 1 vol.   977.201 W589i

Liggett, F.D., [Cemetery records...]. 1963. v.p. (Bedford, Lake Shafer, Wilson family cemetery).   977.201 W589L

Stotler, Frank, Cemetery inscriptions...all military and some civil individuals. 1972. 47pp.   977.201 W589s

Comingore, Charles E., [Brookston, Smelcer and Carr cemeteries, Prairie township...]. [1954]. n.p.   p.f. 977.201 W582 no. 2

White Co. Gen. Soc., The Davis or Winegardner cemetery. 1974. 70pp.   p.f. 977.201 W582 no. 4

Paulus, Margaret, Hemphill private cemetery....1949. 3pp.   p.f. 977.201 Wuncat. no. 2

Stuart, Robert K., [Records of] the Clark cemetery of the Old Scott settlement. (From IMH, vol. 36, 1940). 5pp.   p.f. 977.201 Wuncat. no. 3

Statistics: Rothrock burial ground: Monticello, Indiana....2pp.   p.f. 977.201 Wuncat. no. 4

Brookston, Indiana, centennial, 1853-1953....93pp.   p.f. 977.202 Buncat. no. 1

WPA, Index to supplemental record, registered voters, 1883-1931.   977.201 W589u

Tract books, 1830-1854, 1829-1854.   microfilm

WHITLEY COUNTY

Formed 1835; organized 1838 from Elkhart, Allen County Seat—Columbia City

Deaths:
Williamson, Wallace, Index to deaths...1882-1907. 1965. 261pp.	977.201 W613w
Pence, Mildred, Index to death records...1908-1920. 1966. 230pp.	977.201 W613p

Deeds:
General index patents, 1813-1884.	microfilm
Original entries, 1835-1853.	microfilm
Deed indexes, 1835-1899.	microfilm

Marriages:
Marriages, Sept. 1838-1850 (THG, vol. 19 #3, Sept. 1979).	977.2 H789
DAR, ...Marriage records, 1838-1860. Comp. by Velma W. Moeller. [1946?]. n.p.	977.201 W613
Marriages, 1838-1900.	microfilm
Marriage affidavits, 1864-1885.	microfilm
Raber, Nellie M., Marriages...1860-May 11, 1884. 1973. 412pp.	977.201 W613
Stultz, Marguerite, Marriage records...April 1891 to September 1898. 1971. 130pp.	977.201 W613

Probates:
Probates, 1839-1852; indexes, 1853-1897.	microfilm

Wills:
Carver, Bernice, Some...will records [1839-1895 incomplete]. 1955. [35pp.]	p.f. 977.201 W613 no. 3
Wills, 1839-1897.	microfilm
Pemberton, Dorothy G., Everyname index to abstract of wills...1839-1913 by Nellie Raber. 1979. 53pp.	977.201 W613r

Others:
DAR, Records of cemeteries....1958-59. 2 pts. (pt.2, South Park cemetery).	977.201 W613dc
———, First tax duplicate...1838. 6pp.	p.f. 977.201 W613 no. 1
Tax duplicate 1838 (THG, #5, Sept.-Oct. 1962).	977.2 H789
Circuit court records, 1839-1900.	microfilm
Common pleas records, 1849-1858.	microfilm
Williamson, W., A list of voters of Smith township...1848. 1965. 2pp.	p.f. 977.201 W613 no. 4
———, ...Cemetery inscriptions. [1982?]	977.201 W613wc
DAR, South Whitley, Cleveland twp., cemetery....1967. 185pp.	977.201 W613dd
Harter, Stuart, Original land entries....1981. 1 atlas [12]pp.	f977.201 W613h
Kite, Marjorie J., Cemetery inscriptions....[1980?]. 107pp.	977.201 W613kic
DAR, Grace Lutheran church, Columbia City, Indiana, its organization, its achievements and progress in each ministry, published 1892....[1948]. [19pp.]	977.202 C726g
Raber, Nellie M.R., Greenhill cemetery, Columbia City, Indiana with index. [20], 96pp.	977.202 C726r
Kite, Marjorie J., Obituaries from the South Whitley area, 1885-1930. [19—]. 248pp.	977.202 S728k
Ind. Hist. Soc., [Cemetery records...]. 9pts.	p.f. 977.201 W613 no. 2
Williamson, Wallace, ...1840 census index. [1964]. 5pp.	p.f. 977.201 Wuncat. no. 1